UTOPIA

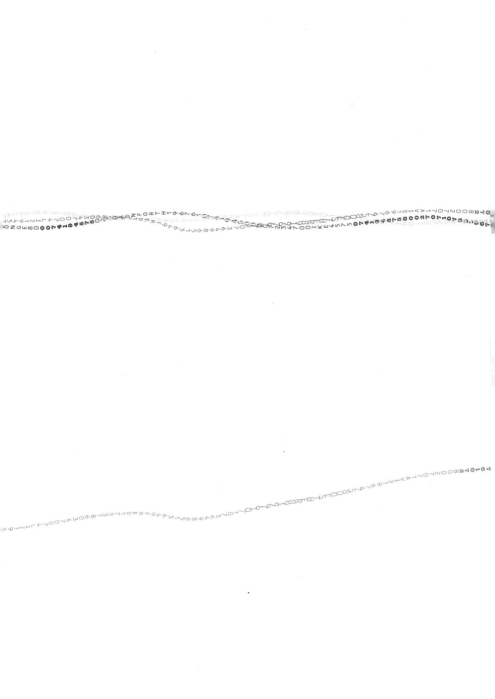

uTOpia
TOWARDS A NEW TORONTO

JASON MCBRIDE
ALANA WILCOX
EDITORS

COACH HOUSE BOOKS
TORONTO

First edition

Published with the assistance of the Canada Council for the Arts
and the Ontario Arts Council. We also acknowledge the financial
support of the Government of Ontario through the Ontario Book
Publishing Tax Credit Program and the Government of Canada
through the Book Publishing Industry Development Program.

Library and Archives Canada Cataloguing in Publication

UTOpia : towards a new Toronto / editors: Jason McBride and
Alana Wilcox.

ISBN 1-55245-156-9

1. Toronto (Ont.). 2. Toronto (Ont.)--Social conditions--21st
century.
I. McBride, Jason, 1968- II. Wilcox, Alana

FC3097.3.U86 2005   971.3'541
C2005-906345-9

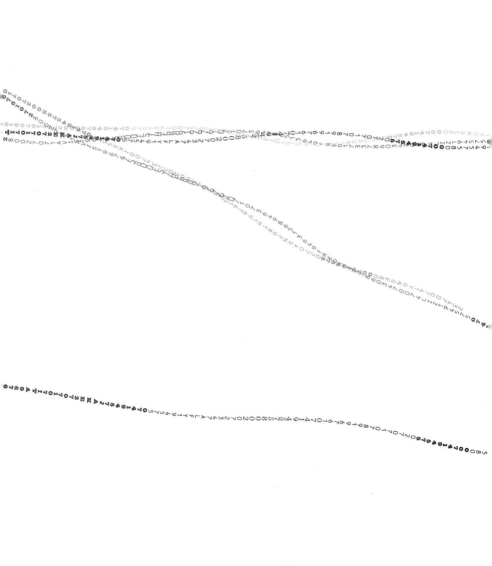

CONTENTS

FOREWORD

It isn't easy to reinvent a city. Cities are made of reinforced concrete, brick and metal. Office towers and subway tunnels don't yield readily to the forces of change. Highways and sewer systems don't lend themselves to metamorphosis.

The biggest impediment to transforming a city, though, is not a physical limitation; it's the inertia that comes from historical legacy and a mentality of resignation. In other words, if a city is perceived in a particular way, it takes a tremendous amount of energy and inspiration to reimagine it as something radically different and better.

I have my own beliefs about what will transform this city – a new waterfront, new governmental powers, new investment in the public realm, new art and architecture – but my vision alone isn't enough. That's why I welcome this book, which encourages people to challenge all their assumptions about Toronto, and to picture the city not as it is but as it can and should be.

I believe that there is more than enough energy and inspiration among the people of Toronto to make this city into something new and spectacular. The volume you now hold is evidence of that.

Mayor David Miller
City of Toronto

INTRODUCTION

Neither of us was born in Toronto, but we have, both of us, lived in the city for more than fifteen years. It is, for better or worse, home. And in the fifteen years we have lived here, we have never felt about Toronto what we do now: we adore the city. Even while recognizing Toronto's many limitations and inadequacies, we appreciate how much it has to offer – culturally, economically, socially. It now seems a city of extraordinary possibility.

We certainly have not always felt this way, and, in fact, we can roughly pinpoint, without too much effort, the moment we truly embraced Toronto. It was the day David Miller was elected mayor. Miller wasn't, *isn't,* perfect – what politician could be? – but he's a far cry from the elected officials who had previously governed the city. He seems like a genuinely decent person, with an authentic love of the city and a respectful vision for its future. He made mistakes as a councillor and will make many more again as mayor, but he offers us something we have rarely felt before: hope. Hope that the city can grow and prosper in a way that includes every Torontonian. Hope that the enormous potential the city possesses will be exploited and not wasted. To attribute so much promise to one elected official is certainly naive, and it would be misplaced optimism if his election hadn't coincided with a wellspring of cultural and ideological activity that has gushed forth from an infinite diversity of wells. Perhaps it seems new only because many of our peers, friends and colleagues are involved in this activity. Or perhaps we're simply getting older. But for the first time, it feels as if the city is becoming *ours.*

When we speak of ownership, we are speaking in an ideological or rhetorical sense, not an economic one. A city, by its very nature, is not owned; it is shared. Public space is public property. Especially for those of us – and there are many – unable to afford private property, a condo or house to call our own, public space is extremely important. Increasingly, our homes are outside: in the streets, on patios, in bars, on concert stages, in bookstores, in parks. Family extends beyond living room walls and includes the people who are in your band, who are on your basketball team, who help design your website and who are part of your burlesque act. The public is the private and vice versa, always.

Ownership also implies responsibility, and responsibility begets contribution. Contribution, in turn, engenders growth. And we are contributing to Toronto's growth by refusing to accept its limitations – or, rather, by turning those limitations into virtues. We are creating culture. We are reclaiming public space. We are transforming neighbourhoods. We are rediscovering or recovering history. We are trying to make home feel more like home. We are telling people that we live in Toronto with a proud smile instead of an embarrassed titter.

The people involved in this transformation are artists, activists, journalists, historians, students, musicians, architects, writers, engineers, publishers, restaurateurs, bartenders, gardeners, scientists. They are, as Edward Keenan points out in his essay, involved in things like *Spacing*, the Lexiconjury reading series, tours of the city's hidden laneways, *Broken Pencil*, the revitalization of Dufferin Grove Park, the Trampoline Hall lecture series, blogs, the Toronto Public Space Committee, the Images

Festival, Arts & Crafts Records, the Community Bicycling Network, the Wavelength music series, *This*, the City Beautification Ensemble, OCAP, Diplomatic Immunities, the Toronto Psychogeography Society, [murmur], the Toronto Free Gallery, Planning Action, the Liaison of Independent Filmmakers of Toronto, to list but a few. They're all discrete projects, but a flow chart of the people involved would be a tangled one.

At Coach House, we have cultivated relationships, both formal and informal, with many of these individuals and groups. For forty years in fact, from our garage on the outskirts of the University of Toronto, Coach House has served as a kind of cultural hub, where writers and artists of all stripes have found a home – a microcosmic version of this larger utopian web. Who better then to document this current civic enthusiasm than us? We wanted to capture and preserve and encourage this energy and inventiveness, to put it on paper and between covers.

It is easy to recognize the problems of a city, and Toronto has its fair share. Our roads are in disrepair. Violent crime seems to have escalated. Affordable housing and an inefficient public transit system remain constant obstacles. But in compiling this anthology, we asked our contributors to focus on the positive aspects of the city, what it had done and was doing right, and how that activity could lay the groundwork for an even better city. We encouraged optimism. We insisted on imagination. The pieces in this anthology could be called essays in a broad sense, but they could also be described variously as reportage, memoir, art installation, manifesto, rant, battle plan, lecture, musings – there are even two maps (in the back pocket of the book) reimagining the city. They are all illustrative of just how important and exciting this moment in the city's history is.

We have no illusions that *uTOpia* is a comprehensive portrait of Toronto in 2005. It is necessarily just a small cross-section of the city's inhabitants, and just a small cross-section of the things our city needs to think about. These are a few ideas. We know that there are thousands of other ideas about the city's future, and we hope that this might be, as Bert Archer urges, a way of getting the conversation started. We hope to see many more *uTOpias*, many more books and maps and CDs and conversations in print and in coffee shops.

To this end, we invite you to join in the dialogue; we've started an online discussion forum at www.chbooks.com/utopia/forum. Please add your two cents.

To quote the writer Matthew Stadler, this book is a tool for the future, which is here. You can use it. The language of the future is more beautiful than we know.

Jason McBride and Alana Wilcox

TOuchstones

Erik Rutherford
Toronto: a city in our image

Here in an Irish pub on the trendy rue Montorgueil, my friends and I have gathered to share a last drink. After seven years in Paris, I am moving back to my native Toronto. In only a few days, in a similar bar on College Street, I will be asked, sincerely or out of courtesy, why I have renounced life in Paris to come to 'dreary' Toronto. And yet for my friends here – most of them young expatriates from the U.K., Canada and the U.S. – no such explanations are needed. On the contrary, they spend my farewell evening sheepishly justifying their own reasons for staying behind and repeating the refrain: 'You are right to go.'

Like them, I feel that life will be better in Toronto, not because I have better friends or a better job there, but because the city itself will allow things to happen. Why this sentiment should be so strong, especially when set against Paris, one of the world's most envied and prestigious cities, has much to do with the very aspect of Toronto that shames many Torontonians: its physical landscape.

In Jonathan Raban's classic study of urban living, *Soft City*, he says that 'Cities, unlike villages and small towns, are plastic by nature. We mould them in our images: they, in their turn, shape us by the resistance they offer when we try to impose our own personal form on them.'

Paris strongly resists our attempts to 'impose.' As we sit in its cafés, wander its manicured gardens, or stream down its corridor streets from one monument to the next, we bend to its dictates. Arrows and signs tell us how to look. The city poses and struts, flaunting its grand perspectives and elegant architecture. We, in turn, feed its vanity, move and dress our bodies to please it, submit to its geometry.

Toronto does not require us to adopt its shape, to move as it prescribes. Its porous streets spill into back alleys and parking lots or descend into a labyrinth of underground passageways. New glass condos rub up against arterial highways and old warehouses; low-rise subdivisions and office blocks make way for advancing armies of electrical pylons; Victorian houses border drive-in doughnut shops and gas stations, lonely schoolyards, ravines, strip malls and industrial zones. It is a city in which you walk in quiet solitude, pulled into its folds and crevices, whimsically cutting your own path.

Paris is so seamlessly put together, so uniform in its edifices and furnishings, you feel you could drive in a wedge where the city comes up against the highway that encircles it and pop it out in one piece – like a jewel that has been superficially encrusted in the earth's surface. Where would you drive in the wedge in Toronto? And how deeply would the wedge have to go?

In Toronto, we work in buildings that are younger than our parents. We shop in practical, matter-of-fact constructions that have a makeshift quality about them; we can almost see the wrecking ball waiting in the wings. Everywhere there is the presence of demolition and construction, the sense that what surrounds us is not the product of careful planning, of a contract between the generations, but rather the caprice of chance and private interest. It feels, as Robert Fulford has said, *accidental*, as if what remains has simply survived – a residue of the past, and a recent past at that (in 1793, while the revolutionaries were leading their king to the guillotine in Paris, an advance party of Rangers had just begun clearing virgin forest on the shores of what was to become Fort York).

Paris is anything but accidental. What you see is what you were meant to see. It is the slow accumulation of selected symbols, an anthology of French heritage, a model of fastidious urban housekeeping. Its edifices appear to us as inviolable and timeless, not because of their beauty (though, as Zola said, 'Paris is art, all around us'), but because they are the physical embodiment of the mythology, history and values of France. Otherwise functional buildings – hospitals, law courts, police stations – are monuments and memorials in themselves, vectors of cultural identity. 'Liberté, Egalité et Fraternité' is engraved into their stone. The reason for their existence is written onto plaques that stand next to them. The city's parks, squares, bridges and subway stations bear the names of momentous events from French history – its military victories and ideological triumphs. Street signs include mini-curricula vitae of the *grands hommes* they are named after – year of birth, year of death, profession and achievements.

Little has changed since Baron Haussmann, the infamous city planner working under Napoleon III, completed his massive reconstruction of Paris in the middle of the nineteenth century (with notable exceptions – the Centre Pompidou or Mitterrand's Grands Travaux). Impracticable buildings that cannot be rescued are torn down reluctantly, but their facades are preserved, held up by wooden scaffolding until a new construction is built up behind them. Throughout Paris, these facades (paper-thin against the sky) stand forlorn, reminding us of the Wild West towns of a Hollywood movie set. Meanwhile, monuments like Notre Dame Cathedral and Tour St. Jacques are sandblasted and refurbished. They emerge looking unfamiliar, artificial, like restored paintings – clearer, more distinct, and yet the lines of experience gone from them along with much of their character. Little by little, Paris is becoming a pastiche of itself, an airbrushed city of reconditioned stone. How could it be any different? Each new generation of city administrators and architects labours under the restraints of historical and aesthetic continuity. Theirs is, in many ways, the work of curators: taking inventory, maintenance, merchandising, applying the finishing touches – new street fixtures, improved signs, better access.

Torontonians live in a city where the beginning is forgotten and the end is unknown, and so whatever happens can only surprise and surpass. Tremendous historic events do not resonate in its cement, glass and brick. The city was not built upon sturdy founding mythologies, and only historians and enthusiasts know the names on its street signs, who designed the CN Tower, what the Aboriginal word 'Toronto' means, or what any of the mysterious little Discovery Walk signs that dot the city might refer to. Distinctive monuments are few and far between, as attested to by the souvenir shops (how would you pick Toronto out of a crowd without the CN Tower?). And Lake Ontario, the city's most important feature, is a strangely discreet presence, making only fleeting appearances, peeking up now and then from beyond the streaming expressway. The result is an undemonstrative, secretive city, unsure of how to represent itself, with no identifiable brand of metropolitanism. No wonder it is 'accommodating' to novelty and newcomers, to renovation and ugliness, to bold idiosyncracy. In Paris, 'beginnings' are so manifest that what happens bears out only what is meant to happen. Its values are well defined, and so its buildings – even the new ones – are the means to an end that is already known. Thus the overwhelming sense that life is happening elsewhere. As Marx puts it, 'The tradition of all the dead generations weighs like a nightmare on the brain of the living.' How heavy the weight of iconic, self-regarding Paris.

The pub is now dense with cigarette smoke. Trevor, a Dubliner with a fledgling career as a literary translator, stares into his empty pint glass and sighs. 'I was going to leave this year, I really was.' He has been saying this ever since I met him five years ago.

'No need to explain,' I say.

'You're a passenger in this city. You don't have to make an effort. And it's not as if you feel like you belong, but in time you just feel it's harder to belong anywhere else. You lose your will to advance and accumulate.'

Keith jumps in: 'You'll never go,' he says. Keith is a journalist who left London in the early nineties to be with his French girlfriend. Together, they now have two boys and live in a chic neighbourhood near the Parc Monceau. 'You've coasted for too long, Trevor. You're here to stay.'

'I'm just waiting for the cash,' Trevor says.

'You're waiting for the courage.'

This nagging feeling that living in Paris is somehow a failure to engage with life, a kind of cowardly evasion, has much to do with being an expatriate. But there is also the effect of the city itself. Whether tall buildings break open the sky as they do in Toronto or cut the sky into ribbons as they do in Paris; whether we have space or feel someone at our back as we walk down the sidewalk; whether cars circulate haltingly or flowingly; whether we feel scrutinized or ignored; whether there are places to congregate; whether in parks we can sit on the grass; whether it is noisy or polluted; whether there are horizons – all these things inform what we believe to be worthwhile, or possible, or necessary, both as citizens and individuals. Paris seems to inhibit the natural process of making the city one's own, that process in which shops and street corners become mnemonic for the people we know and the experiences we live. The walls of the great city have no need of our yearnings and judgments. They are already blackened with stories, like carbon applied to paper an infinite number of times.

We are all latecomers, and as latecomers we let the city assign a role to us, write a story on our behalf. If we allow it to, Paris *completes* us, making up for what we lack as individuals by turning us into citizens – public property. It requires only that we perform our civic duty. And so the brain of the living, straining to express itself, grows weary or complacent.

As urban people, we yearn for crowds, but our stronger instinct is to be free of the crowd, to be alone in our own secret places in order to experience our uniqueness. In Toronto, our solitude is dense. Whereas in Paris a tree is decoration, symbol or artifact ('Under this tree, Victor Hugo used to write...'), in Toronto a tree might just be a tree – barely noticed, forgotten in the corner of someone's yard, home to a family of birds. Toronto's houses bind you to the instant; they do not draw you away along a chain of aesthetic and historical associations. We are in the domain of the intimate and the appropriated rather than the public and the designated. Wooden telephone poles punctured by thousands of staples – the trace of countless homemade messages – are totems in a city that has not institutionalized every human interchange. These same telephone poles hold aloft a tangle of wires that form a patterned ceiling above the street, itself cluttered with mismatched street furniture. Everything tells us that Toronto is a bricolage of atomized privacies, that we have few obligations to it and, equally, little guidance from it. Jan Morris called Toronto a city 'conducive to self-doubt and introspection.' Toronto is also conducive to self-realization, brimming with opportunities to mould its malleable stuff in our own image.

When we move to a new city, the sediment of the soul is stirred up as new waters flood in. These new waters slowly evaporate, leaving behind that same sediment, dried into the patterns of the city we have lived in. In Paris, the sediment maps Haussman's streets. In Toronto, it maps not merely the city but also some part of our elsewhere selves.

Pierre the bartender has been listening in. He decides to defend his city. 'I don't understand you people. Paris is the most beautiful and brilliant city in the world. Do you condemn a woman for being too brilliant and too beautiful?'

Trevor, with a hint of drunken slur, offers an answer: 'She *was* brilliant and beautiful. Now she's well past her finest hour, but because she thinks she's still got it, she bores you with stories of how she used to be the life of the party. She shows you her photo albums, all scrupulously indexed and labelled. And when you offer to take her memoirs home for a read, she forces them into your hand and makes you read aloud.'

'Okay, then,' says Pierre, slapping his towel on the countertop. 'What is Toronto? *Une jolie jeune fille?*'

Everyone turns to me. I have never considered the question, but the conversation has conjured an image: 'Well, I suppose Toronto is a young man, just out of university. He's done a degree in commerce with a minor in the humanities, where he shows surprising talent. He's always been an A student and done what is expected of him. When you praise him, he doesn't believe you; when you criticize him, his pride is wounded. He's still a little inexperienced, poorly dressed, a touch diffident, but full of youthful energy and ambition. And though he doesn't yet know the best way to achieve glory, he makes you feel he will.'

And so I return to rekindle my friendship with him.

Edward Keenan
Making a scene:
a bunch of youngish indie rockers, political activists and small-press literati are creating the cultural history of Toronto

It was pouring rain in Toronto the night of November 3, 2003. Still, several hundred people queued up for more than an hour along Queen Street West, some huddled under umbrellas, others sopping wet, stretching in a line from the doors of the Gladstone Hotel east to Beaconsfield and around the corner. There was an un-Parkdalian giddiness in the attitude of the crowd, an expectant optimism that had been spreading throughout the city for the previous few weeks as left-ish reformer David Miller – once considered an unthinkable long shot – had emerged as the leader in the dwindling fall mayoral election campaign. One grey lady from the Annex, wearing a yellow rain slicker, surveying the architectural glasses and purposefully unkempt hair of the predominantly twentysomething crowd, asked, 'What the heck is Trampoline Hall? I've never seen a crowd like this for an election speech before.' It's unclear whether she was referring to the assembly's size or its fashion sense, but she could easily have meant either, or both. She'd likely never been turned away at the doors of a political speech before, either, but that's what happened around eight o'clock, as word trickled down the disappointed line that the Gladstone Ballroom had reached capacity and no one else would be allowed in.[1]

Indoors, 150 or so people witnessed a most unusual campaign event. One

1 Citing a journalistic obligation as a reporter for urban news and entertainment thingy *Eye Weekly*, I managed to sneak in. A surprising number of others also refused to take 'go home' for an answer, with less success – several dozen shivered in the rain, while a gradually shrinking crowd stood, like candidates for a Zen monastery, outside the closed and locked doors of the event, expecting their patience to be eventually rewarded. As far as I know, it was not.

week to the day before the election,[2] David Miller had taken three and a half hours out of his schedule to share the stage with an assortment of writers, thinkers and artists (including playwright Deanne Taylor, novelist Nino Ricci and urban-planning guru Jane Jacobs[3]) to discuss a topic assigned to him by Trampoline Hall lecture series curator Sheila Heti: 'Beauty and the Aesthetic City.' The event was billed – misleadingly, since Millermania had very clearly taken hold of the crowd – 'Trampoline Hall vs. David Miller.'

But what left an impression on me most is not anything the candidate said[4] but a point Nino Ricci made early on as part of a panel discussion. I forget the question, but it concerned what he liked about Toronto. As a child of immigrant parents, Ricci explained, he'd grown up feeling like an Italian – an outsider – in Canada. But when he went 'home' to Florence to study, he was, of course, an outsider there too, not a real Italian. Furthermore, he found there was a very rigid definition of what it meant to be Italian – and of what it meant to be Sicilian or Roman or Florentine. Thousands of years of history had gone into creating the Italian identity, its customs and architecture and art and literature, its cuisine and politics. 'The mythology of Florence had already been written,' he said.[5] It was an atmosphere he found smothering. Nothing one could do could have the smallest hope of contributing to or evolving the cultural life of the city or the country.

2 On election night, Miller would hold a broom over his head in the now-famous celebration of his victory, earning himself the nickname 'Broom-Broom.'

3 She held one of those big horn-type hearing devices you see in cartoons next to her ear to field questions from the audience.

4 Though he did impress me, as was evident from the cover-story back rub I filed for *Eye Weekly* the next day. It's called 'What a Mayor Can Be: David Miller Thinks More, Calculates Less,' and ran on November 6, 2003. It's online, in the unlikely event that you're interested in looking it up.

5 Or so I remember. Here and following, I am paraphrasing from memory, as my notes of the night's events are distressingly Miller-centric.

Toronto, by contrast, is a young city in a young country, famously grappling with its identity. It is populated largely by a diverse collection of first- and second- and third-generation immigrants from other cities and provinces and countries. This is what Ricci found exciting about this city. 'Toronto,' he said, 'is still deciding what it will be. We're still finding out what it means to be Torontonian. Our mythology has yet to be written.'

It was hard, that night, not to agree. For in a sort of corny but real way, it felt like those of us in that room were in the middle of writing a chapter in the mythology of Toronto: in the half-renovated, half-gutted charm of Toronto's oldest continuously operating hotel, with those who couldn't fit inside congregated outside the windows in the rain, the crowd inside was enraptured by an hours-long discussion of civic identity and city planning and (briefly, as it was a topic supposedly off limits) electoral politics. A group of normally alienated independent artists suddenly realized that a candidate they had something in common with, a politico they could actually root for, was about to be elected. Long-time fans of the Trampoline Hall lecture series – described that week by *NOW* magazine as 'oddball popcult'[6] – all at once awkwardly found themselves important enough to occupy valuable final campaign hours and to dictate terms to the man who would be mayor of the city. Later in the evening, a woman in the back of the room stood up and cried as she explained that she'd hated Toronto since moving here from Montreal, but finally, tonight, she suddenly got it and was in love with the city and wanted to thank everyone for sharing it with her. It was that kind of night. We, in that room, were shaping the future history of Toronto. At least a little bit, we were writing our own mythology.[7]

There's been a lot of that going around lately – the feeling that this is an important moment in Toronto's history, that we're in the midst of shaping what the city will become, of defining what Toronto will come to mean. That ever more widespread perception is, I can only assume, the reason someone would decide to put

6 *NOW*, listings, Oct. 30, 2003.

7 Some of us (ahem) maybe more literally than others.

together a book devoted to considering the city's present and future. The intersection with Miller – and the traditional institutional structure of city building he represents, by virtue of his being in electoral politics – was significant but atypical. The feeling I'm describing occurs more often at smaller events that are still, if ever less so, on the fringes of mainstream city life. It exists most noticeably in three growing and increasingly overlapping scenes, which can be loosely grouped together as literary, musical and political. In the Trampoline Hall lecture series, the city's independent literary crowd has found a gathering place and a governing aesthetic. The Wavelength music series (and the on-again, off-again magazine that accompanies it) has become more than a weekly live-music event, more, even, than a home base for a community of music fans; it's barely an overstatement to say that Wavelength is the Toronto indie-rock scene. Meanwhile, the Toronto Public Space Committee and its affiliated magazine, *Spacing*, have served as an umbrella for a legion of political activists who express their love for the city in any number of unconventional ways and have, in the process, accomplished the near impossible task of making politics seem cool.[8]

These three broadly defined circles have grown over the past four or five years, both in size and in influence, and have recently been overlapping and cross-pollinating in varied and interesting ways.[9] They appear sometimes to be coalescing around shared interests and aesthetics in a way that multiplies the excitement attached to each. I'd hesitate to call what they're collectively becoming a 'movement,' but it certainly is, as Misha Glouberman told me in conversation, a moment: 'Cultural history is happening.'[10]

8 This may be as good a place as any to acknowledge the awkward fact that people closely involved with all these events and organizations I'm writing about have also contributed essays to this anthology – Jonathan Bunce (or Jonny Dovercourt, as he's known in indie-music circles) of Wavelength, Sheila Heti and Misha Glouberman of Trampoline Hall, Dave 'Mez' Meslin of the TPSC. This may appear incestuous, and maybe it is, but I'm afraid it's impossible to write about this moment in Toronto without focusing on these people. It's also impossible to put together an anthology about this moment in Toronto without including submissions from these people. So here we are. Deal with it.

9 I should maybe also point out that I have some sort of personal connection to many of these people. I work as a writer and editor for a magazine that covers their work, and I travel in social circles that overlap with theirs. I can't help it. For your conflict-of-interest tracking pleasure, I'll try to document any relationships as I go. So far: I voted for David Miller; I have once been the editor of an article Sheila Heti wrote for *Eye Weekly* and have attended parties in the former home of her husband, Carl Wilson; Misha Glouberman also wrote something for me at *Eye* and came recently to my birthday party; Jonathan Bunce plays in a band with Kate McGee, who is a something-removed cousin of mine (though I did not meet her until a few years ago); and I have written three times for *Spacing* magazine (once they paid me about ten cents a word).

10 This conversation took place in Kensington Market, while I was taking notes for this essay. He later told me that he'd decided he hated being quoted. Oh well.

Wavelength came first. As *Eye Weekly* Senior Editor Stuart Berman[11] wrote on the occasion of Wavelength's fifth anniversary:

11 One of several authorities on indie music in Toronto – also, inconveniently, my direct supervisor at work.

> Before the weekly Sunday-night indie revelry made its modest debut on Feb. 13, 2000, ... [T]he community was a disconnected cabal of locally recognized but internationally neglected warriors ... each fighting their own wars, trying to crash through a glass ceiling clouded by a fog of apathy that historically confined bands to within city limits.
>
> What Wavelength founders Jonathan Bunce, Duncan MacDonnell and Derek Westerholm realized was that, in order to smash that ceiling, you needed a united push from all corners of the underground: the indie rockers, the punks, the jazzbos, the tech-heads. Wavelength's agenda was as universal as an ABC after-school special: be proud of what you've got. Don't worry about being cool. Don't resist the unknown; learn from it. And please, don't be afraid to dance.
>
> ... Before Wavelength, Toronto simply lived; after Wavelength, we loved, proving hippie hearts and Converse soles are not incompatible.[12]

12 'On any given Sunday,' *Eye Weekly*, Feb. 10, 2005.

As Jonathan 'Jonny Dovercourt' Bunce remembers it, that's exactly what he and the other founders of Wavelength set out to do when they created the series. Sitting on the patio of the 360 on Queen just east of Spadina[13] in the spring of 2005, Bunce says that in 2000, while he was working a day job as listings editor of *Eye Weekly*, with hopes of becoming a rock star, the Toronto music scene was 'splintered into little cliques and enclaves.' After more than a decade of playing gigs in Toronto in various bands, he and his friends were finding it hard to create any kind of buzz. There wasn't much of a sense of a musical community – there was no central record label, magazine or venue to bring the indie crowd together. Everyone was just doing their own thing in hopes of moving on to New York or Los Angeles, where they might get some attention. 'We wanted to see something happening in Toronto,' says Bunce. 'There was a lot of good music, but there was no one around to celebrate it and raise it up.'

13 One of Toronto's great dives and best music venues until it was shut down by the Ontario Command of the Royal Canadian Legion – the regulatory body that oversees the Canadian Legion Ukrainian Branch, which owned the club – on June 7, 2005, just a few weeks after my chat with Bunce. That it was operating mainly as a music venue instead of a legion hall was the main reason for the RCL's decision.

On September 11, 1999, he and his then bandmate Alex Durlak[14] called a 'heads of state meeting' at the Green Room, a pleasantly shabby back-alley coffee house and bar in the Annex. There, Bunce, Durlack and various friends from bands around Toronto – Duncan MacDonnell of Folk Festival Massacre, Greg Chambers of Mean Red Spiders, Derek Westerholm of Parts Unknown and Paul Boddum of Neck, among others – discussed their frustration with the Toronto scene and came up with a three-pronged plan to address it: they'd start a music zine, a website and a weekly concert series to give themselves and the bands they liked a platform. Wavelength, which encompassed all three, was born.

14 Their band, for the record, was called Kid Sniper.

The debuts of the weekly music series at Ted's Wrecking Yard on College Street[15] – featuring Mean Red Spiders and Neck – and its accompanying photocopied and hand-stapled zine came together in February 2000. Fifty people attended the first show, and Bunce doesn't remember having the sense that they'd created something monumental in the early months. Still, the editors' letter in the inaugural issue of the zine laid out their ambitions fairly clearly:

15 Like the 360, another seminal music venue now shuttered and, in this case, half-demolished to make room for a boutique hotel that went broke midway through construction.

> Wavelength is a loose collective of friends and fellow musicians who got together last fall to figure out how to boost our own scene. This is what we came up with – we hope you dig it. We all feel that Toronto is on the cusp of something, something exciting and potentially big. The music being made here – in all genres – is unparalleled on an international scale. We want to let people here, and in the rest of the world, know about it. And we want everyone to come out, get loose and have some fun.

A couple of gigs now remembered as seminal moments in the creation of today's thriving and increasingly internationally recognized scene followed, among them the December 17, 2000, first-ever gig by what was then billed as John Tesh Jr. and the Broken Social Scene and the February 4, 2001, Toronto coming out of Guelph band the Constantines. But it was a week after the Cons shook the foundations of Ted's, at Wavelength's first anniversary show, that Bunce first really got the sense that he was at the centre of something big. 'For the first six months or more, it was really just us and our friends... At the first anniversary show, we had bands on both floors over three nights,[16] and there were a whole bunch of new faces – faces of people we didn't know. It was really dawning that people felt we'd created a welcoming space for everybody.'

Since then, the series has moved from Ted's to the cavernous Lee's Palace and then on to its current home at Sneaky Dee's, and has played a pivotal role in the success of many of Ontario's now celebrated rockers – Broken Social Scene (and the solo and side projects of that ungainly group's various members: Jason Collett, Gentleman Reg, Leslie Feist, Do Make Say Think, Metric, Raising the Fawn ...), the Hidden Cameras, the Constantines, FemBots, the Deadly Snakes, Controller.Controller, Cuff the Duke, Royal City and Bunce's own new band – maybe his most successful yet – Republic of Safety. But more than just providing a venue and a launching pad, Wavelength has become the centre of a community that comes out week after week to see bands known and unknown, gathers to electronically chat on the message boards at Stillepost.ca and otherwise parties and plays together.[17] And, slowly, this scene has moved from the fringes of Toronto's – and Canada's – musical consciousness towards the mainstream.

At roughly the same time as a bunch of local indie musicians were planning a revolution in the musical scene, Dave Meslin was experiencing a revolution in his consciousness. In his early twenties, Mez, as his friends call him, had become a successful entrepreneur, running a T-shirt-printing factory in an industrial building in Leaside that doubled as a clubhouse for him and his pals. But by 1997, he'd become interested in, and troubled by, the politics of cotton. The fibres that made up the shirts that made up his products were often produced in horrible conditions in developing economies and then manufactured in sweatshops before arriving in his hands.

Getting out of the T-shirt business, he spent a few years becoming increasingly immersed in the world

16 Among them the Beethoven Frieze, Christiana, the Co-operators, the Connoisseurs, the Dinner Is Ruined, Fembots, GUH, It's Patrick, Kid Sniper, Mellonova, Mean Red Spiders, More Plastic, Picastro, Rhume, Someone Is Flying and Zebradonk.

17 The May 2005 wedding of Katarina Gligorijevic of Barcelona Pavilion and Republic of Safety to Matt Collins of Ninja High School was one of the scene's social events of the year. Music columnist, Trampoline Hall doorman and blogger Carl Wilson described the reception on his blog Zoilus.com as follows: 'We did go to the most indie-rock wedding reception ever, last night at Sneaky Dee's, featuring a welcoming barrage of silly string for the newlyweds, then Steve Kado and Greg Collins (of Ninja High School, Blocks Recording Club and dozens of other local bands between them) as MANSHIT playing Elvis and Bruce Springsteen covers for slow-dance shout-alongs to start the night, and then the electro-make-out music of Kids on TV and a whole helluva lot of fog machine, climaxing with a mass half-naked, half-drunk audience-on-stage dance frenzy (followed by more dancing courtesy of DJ Jonny Dovercourt). Plus indoors smoking, and cake.'

of culture jamming. Under the banner of the Toronto Public Space Committee, Mez founded an e-mail newsletter in the spirit of the Reclaim the Streets movement, which was then picking up steam. A set of events in cities around the world, Reclaim the Streets was a vaguely defined group of anarchists, socialists and others who opposed globalization, pollution and automobiles and held events intended to clog streets with pedestrian protesters costumed and dancing in a celebration of disrupting traffic.

This awakened sense of the politics of global trade led Mez and his friend Matthew Blackett – then a *Hockey News* graphic designer and zinester cartoonist[18] – to travel to Quebec City for the demonstrations against the Summit of the Americas conference on free trade in April 2001.

As Blackett remembers it, the two came back with a sense of determination fuelled by the remembered smell of tear gas. 'It started with the anti-globalization movement, but we really took the phrase 'Think globally, act locally' seriously. We wanted to be part of the movement here at home, affecting our home – helping shape Toronto into something better.'

Soon, the outline of a new kind of political movement took shape: the TPSC brought together whole groups of until then disparate activists – environmentalists, cyclists, indie rockers who depend on postering, graffiti artists, anti-consumerists – under a galvanizing central concern: public-space issues. The TPSC has approached its campaigns with a certain rock'n'roll playfulness, from Guerrilla Gardening campaigns, in which members plant flowers on roadsides and patches of dirt, to the Toronto De-fence project, in which the TPSC will provide free labour to remove chain-link fences from private property at the owner's request. At the core of their work has been an apparent paradox: rigid opposition to the growing use of public spaces and sightlines for commercial advertising, such as transit posters, billboards and garbage cans featuring corporate messages on the side; and an equally steadfast defence of small-scale postering on utility poles

18 His strip is called M@B (pronounced 'Matt Bee'), and the title doubles as a nickname, by which Blackett is widely known. And, of course, in the interests of transparency, please note that M@B is published in *Eye Weekly*, Matt is my editor at *Spacing* magazine, and I consider him something of a friend.

of the sort used to promote local bands and lawn sales or to plead for help in finding a missing pet.

It was in the service of the latter concern that the TPSC really came into broad public view when, in 2002, it successfully galvanized various activists and the local music community to fend off a proposed bylaw that would have outlawed postering on public utility poles.

In December 2003, the TPSC took another step in what Blackett calls its 'maturation' when it launched the first issue of *Spacing* magazine. Devoted to chronicling, pondering and proselytizing on issues of public space – in Toronto in particular – and how people interact with it, the magazine was perhaps surprisingly successful from the start. Running calls for action on issues such as billboard advertising in Dundas Square and the threat to free speech posed by anti-postering bylaws next to meditations on getting lost in the city and making eye contact, and finding rich photography from the growing community of photo-bloggers, the magazine found a ready audience among urban planners[19] and politicians, among activists around the city and in an arts community that's recently begun looking less frequently to New York for success and instead taking pride in its hometown.

By 2005, the TPSC and *Spacing*[20] have become major players in Toronto politics – Meslin, Blackett and *Spacing* editor Shawn Micallef are ubiquitous interview subjects whenever advertising and public-space issues arise in the media, and leftist politicians such as Joe Mihevc and even the mayor often seem in a rush to align themselves with the group.[21] From its origins as an e-mail newsletter, the TPSC has become an influential player at city hall and a leader of public debate on how the city should be shaped in the years to come.

One of the earliest high-profile contributors to *Spacing* was Sheila Heti, who had by that point spent a couple years making her own contribution to the city's growing cultural renaissance. In 2000, the then twenty-four-year-old University of Toronto undergraduate exploded into the Canadian literary consciousness when *McSweeney's*[22] published six of her stories as a chapbook and *Toronto Life*

19 I found this out first-hand at a recent *Spacing* fundraiser thrown by ERA Architects, where I witnessed a series of planners and architects in very expensive glasses behave like teenybopper groupies in the presence of the magazine's editors.

20 They are now separate but affiliated entities, the TPSC driven by Meslin as a sort of loudmouth activist and lobbying organization, *Spacing* run as an interested but less agenda-driven forum for discussion and meditation.

21 Such as when the mayor wore a *Spacing*-produced lapel button bearing the name of a local subway station into council chambers when he threw his support behind a TPSC-backed push to kill a revised postering bylaw in May 2005.

22 Dave Eggers's then Brooklyn-based literary journal phenomenon, which was successful in the realm of literary journals to an unheard-of extent; magazines such as *US* and *People* were noticing it, and its founder was propelled to appearing-on-Rosie-O'Donnell's-talk-show-level stardom.

published another of her stories in its summer fiction issue. A book deal with House of Anansi followed and, with the ecstatic reviews that accompanied the release of her short story collection, *The Middle Stories,* in April 2001, a bona fide literary celebrity was born.[23]

On the heels of her successful book, she created the Trampoline Hall lecture series in December 2001, a monthly gathering (originally) at the Cameron House at which three lecturers would discuss subjects about which they are not professionally expert. Question-and-answer sessions would follow, moderated by host Misha Glouberman. Every show featured a set designed by Leah Walker. And the man who would become Heti's husband, Carl Wilson, collected the cover charge at the door.

The range of topics was quizzically diverse. Matthew MacFadzean lectured on the number 32 in January 2002, Ruby King lectured on temping in September 2002, Kate Rae spoke about dry humping in February 2003 and, in May 2004, James O'Reilly discussed his hometown of Uranium, Saskatchewan. Sometimes lectures were well researched and professionally presented; sometimes they were entirely made up or a confusion of mumbles. Along the way, special events were thrown in: the 'What Is Beauty?' pageant in May 2002, the night devoted entirely to lectures on Heti's friend Patrick Roscoe in August 2002, and the 2003 Trampoline Hall vs. David Miller political event mentioned earlier.

The mixture of elements was a tremendous success out of the gate; every Trampoline Hall in Toronto[24] except one (held at Club Rockit on Church Street during the 'venue tour' of 2004) has been sold out, often with queues of disappointed hopefuls stretching out into the street.

This was, Glouberman told me in Kensington Market in May 2005, the plan: 'It was clear from the inception that the project was bigger than a party; we were creating a scene, and we were very aware of that.'

There were a few things that set Trampoline Hall apart from the run-of-the-mill reading series it might have resembled: the quirky subject matter, for one, and the interesting interaction between Heti's selections of

23 Do you doubt this? Consider that in 2004, when she had only the one book under her belt, the Canadian Magazine Publishers Association took out ads that read: 'Atwood. Coupland. Davies. Heti. Ondaatje. Quarrington. We have our own library, we have our own magazines.'

24 After a successful tour of the U.S. in late 2002, a New York edition, also hosted by Glouberman, was started and continues to run today.

lecturers with their chosen topics and Glouberman's mastery of the ceremonies, for another. But the most remarkable thing about Trampoline Hall is the interaction between the audience and lecturer – the question-and-answer sessions that follow lectures are routinely the most interesting part of the evening. Often a crowd is charitably supportive of an unsure lecturer, and nearly as often they'll antagonize and get outright belligerent. In either case, the lectures seem more an excuse for the audience to interact than anything else: certainly no one I've ever talked to has attended the lectures for their informational value.

Again, Glouberman says, that's happened by design. Trampoline Hall is about getting a group of people together and interacting with them – the audience is a part of the show, not merely witness to it. 'Trampoline Hall is about the city,' he says.

And though he says he was slightly disappointed with the result, that connection between Toronto broadly and Trampoline Hall was never clearer than the night the mayor lectured.

These three elements of Toronto's current cultural/political landscape share some broad traits: a passion for quirkiness, for a start, and a small-is-beautiful, DIY aesthetic (aside from the TPSC's hate-on for corporate advertising and love of indie postering and *Spacing*'s advocacy on behalf of the beauty of laneways and overlooked areas of beauty in the city, witness that both Trampoline Hall and Wavelength rejected larger venues after experimenting with them[25] because they felt intimacy was essential to their events).

They also share an aversion to commercialism that borders on the fanatical. In the case of the TPSC, with its *No Logo*, anti-corporatist roots, this is explicit. But Trampoline Hall has always operated with a money-losing cover charge of $5,[26] and not only is there no merch table, but lecturers are forbidden to sell their latest book or album – or even plug it – from the stage. Wavelength, for its part, has always been Pay What You Can.

25 And both, curiously, now find a home in the upstairs of Sneaky Dee's.

26 Except twice when they had to rent chairs at Club Rockit, when it was $6.

Up until this point, I may have implied that Wavelength, Trampoline Hall and the TPSC exist as solitary signposts. Far from it. They are merely the most visible and representative of tens and possibly hundreds of projects taking place within these three increasingly overlapping communities. Alongside Wavelength, there are a few influential record labels – Arts and Crafts, Paper Bag, Three Gut[27] – driving the Toronto indie-rock scene, and many music/dance/performance-art event series in roughly the Wavelength mould: the annual Fake Prom; Vazaleen, Will Munroe's celebration of Alt-queer culture[28]; Jason Collett's Radio Mondays songwriters' night at Supermarket in Kensington; Tyler Clark Burke's[29] Santa Cruz, a night of live music, slow dancing and fun art projects like the 'video make-out booth.' Trampoline Hall seems to be of a piece with Emily Schultz and Brian Joseph Davis's[30] Pocket Canon series of anonymously authored chapbooks, Paola Poletto and Emily Pohl-Weary's *Kiss Machine* literary magazine, the live 'magazine' run by Damian Rogers[31] called Pontiac Quarterly, and Glouberman's own Room 101 game nights, at which people play games like Scrabble and charades. And, finally, the TPSC soldiers alongside people like the City Beautification Ensemble, who paint such things as concrete curbs and metal bike posts in bright colours; the [murmur] project, which records neighbourhood history for people to access by calling phone numbers posted on signs; the urban-exploration movement[32]; the Pedestrian Sundays in Kensington crew; and the New Mindspace collective, which has organized games of Capture the Flag in city streets and parties on subway cars.

Sometimes the events are hard to categorize. Take Manhunt, a weekly game organized by Ninja High School singer Matt Collins. It's a game of tag played in public places – such as the financial district – every Thursday night. Most of the players are indie rockers who know each other from the Stillepost message board, but increasingly it's attracting people from various other areas. It's interesting to psychogeographers like the *Spacing* crew because it repurposes commercial space for recreational

27 Which, sadly, folded up shop in summer 2005.

28 Which predated Wavelength by a few months. I don't mean to suggest that any of these are copycats, just that they share the same sensibility and excitement – and serve the same community – I've been discussing.

29 I have worked with Tyler at *Eye Weekly*, where she's done design work.

30 Both have written for me at *Eye*, Emily once published a short story of mine in a magazine she edited (for which I was not paid) and I consider both friends.

31 Damian is the arts editor of *Eye Weekly* and is a close friend of mine. I've also read at every installment of Pontiac Quarterly.

32 Led by the recently deceased Ninjalicious of www.infiltration.org.

use – who says the PATH system is okay to work and shop in but not to play in? And, of course, it's lots of fun.

This points to another element of what's happening in Toronto right now. Not only is the scene larger than I have portrayed it, it's also less distinctly defined, and increasingly less so. Like the Catholic Trinity or a shamrock, there are three parts, certainly, but they form one whole. Many Wavelength performers have lectured at Trampoline Hall, for example, and indie-rock bands routinely play TPSC and *Spacing* fundraisers. In fact, Maggie MacDonald of the Hidden Cameras and Republic of Safety shared a house until very recently with Matt Blackett and Dave Meslin. Blackett has written for the Wavelength zine, and Sheila Heti was among the earliest contributors to *Spacing*. And on and on.

This is a community that's marked, above almost all else, by an irreverence that is notably lacking in cynicism. In fact, these groups I've been writing about are defined by an almost naive positivity about all of their events and undertakings, a desire to celebrate the communities they serve and the city at large.[33] It's one of the things that leads those in attendance at a concert or lecture, or those flipping through a copy of *Spacing* magazine, to begin to have the feeling I had at Trampoline Hall when Nino Ricci was speaking: the feeling that we are participating in something larger and more exciting than simply a cultural event, that we're actually a part of cultural history, of a mythology in the making. Because, very consciously, all of these things are meant to be something more than what they are on the surface. A concert. A night of lectures. A political protest. A magazine. In every case, the sense of community is primary and the performers or writers are almost secondary. And the community feels a tremendous sense of ownership. When Jonathan Bunce talked to a young Wavelengther about the possibility that it was time to retire the series, she told him he should just hand it over to another generation. The institution (his word; she compared it to a church) he and his friends had created in five years had become vastly important to hundreds of others in the city.

33 This is sometimes very explicit, such as in the case of the CD *Toronto Is Great!!!*, put out by Steve Kado's Blocks Recording Club and recorded in part at Wavelength, and Kado's Torontopia shows. Also notice the title of this book, and its contents.

It will be interesting to see, in the coming years, as the participants of this thriving arts and cultural circle mature into ever more prominent and influential demographics, how the Toronto of the future will look when people like Heti, Bunce, Meslin and their friends and followers – now almost all in their twenties and early thirties – move into a position to run things. In a way, with the election of Miller, the Torontopia movement already has one of its own in office. It's hard to predict how a Toronto built on the principles I've been describing will look – it will be, perhaps, a city in which the small, often overlooked details are celebrated, in which corporate wealth is suspect and a bizarrely irreverent playfulness is the prevailing ethos.

Perhaps, as Misha Gouberman told me, it's better not to play the dangerous utopian game of looking at how we can transform Toronto in the current scene's image; there's really no need to sit down and try to map out a strategy for a movement. The question of what this generation of Torontonians will do is already being answered. At concerts and in magazines and through political actions, tomorrow's history is being written right now by people who, for once, are not glancing south to New York or San Francisco or across the Atlantic to the Old World to gauge how we measure up against what a former mayor of ours always considered real world-class cities. This chapter of our mythology will feature a crowd of people who think there is no better place in the world to live than Toronto, people who are making Toronto a better and better place to live all the time.

Shawn Micallef
Psssst. Modern Toronto just wants some respect.

Queen Victoria and her son King Edward still rule Toronto – the city's older neighbourhoods are full of houses built in the style of their respective reigns. It's a comfortable style, and a lot of us live on those streets and in those houses. But an outsider, or even a Torontonian, might be surprised to find out that Toronto contains a lot of buildings built in the modernist era. Some of them are grand and stand out, like the TD Centre, while others are quiet and go unnoticed, maybe tucked away in a cul-de-sac in Don Mills or North York. Even as we make a lot of noise about gingerbread and white picket fences, Toronto is still a relatively new city, and these modern buildings are just as much a part of our civic and geographic ontology as those neighbourhoods we revere because they're a little bit older.

The mixed bag of architectural styles and the surprises we encounter as we walk through Toronto makes this city unlike any other. Toronto was once described to me as a cyber-punk city because of the way its glass sky-scrapers blend in with those Victorian and Edwardian buildings. It's new and old co-existing, a city built with *Blade Runner*'s production values, minus much of the filth, squalor and darkness. Instead, Toronto is filled with trees, parks and ravines. And while Toronto may not be a leader in historic preservation, the modern city hasn't completely obliterated the past yet. The old stuff is still around and in use, so the cyber-punk anal-ogy makes sense to me. This was the Toronto I saw on my all-too-brief visits to the city when I was a kid. In particular, I would notice the way bits of modernism stuck out from the older fabric of Toronto. Few things are as beautiful as seeing an Uno Prii apartment building, with curving concrete soaring to the sky, rise above the Annex. Better yet, the proximity of some of these urban, big-city buildings to some of Toronto's wild and natural ravines makes our city of contradictions all the more striking. If

Toronto is a 'City Within a Park,' then these buildings are Le Corbusier's 'Tower in a Park' ideal writ large – and more exciting and populated than he may have envisioned. We've only just begun to celebrate these places, perhaps because we're not done venerating the pre-war era yet. Because we've focused on the old, we've let some of our truly optimistic places, in the modernist sense, slide into disrepair, neglect and, most shamefully, disrespect.

Toronto's modern 'revolution' sort of snuck upon us. Canada came of age in Montreal with Jean Drapeau, Expo 67 and Trudeaumania. Montreal was our most important city, so that's where the big stuff happened, while Toronto was still a dirty provincial town. But while the nation was focused on Montreal, Toronto built itself up with little fanfare – bits and pieces here and there, scattered throughout the city like little modern utopias.

Certainly the biggest concentration of our optimistic modernism is found at the CNE and Ontario Place. Here our past and present are most at odds. As our values change like fashion, the modernism we built in the 1950s and 1960s is not being accorded the same respect as some older parts of our city. Ontario Place was our answer to Expo 67, but without the cultural importance. I've visited Ontario Place only once in the past sixteen years – and yet I've walked through the empty Expo 67 site numerous times, looking for relics. The white pods suspended over Lake Ontario are certainly the most striking part of the place, yet I'm not sure what they were used for, then or now. Toronto's Ministry of Hopefulness should be housed in them because they look as if they're waiting for just such a noble purpose.

My parents went there when it opened in 1971. The album that held pictures of that vacation was one of my favourites. I thought all of Toronto must be like this: young, happy, clean, modern and undivorced. In the pictures, the people working there seemed to be very Ontario-proud, decked out in lime-green miniskirts with trilliums on them. A choir sang outside the Cinesphere. I don't think they do that anymore – singing probably isn't in Ontario's present-day budget or sensibility.

Though it's supposed to be happy, Ontario Place is a sad place. The sense of idealism has evaporated as the site is allowed to either fall into disrepair or be used in ways at odds with the original design. The Forum has been replaced by the Molson Amphitheatre, a generic outdoor concert venue, complete with frightening signs warning of 'Disallowed Items.' Toronto folk could see concerts in the round at the Forum, relaxing under the tent-like roof, surrounded by trees, with the city in the background. But what was a casual affair is now an overly regulated, secure, plastic-cup-only experience.

Across Lakeshore Boulevard, the CNE hasn't fared much better. We still have wonderful structures like the Better Living Centre, complete with the multicoloured Piet Mondrian/de Stijl–inspired ornament on top, and the Queen Elizabeth and Food buildings, as well as various fountains and monuments nearby. These buildings – like Gothic churches before them – were designed to lift our spirits and make us think of some kind of higher power (in the CNE's case, peace, order and good government perhaps). The Better Living Centre's north elevation remains as intended, but the south side, with its grand and wide staircase that looks as if it could float up to some Bauhaus heaven, now leads majestically to a chain-link fence and Lakeshore Boulevard's six lanes of arterial traffic. There's no reason to enter or exit here anymore. It's painful to see such design thwarted, either by lack of care or by redesigns that take structures out of their original context.

Perhaps the greatest blow to this optimistic age was the 1985 destruction of the Bulova Tower (originally the Shell Oil Tower), the first example of a welded steel and glass structure in our city when built in 1955. It was in the way of the Molson Indy. In fact, Molson paid the $150,000 it cost to demolish it. Many didn't see an architectural value in it, including then mayor Art Eggleton, who told the *Toronto Star*, 'I think the money could be better spent on the other fine old buildings on the site.' Though Eggleton speeds towards the dustbin of history now, we're still without our tower and stuck with the Molson Indy. It's because of the Indy, and the need for empty space for its grandstands, that there is so much empty, treeless, underused space at the CNE.

Exhibition Stadium used to fill up some of that parking lot. Just to the east of the Better Living Centre is a plaque in the ground that outlines the footprints of the old grandstands, as well as some of the old seats from the stadium. In 1988, on our Grade Eight class trip to Toronto, the bus dropped us off in this spot. We sat in the outfield, right behind George Bell. The Jays lost that day, but I was in awe of it all. The whole site is a landscape of our collective memories, the best days of all of our lives, memorialized in a parking lot.

As much as I would miss it, I almost think it would be better to tear down this wonderful stuff if it isn't going to be treated right. In 1893, Chicago built a magnificent 'White City' of pristine Beaux Arts buildings for the World's Fair. As the fair came to a close, people began to wonder what might happen to these buildings; the fear of letting them fall into disrepair was a worry even then. In *Cosmopolitan* that December, after the fair came to a close, Norwegian-American writer Hjalmar Hjorth Boyesen wrote: 'Better to have it vanish suddenly, in a blaze of glory, than fall into gradual disrepair and dilapidation. There is no more melancholy spectacle than a festal hall, the morning after the banquet, when the guests have departed and the lights are extinguished.' I felt that melancholy in full one quiet night last year, when a friend and I were wandering around the empty grounds after the CNE was over. We climbed up the back of the Music Building, an older building with a glass dome. We sat on the roof for a while, looking at the city rise above the empty land, listening to the hum of the Gardiner.

I'm not ready for a blaze of glory here. For me, the lights at the CNE, or even Ontario Place, haven't been extinguished yet, but I wonder if it's just my imagination filling in the blanks, and my love of these buildings, that causes me to feel good when I'm near them, even while they are being treated so poorly.

These modern utopias are scattered throughout our city. When our crown jewel, the new City Hall, was opened in 1965, it was one of the indications – maybe even the exact moment – that the city was evolving from its uptight 'Toronto the Good' reputation to something else – something Victoria or Edward could not have dreamed of. Even as heavyweights like Ludwig Mies van der Rohe built the TD Centre, Toronto architects were quietly filling our city with new buildings. Peter Dickinson built structures like the Benvenuto Place apartments at the top of the Avenue Road hill, the Continental Can Building on the southwest corner of Bay and College, and the Juvenile and Family Courts building on Jarvis. John B. Parkin Associates designed the Ontario Association of Architects building at 50 Park Road, Don Mills Collegiate Institute and the Sidney Smith Hall at the University of Toronto. Unsung Toronto modernist Peter Etherington designed the bank building on the southeast corner of College and Spadina (now home to a generic Burger King — but notice how its cornice matches the rooflines of the older buildings to the south). The O'Keefe Centre, both New and Massey Colleges, the Colonnade on Bloor and apartment clusters around places like Davisville were all part of Toronto's modern building boom that took place in Montreal's shadow. Even the Pavilions on the Toronto Islands were well done in the modern style, winning a Massey Medal in 1964.

I got to live in one of our unsung modern utopias when I first moved to Toronto in 2000. My roommate, Heather, and I lived at 40 Pleasant Boulevard, one block south of Yonge and St. Clair. We moved from Windsor together, her to be near her boyfriend, me to live in the city I had always wanted to live in. A high-rise tower wasn't where I expected to live; the image I had had of my Toronto life was somewhere in the Annex, maybe on Brunswick Avenue, on the third floor of some old house, with a claw-foot tub and other quaint stuff. But in 2000 we were having trouble finding a house like that because it was the height of a tight rental market, just before the condo glut started opening things up. As a result, we saw mostly apartments in buildings, not in cute little houses.

So we looked up, riding the elevators of some of Toronto's finer mid- to low-end buildings. On an overcast day we went to see a place in the horrific-looking building that sits in the wedge of land at Vaughan Road and Bathurst, just south of St. Clair. Though it's an ugly building, the view from the apartment we saw was stunning. People who disdain apartment buildings forget that the view from the top is often pretty good. With the open vistas and sprawling views, it's almost like living in the country.

We had one more place to see, but Heather and I agreed we would take this place if the next one wasn't better. That place was 40 Pleasant, the left half of two connected buildings called Commonwealth Towers. The thin white buildings, built in 1968, rise from one shared eight-storey-high rectangular parking garage podium. On the eighth floor, in between the two buildings, there is a grassy park with little earthen mounds and paved paths. In the middle, there's a small swimming pool.

The Serbian superintendent showed us the apartment on the nineteenth floor. After we saw the place, we went to the Timothy's on the corner to figure out what to do. In the bathroom, I decided that this was the one to take. It wasn't an old house or in the Annex, and it was sort of expensive, but I couldn't say no. It was that childhood vision of modern Toronto, and it seemed like what big-city living was all about.

The building became home, and I got a kick out of showing off some of the features to visitors. The lobbies of 40 and 60 Pleasant each have an identical fountain that looks like a Sputnik spraying water into its own little pool. Urban-planner types now call this sort of thing a 'water feature,' an underwhelming term for a wonderful thing. Unfortunately, they are behind locked iron fences, so I called them the 'caged Sputniks.' I still bring people by the buildings when we're in the neighbourhood to look at the fountains behind the glass.

The area around the elevators has big rectangular couches underneath square wooden tubes with lights installed in them; the lighting is directed down so it's soft and low. The colours are various shades of dark brown. It's all vaguely Japanese, or what I think of as 1960s Japanese: the kind of place where Kurosawa would have shot one of his modern epics. On a completely different cultural note, one of the walls has a Mayan-like concrete mosaic. It's exotic ethnic appropriation at its best. This place must have really been swinging when it was built, so much so that people wouldn't worry about the mixed metaphors used in the design. That our building was attached to the St. Clair subway station made it seem extra cosmopolitan – as if the building were part of the infrastructure of the rest of the city. I could count the steps from my bedroom to the subway platform.

The apartment itself was standard building fare, but there was lots of glass and we could see the CN Tower, the lake, and even St. Catharines on the few smog-free days Toronto gets. In fact, with the doors open, the bathroom had a clear view of the tower – the mark of any good Toronto home, I figure. It could have met the sidewalk in a better way – there is too much parking garage there now – and the rooftop park is private rather than public space, but the demographic is still fairly heterogeneous, making it an interesting place to live.

There is a cluster of similar apartment buildings in the area, built in the same era as our building. A fine place to see it all was from the Rosehill Reservoir Park, just to the south. The reservoir has been covered over with grass and reflecting pools. The grass is often soggy because the soil isn't deep enough to absorb big rainfalls. The park is surrounded by buildings on two sides, with trees around the other two. I would sometimes walk the dog in the park and watch the sun set behind those buildings, casting long, perfect shadows across the grass. In the middle of the park is another space-age fountain – this time a big atom-like structure. There are plaques around dedicating it to the anniversary of Confederation in 1967.

To the east of the park is a deep ravine. There's a path off Avoca Avenue that descends quickly into the ravine. The sounds of the city disappear, replaced by cool humidity and mosquitoes. I would often go running through the park, under the road and railway bridges high overhead, along the stream that flowed beneath the Rosedale mansions perched at the top of hills. Abruptly, the stream disappears into a culvert, reappearing on the other side of Mount Pleasant, on its way to the Don River. Toronto is firmly in control of nature here.

There's something particularly magnificent about the way clean modern lines rise up out of both the natural and older parts of the city. I'm glad this was my first Toronto apartment. I think I'd have always wondered what it was like had I not lived at a place like 40 Pleasant. And maybe I understand, or appreciate, a place like Ontario Place better for having lived in a building of that era. Where you live affects the way you view the city. Right now I do live in one of those three-storey Annex homes on Dupont. I can hear sidewalk conversations from my kitchen window as people walk by. When I lived up in the air, I didn't get such a street-level show, but I felt a little more connected to the city in a wider sense. I watched thunderstorms cross the city from west to east, and on Victoria Day I saw hundreds of backyard fireworks displays in one glance.

I like that our modern experiments remain with us, and if some of us choose to, we can still live in them, or visit on occasion. We have a complicated relationship with these buildings; I feel as if we've let them down for the time being. But when fashion comes around and we decide these are valuable parts of Toronto, we'll take down the chain link fences and give them new coats of paint worthy of the utopian visions that created them.

Nicole Cohen
**The Zeidler effect:
how one family transformed Toronto**

If Eberhard Zeidler had gotten his way, many of us would live in townhouses in Harbour City, rings of human-made islands dotting the shore of Lake Ontario. We'd have lake views, scoot around on water transit and lead mostly car-free, sustainable lives. This antidote to suburban sprawl could have added thirty kilometres of public park to Toronto's waterfront and, back in the early 1970s, would have given waterfront development a significant boost. If three levels of government and the Toronto Harbour Commission could have agreed on Zeidler's project at the same time, there might be 60,000 people living in a mini-city at the foot of Toronto.

Though he sounds like a utopian visionary, Zeidler is an architect grounded in reality. Through his work – Toronto Eaton Centre, Ontario Place, Vancouver's Canada Place, among many, many others – he creates what he calls livable urban environments, multi-purpose buildings that are nice to look at and provide plenty of space for people to interact. His vision for planning and building is in the spirit of urban planning expert and close family friend Jane Jacobs: mixed usage, urban density and lots of public space.

Zeidler is concerned with more than just how a building looks. How people relate to spaces and the way those spaces function in the city has been a major part of his thinking and work, from restoring an old warehouse to create the mixed-use Queen's Quay Terminal, to reinterpreting a suburban archetype – the shopping mall – to help rejuvenate downtown. As an architect, Zeidler has planning on his mind, and as a developer, he takes architecture seriously. But above all, his social conscience drives his work.

A 1971 sketch of Ontario Place gives some insight into his development philosophy. It shows an industrial wasteland of a waterfront crossed out and a prettier version with sailboats and trees drawn in its place. Across the top, Zeidler scrawled 'Reclaiming shoreline for people.'

Zielder's fingerprints are all over the city, in the form of giant structures that have shaped Toronto's development over the past few decades. And his progressive, innovative vision has inspired the work of two of his daughters, who are both doing their part to shape Toronto's future: Margaret Zeidler, developer of restored buildings 401 Richmond and 215 Spadina, and Christina Zeidler, who is running the family-owned historic Gladstone Hotel. Through the family's work, Toronto has become a city known for creative spaces, one that has learned to respect its heritage while moving forward. It has become an artist-friendly city where people can live and work downtown. And though Harbour City was never realized, those same planning principles are present in spaces across Toronto. Call it the Zeidler effect.

Born in Braunsdorf, Germany, Eberhard Zeidler grew up in the part of Poland then known as Silesia and studied at the famed Weimar Bauhaus in East Germany and the Universität Karlsruhe. He came to Canada in 1951 with nothing but a suit, a cane and a little English. ('He spent all his money on that suit,' Christina says. 'They called him The Duke.'). Immigration officials sent him to Peterborough to work at architecture firm Blackwell and Craig, where he was soon made partner and, by 1953, chief designer. The firm evolved into what is now Zeidler Partnership Architects, headquartered in Toronto, with offices in Beijing, Berlin, Calgary, London and West Palm Beach, Florida. The award-winning firm has designed major projects around the world, including Canada Place at London's Canary Wharf, the fifty-storey Torre Mayor in Mexico City (the tallest building in Latin America) and Cinedom in Cologne, Germany's MediaPark. Though there is hope the current celebrity-architect boom will cement Toronto's status as a world-class city, it's Zeidler's dozens of structures, the buildings in which we live, work, play, eat, learn and shop, that have played a role in shaping how we regard our city. Walk through the city and take note of the buildings and spaces you interact with every day. There's a good chance Zeidler's influence is there.

It was Zeidler who, in 1973, made what remains the single greatest leap forward in our perpetually stalled waterfront when he took on what is now Queen's Quay Terminal. At the time, it was a dead area: railroads and a run-down warehouse that was slated to be demolished. Zeidler convinced the developers to restore the eight-storey warehouse and incorporated it into a modern design for a mixed-use complex, with office space sandwiched between retail and housing.

When it comes to new buildings, Zeidler pushes for his vision of Toronto as a dense, transit-reliant city. When his firm took over a condo project at Yonge and St. Clair, area residents were not pleased about the increased density, Zeidler recalls.

'There was a great howl because people said, "Not in my backyard." But if you look at the city, not just from the isolated position of "I have a house and don't want to see a condominium there," then it becomes important that people live downtown and on the subway stops.' He believes people won't use the subway if they live more than five minutes from a station, and he emphasizes the importance of not only building on top of subway stops but of creating a mix of retail and residential spaces in those buildings.

His ideas are utilitarian, but they have potential to transform cities. As Stefano Pavarini wrote in an introduction to Zeidler's work, 'Zeidler's architecture is deliberately designed to be a form of art applied to reality, operating on a practical level with market demands, costs, building constraints ... ' The results are buildings that look nice – lots of glass and steel, big curves and wide-open spaces – but are functional and blend into streetscapes.

His Eaton Centre was the first major downtown project designed by a Toronto architect during the building boom of the 1960s and 1970s. It was the first time in North America that the suburban mall was adapted to suit downtown, and Zeidler ensured it wasn't an isolated structure surrounded by parking lots but rather a continuation of the city grid with integrated office space and parking. And though it took some adjustments – at first in the minds and habits of downtown dwellers, and later, in the design process, as modifications to make the inward-looking original structure more outward-looking – the Eaton Centre's function is to draw people to the city's core.

And perhaps foreshadowing his daughters' work with 401 Richmond, Zeidler had planned to turn the square that surrounds Church of the Holy Trinity, behind the Eaton Centre, into an arcade of stores supplemented by housing for artists, who would sell their goods in the stores, making tangible his belief that the creative class has an integral role in the city's development.

That class was on his mind during the 1970s, when then mayor David Crombie was pushing for urban renewal, which divided Toronto architects. Crombie envisioned more housing and less unchecked development. On one side was the younger generation, in favour of a more residential downtown, preservation of old buildings and more thoughtful planning. The older generation was less ready to support an agenda of reform. It was a political showdown, and Zeidler was called a traitor for pushing for his vision of a city where people lived and worked downtown, in beautiful spaces that stimulated creativity. But over the years, his vision has been in part realized, and he has passed it on to his children, who are doing their part to make Toronto a truly great city.

Now that Christina Zeidler is almost finished with the Gladstone Hotel, the historic Toronto landmark is starting to look remarkably like it did when it was built in 1889. Christina, who is a filmmaker by profession, has directed a team of workers and designers on a seven-figure renovation to replicate the former railway hotel's original architecture. Crews worked from old photographs and remnants of the past to recreate the plaster mouldings, restore the curved glass windows on the second floor and replicate the hotel's tall baseboards. The space is beautiful, more demure and timeless than the other famed hotel renovation: the Drake, a few blocks east on Queen Street West.

The Zeidler family, spurred on by developer and oldest daughter Margaret (known to most as Margie), bought the Gladstone in 2000 for $2.3 million (with developer Michael Tippin, whom she later bought out in a complicated arrangement involving a lapsed insurance policy), and Christina runs the show. She worked closely on the design with her father, whose firm did the restoration.

Like all Margie Zeidler projects, the hotel's historic retrofit is inspired by Jane Jacobs's maxim that 'old ideas can sometimes use new buildings. New ideas must use old buildings.' So, in true Zeidler fashion, this hotel will be more than just a place to sleep.

Christina wants to give a variety of people access to the space. Rooms range from budget to what she calls budget glam. There are rooms for the hotel's long-term tenants, and the second floor is designated for mixed use: private rooms, artist live-work space and exhibit rooms.

'The architecture of this building is special,' says Christina. 'It's built differently; the emphasis is on public space.' Each floor opens onto large, open areas that Eb calls living rooms – valuable, rentable space that other hotels would likely turn into rooms.

The Zeidlers' vision for the Gladstone, similar to their work on 401 Richmond West and 215 Spadina Avenue, is to create a social, creative hub. By purchasing old buildings, restoring them and renting affordable office space to artists and non-profits (space at 401 Richmond goes for as little as twelve dollars a square foot, compared with the eighteen or twenty dollars other nearby buildings charge), the Zeidler sisters have helped to turn many arts organizations into institutions.

The idea was to provide small businesses, not-for-profits and artist-run centres with affordable office space. 'These are people who appreciate being invested in,' says Christina. And in return for a ten-year lease, artists and companies have invested in the buildings and their spaces. 'Diversifying tenants and investing in people who will invest in you will put energy into the building and is great for business,' she says.

George Baird, dean of the University of Toronto's Faculty of Architecture, believes that what the Zeidler sisters are up to is very important. He describes their ventures as enlightened micro-capitalism. 'It's an idea that you can create enterprises that involve a lot of people, none of whom have a lot of capital, and modulate the cash-flow arrangement to allow people to get a foothold,' he says. 'It's a very creative economic and urban activity and a very precedent-setting one.'

In 1994, Margie and her father purchased 401 Richmond West, a historic building slated for demolition, for $150,000. She was partly inspired by her time on the board of Artscape, a non-profit involved with real estate for artists, which convinced her that creating affordable, multi-tenant centres and working with artists could be a good business model. At the time, it was a radical idea. Now, as Christina says, everyone wants an artist in their basement.

Though it seemed to many to be overly idealistic, 401 has been a huge success, lauded for its restoration and community spirit and visited by developers from around the world. The waiting list for tenancy is a hundred names long, and the model has been used by Cityscape Holdings, Inc. to develop the Distillery District.

Tenants have praised the Zeidlers for their inclusive and integrative approach to planning 401, creating a daycare for tenants and neighbours that's a central, visible part of the building (and providing space rent-free) and creating naturally lit, oversized hallways to encourage interaction. It's an office building where people aren't pigeonholed in their offices, one where the owners would rather spend more money on restoring old windows than replacing them with new ones. There is public art on the walls. The restaurant and rooftop garden have become important meeting spaces, and they encourage collaboration between tenants. It's a different way of doing business, one that's about more than boardrooms and conference calls.

By 2002, Margie had her eye on the Robertson Building, a large Edwardian warehouse built between 1911 and 1913 at 215 Spadina Avenue, just north of Queen Street. She wanted to provide space for larger tenants and try new ideas, such as enabling small organizations involved with social innovation to share offices, meeting rooms and resources, giving them space they couldn't otherwise afford. This has given a boost to many foundations and charities. Like 401, 215 is fully leased.

Since he began working in Toronto in the 1960s, it's been important to Eb Zeidler to encourage the creative class to live and work downtown, and he has passed that philosophy on to his daughters.

The family grew up thinking about planning. Eb's wife, Jane, is an art consultant who works only with living Canadian artists. The middle daughter, Kate, is a prominent interior designer and is helping with the Gladstone. The brother, Robert, is in the Canadian army reserves and has also worked as a developer.

Though Christina calls herself an accidental hotelier, it was inevitable she would get involved with the Gladstone. She has worked on many of the behind-the-scenes aspects of Zeidler projects, advising Margie on artists to bring into spaces and guiding the visions for projects. She has let the Gladstone take over her life, and has moved back to Toronto from Port Hope to be closer to the project. Ask her why she took on such a massive project, and she'll say, 'I feel a responsibility to this city and to my family.'

For this family, work is about more than architecture or development or even restoring old buildings. The Zeidlers believe in a larger goal, in using their privilege and experience to make the world – in this case, Toronto – a better place.

Eb Ziedler may not have gotten his way with Harbour City, a place that could very well still help Toronto get out of its muddled waterfront fix. But his ideas about urban life live on. They're there in the current surge of support for public transit, in the old warehouses and spaces being restored for mixed use, in the new respect developers have for artists. They're in the buildings that define how our city works, in the way his daughters Margie and Christina are making their mark on the city. After all, it's hard to forget ideas that have utterly transformed Toronto.

A version of this piece originally appeared in *Eye Weekly*.

Derek Murr
The history of Toronto's future

You could say that all cities are utopian acts. Not perfect places, no, since there's no such thing as perfect, but utopian in intent, surely. The very act of founding a city betrays a certain foolhardy optimism. No one would embark upon such a complex project without faith that, in the end, all will be well, yet no idea will ever encounter the real world without being changed. This collision between the perfect plan and uncooperative reality happens in every city, and Toronto is no exception.

We have in our history our fair share of unrealized visions of the future, going back almost to its founding: for example, Captain Gother Mann's 1798 'Plan of Torento [sic] Harbour with the Proposed Town and part of the Settlement.' A commander of Upper Canada's Royal Engineers, Mann put to paper a model British colonial town: a central public square, bordered by government and military buildings and surrounded by streets in a perfect Euclidean grid, their straight lines untainted by petty details like geography. Toronto's rivers, ravines and hills made it quite impossible to build Mann's Platonic ideal of a colonial town – in fact, it was never even attempted – but though they didn't fit within his plan, those same troublesome areas shaped some of the most beautiful parts of this city, and what could have been a generic anytown grid was forced to take a more uniquely charming shape.

There is always a gap between a vision of the ideal and the reality of what's possible, and this gap is the space where cities live; the particular personality of a place comes through in those parts of town where all did not go according to plan. You can see that different visions of the future collided in those areas on the map where the perfect street grid breaks down, whether because of geography or culture or economics or blind chance. You can see it in Toronto in areas that didn't quite work out:

the unwieldy density of the St. James Town apartment towers, the uncomfortable segregation of the original Regent Park housing development. You can see it in those landmarks where dreams burst through our stereotypical Canadian reserve: the retro-futuristic structures of Ontario Place hovering over the lake, or the CN Tower, still the world's tallest free-standing expression of optimism, or more recent landmarks like OCAD's whimsical expansion, stilt perched and Dalmatian spotted. These are all artifacts from the history of our future: examples of what the future might have been like, or may still be like – shining and different – if only, if only.

This is not to say that all big plans are motivated by idealism; many are the result of baser motives. Ambition must certainly have helped drive the various early incarnations of Project Viking, an attempt to dramatically increase downtown office and retail space. Many design proposals were put forward for this project, most of which required building enormous towers that ignored all sense of place and scale, and *all* of which required razing the Church of the Holy Trinity and Old City Hall, destroying valuable parts of our city's past in favour of maximizing valuable real estate. (A later version of Project Viking, one which better respected the scale of the area and which preserved those historic buildings, eventually evolved to become the downtown Eaton Centre.) Other pie-in-the-sky plans are motivated by hubris; how else to explain a 1911 proposal for the Toronto Union Terminal, a technologically and economically impossible forty-million-square-foot (!) combination of offices, warehouses and a shipping terminus, looming over the city at Yonge and Queen. Still other plans in the history of our future arose from a blind faith in unworkable theories, such as the series of highways included in the City of Toronto's plans up until the early seventies, whose proponents insisted that a modern downtown could not function without several highways driven through the heart of it – five highways, in fact, cutting through neighbourhoods from Chinatown to Rosedale, Eglinton to Christie Pits and West Queen West. This was the established city-building wisdom of the day, fuelled by cheap petroleum and, perhaps, boyhood memories of Gernsback science-fiction pulp covers, all rockets and mile-high skyscrapers and twenty-lane superhighways. It was, in its own way, a version of an ideal city, albeit a vision of the city as nothing more than a method of shuttling people and goods from A to B as quickly as possible. The skeleton of that dead vision can still be seen in the city's southeast corner, in the empty trestles of the unmade eastern Gardiner Expressway, rising out of tall grass.

The most infamous of these highways, the Spadina (or Allen) Expressway, met with fierce grassroots resistance; under tremendous pressure from local community groups, from public intellectuals like urban theorist Jane Jacobs, from environmental groups and business improvement associations, then premier Bill Davis cancelled the freeway. With public opinion so effectively mobilized against them, the other highways were, one by one, cancelled and stricken from the city's official plans: another example of people struggling to build their own vision of the future Toronto. It is these tensions – between what people want from their city, between differing motives, between differing visions of the future, between what is dreamed and what is simply, palely, *possible* – that characterize the built fabric of Toronto; it is the balance between these tensions that makes Toronto actually work. It might be part of our national character: Canadians tend to put the collective good ahead of the individual vision. This means that realizing any dream of the future can be a painful, committee-ridden process (witness the interminable debate over how best to redevelop the Port Lands and waterfront) but, on the plus side, it saves us from missteps. For every project that gets built, there are twenty in the archives (Floating airports! Geodesic domes over the downtown core! City Halls shaped like big glass pyramids! Artificial island communities!) that did not, and with good reason. And for every project in the archives, there are dozens more that have not been recorded at all.

I've been talking mostly about the built environment of the city – buildings and streets – only because they're the most visible artifacts from the history of our future, but they're not the only ones. Even seemingly ephemeral projects, like declaring an area a car-free zone for a day, or organizing a community trash clean-up day are also, in their own way, attempts to realize alternate versions of an ideal future Toronto. Every intervention into public space by one of its citizens, no matter how small, is an act towards creating a different future for that space, and it's the sum total of all these possible futures, large and small, successful and not, the sheer uncountable number of acts and the impossible, beautiful complexity of how they interact and jostle and pull at each other that make a city.

These interactions are so complicated and chaotic that they're probably impossible to understand fully. Happily, in order for a city to work properly, understanding is less important; what's needed most is for *everyone to keep dreaming*. Everything else is built from that. All these schemes and plans – the history of Toronto's future – exist around us, in the fabric of our city: the results, some more successful than others, of so many people trying to make their home a bit better. And as long as there are still people fighting for their vision of their city, then Toronto's future not only has a history but a future as well.

TOPOGRAPHY

Mark Kingwell
Reading Toronto: architecture and utopia

u

My graduate seminar in 2005 investigates the theme 'Architecture and Utopia.' Every week we gather in a fluorescent-washed room, under a cheap suspended ceiling, on mismatched chairs, and discuss big urban dreams, the visions of sprawling hope. Cities transformed into vast Edenic gardens, with sweeping throughways and radial residential blocks as far as the eye can see. Cities razed and rebuilt in futuristic layers, with floating railways stations and razored, hundred-storey office towers. Dreamy cities, with snaking *flâneur*-friendly walkways and arresting juxtaposed street culture. Le Corbusier, Sant'Elia, Benjamin. Visions, images, pictures. We sit under the harsh electrified gas, our heads bent together, a dozen of us, architects and philosophers, probing to the logic of dreams.

Outside, beyond these north-facing windows, the watery winter light of Toronto. The vista is bleak, a scene of nothingness. A parking lot. A snow-covered field where a stadium used to be. To the left, a small daycare centre and playground. Straight ahead, across Bloor Street, the banal concrete brutalism of the OISE building, one of those edifices apparently constructed to convey hatred for the street on which it sits. You must sidle down its edge even to get in. It could be a courthouse or security-conscious consulate. To the left, a windswept and pointless parkette; to the right, a red-brick wall blocking any good view of a private club.

Inside the room, we look at pretty pictures and discuss big ideas. Tales of Paris, Milan, New York, Shanghai. We try not to look out the window, but it's hard, not least because someone has permanently removed the curtains from the windows, something we discovered only when we attempted to screen *The Fountainhead* in class. The dim light, beige and grey structures under colourless sky, undid that dream.

u

The utopian impulse is so often foolish, or dangerous; it is, indeed, a ready shorthand for reckless ideologue, heedless architect of change. Plato called it the lure of Syracuse: the desire to make a shiny political idea real, as Plato tried – and failed – to do with Dionysus the Tyrant. Dionysus was a ruler who, despite his sobriquet, struck Plato as proto-philosophical, mouldable clay for the master of the transcendental Forms. He was wrong, as most utopians have also been wrong.

And yet we need utopia. Its energy and drive, its optimism that things could be better than they are. Once transcendental, as in Plato or Augustine, then geographical or spiritual, as in More or Butler, the impulse now seems largely temporal: the future as the site of our dreams, the undiscovered country, now that there is no physical country left to discover.

Of course, a desire that big is not to be trusted. There is too much associated destruction, too much faith in reason or technology or socialism. Cities, we know, are less planned from the top down than they are grown from the bottom up. Utopian desire is a kind of inner tyrant, a dark, overwhelming form of hope, that peculiar desire to be, as the critic Wayne Koestenbaum has said, 'somehow simultaneously avant-garde and dead.'

In the seminar, we read Jane Jacobs for the usual cure to soaring urban ambition. We note that she lives not far away from where we sit. Also, however, that her ideas, so often celebrated, are actually confused and vague. She celebrates street life, but only at one scale; she doesn't seem to know what inspires or edifies, only what functions. So much here is about blocking things, keeping things from happening, halting the imagined. A distrust of the grandiose pervades. Fine for Boston's North End or New

York's West Village, maybe, but here, looking out, we feel the need for large scale, not small. Big ideas, transformations, something to enliven the dead zone of our gaze.

We cannot ignore the thought, too, that the North End is nowadays a virtual theme park, artificial and tourist addled, gangs of college-logo'd teens lining up for pizza or cannoli. The West Village has become a supermodel haven, priced into the stratosphere by Gwyneth Paltrow and Helena Christensen as they push their babies along Hudson Street in expensive limo-prams. Before her incarceration, Martha Stewart bought a floor in the new Richard Meier buildings at the corner of Perry Street and West. Martin Scorsese too. Good neighbourhoods, kept good, just get expensive. Even the hippie Annex, with its futon stores and used-record shops, is too expensive for any of us, including me, the only one with a job.

I lived in the West Village when I was teaching at the City University of New York, and people would always ask me how I could afford it. The answer was, I couldn't. It was a dream, a wishful thought, a vacation from reality. I used to go running down Perry to the river and see the Meier buildings, the two perfect towers framing the intersection, and imagine myself there, somebody else with somebody else's life.

U

The university blocked a deal to build a new football stadium on the site right outside our classroom. It was considered a great victory for sanity and scholarship, as against money and mass culture. No roiling crowds of drunken Argonauts fans would soil our haven! No overhang of luxury seating would cast a shadow on our quiet streets!

The architects of the original design tried hard to modify their plan to allay these fears. They reduced the number of seats, rejigged the distribution so that more of them stretched over Philosopher's Walk instead of Devonshire Place. They were not the arrogant monomaniacs of the popular imagination, half-pint Howard Roarks designing without heed or scruple. They wanted it to work, it seemed.

They might as well have banged their heads against one of our dark stone walls. The deal was queered, the contract lost, the imagined stadium sent packing up to York University – where, now, the principals are embroiled in lawsuits and an inquiry over shady land deals. This, naturally, makes the stadium's opponents feel even more smug.

Every time I look out the classroom window, I think how great it might have been. To have a genuine downtown stadium, a subway-access park, for the Argonauts and the Blues alike. Sitting in a meeting of the college senate, where the stadium deal was mocked and denounced, I wondered if I was the only one there who had ever sat in the stands of old Varsity Stadium on a dreamy September day and watched a football game. I was usually by myself, because no one else I knew liked football.

I miss the old Varsity Stadium, and I wanted the new one. But here, in this town, victory means keeping things from happening, not making them happen. Not dreaming big, but dashing dreams.

u

It can't be surprising that academics blocked progress, since so many of them see that as part of their job description, at least in the political quarters of life: keeping things from happening rather than making them happen.

In Francis Cornford's satire of academic politics, *Microcosmographia Academica*, published almost a century ago, the classicist noticed the obvious fact that most reasons given in academic debate are not for doing something but for not doing anything.

These include the Principle of the Wedge, which says you should not act justly now for fear of raising expectations that you will act still more justly in future; the Principle of the Dangerous Precedent, by which it is decreed that no thing shall ever be done for the first time; the Principle of the Fair Trial, which argues that the current system, whatever it is, has not been given a chance; and the Principle of Unripe Time, which states that 'people should not do at the present moment what they think right at that moment, because the moment at which they think it right has not yet arrived.'

Time, Cornford adds, 'is like the medlar; it has a trick of going rotten before it is ripe.'

We sometimes forget that Toronto is, among its other identities, very much an academic city. Not as obviously so as Cambridge, Cornford's hometown, but sufficiently to give the political discourse of this city a distinct overtone of academic debate. Reasons given are most often for not doing things, not for doing them. Blockage is progress; resistance is self-evident; ambition is suspect. The old thin-lipped Puritan disapproval of ostentation has merged smoothly with the grievance politics of the multicultural moment, forging an alliance of surprising resilience.

The time is not ripe; the time is rotten. The stadium site is an empty lot of snow and discarded equipment, a *mise en scène* of misery. Thus do we claim victory!

Games, like utopia, offer a dialectic of time and hope. Can I realize my dream of victory before time expires? Can the quirky non-clock time of baseball or cricket grow large enough to encompass my desire? As I look out the grimy window, I think the issue is not so much football as life itself.

The philosopher Bernard Suits argues that games express the highest interests of humankind, the sort of goal-directed activity that is free from use. He means art and philosophy as well as literal games. Here, the prelusory goals of the game give over to the lusory pleasures of the game itself. (*Ludere, lus* – meaning play; a root that is too often forgotten in loose talk of preludes and delusions.) A game is organized play, governed by rules or norms, but never reducible to anything other than the sum of its enactments. The rules are not the game. The pleasure of the game is constraint meeting possibility, tradition under the sign of novelty, knowing that, though many games have come before, this particular one has not. The game unfolds in the playing, in time, purely itself.

Thus, likewise, does art resist reduction to propositions (even as it may be, powerfully, about ideas). Thus does philosophy, at its best, become a sort of impossible profession, whose conclusions are, in a sense, its least valuable achievements, the sloughed-off skin of reflection, which remains a living body, irreducible and itself.

I think of all this, playing another, even less structured game we call daydreaming, looking out on the dead playing field, the denuded ground, bare and lacking its encirclement, the architecture of gamespace, that liminal space separating play from the workaday world, the stadium. Inside my space, a room for reflection, I peer through the transparent boundary, the light-permeable skin, and see future possible games begin to die.

I should really be listening to what one of the architects or philosophers is saying, but I am, as we say, lost in thought. I have lost my way. I am a *flâneur* of the mind. For the moment.

u

That is not all, however. For the unignorable irony is that some of the city's best architecture is part of this very same university that refused to allow the gamespace of the new stadium. Our campus has become a kind of incubator of dreams, a sabbatical space, the way Rem Koolhaas argues Coney Island functions for Manhattan. We have taken risks and scored: Massey College, Graduate House, the Isabel Bader Theatre. And, above all, that indefinable harmony of styles and periods that is impossible to plan or dictate – that must grow, over time.

The university is a strange achievement, a space coherent unto itself, but not closed or opaque. It does not turn its back on the city, the way Yale or Columbia do, or find its identity only via suburban isolation, like York or Calgary or Trent or any number of other places you could mention. Instead, like McGill, arranged along Sherbrooke, or N Y U scattered around the casual drug deals, dog runs, buskers and grungy chess geniuses of Washington Square, the university allows the city to permeate it, to flow into and through our separateness. Down the sweep of Queen's Park, along Hoskin and College, through the jaywalkers on the thin strip of St. George.

Come on in.

u

Nobody can fail to notice, and maybe engage with, the architectural excitement of our city's present moment. There is hype galore, and money, and maybe even some inspired design – though I suspect that we will find, too soon, that it is as if we have woken from a dream and found not the oneiric architecture of our visions but instead the crusted remains of a collective delirium.

Nevertheless, it is a good time to dream big dreams. After so long with so little to show, the city hauls itself out of its pervasive ugliness, its lack of distinction. What will it find? We cannot say yet, but it will, naturally, fall some distance short of utopia. No bad thing, to be sure, at least as a general rule; we don't want, and could not afford, the explosive ambition of a Shanghai or Taipei, those throbbing districts of postmodern futuristic exuberance. Not for the likes of modest, progress-wary us. Anyway, those visions, too, begin to pall: witness the weird neo-feudal violence of ninety-storey shadows falling aslant hovels and dirt, the routine immiseration of twenty-first-century communo-capitalism.

We have, it seems, our own kind of, let us call it, 'modest utopianism.' A calculated conservative ambition, with spurts of radical playfulness, suited to the grey dirty town we remain beneath the slick surface.

One of my favourite things right now is, in the middle of the day, to exit the building that houses the seminar room, also home of my office, and walk along the hoardings and scaffold that dominate Philosopher's Walk. This formerly quiet pathway, once overgrown and dangerous, a no-go zone of potential assignations and assault, is now a building site for the Royal Conservatory of Music and the Royal Ontario Museum. Royalty everywhere. Signs enforce hard hats and steel-toed boots. Crude spray-painted messages indicate an office beyond the sheets of blond plywood. Up the stairs, past the plaque commemorating a royal visit, and out onto the street, the vista opens up. The rusted and angled I-beams of the ROM's crystal design offer a time-stop essay in endocolonization, a kind of slow-motion Borg experiment in which random pieces of steel self-organize and consume the old stone of the Victorian original. The structure is thick with bracing and yet sticks elegant fingers of steel out over the street. I wish it could stay this way, a half-finished piece of genius, order and decay simultaneously conveyed. Stone, steel and rust. The open spaces between the angled beams.

U

My graduate seminar on architecture and utopia was, like many of the utopian projects it examined, an experiment that was more or less a failure, but an illuminating one. That is, its narrative was of an initially large and enthusiastic group of subjects that eventually dwindled to a hard core of devotees, roughly half and half architects and philosophers, who mostly talked past one another even though the stated subject was always the same. Some left because of other work pressure, some because they got fed up with the other students, others no doubt because they got fed up with me.

The students who stayed were a curious bunch. The philosophers, whom I expected to be hard-nosed realists and conceptual myth busters, turned out to be (probably via self-selection) idealists and theoretical high-wire artists in flight from the deadening scientism of academic philosophy's mainstream. The architects who stuck it out were, by contrast, not the firebrand mini-Roarks and Corb clones I had expected but the corporatized pro-capitalist vanguard of the new architectural moment. Their consistent hero was Rem Koolhaas, whose slick collection of essays and images, *Content* (Taschen, 2004), has rapidly become a cult bible for this generation of M.Arch. prodigies. (Koolhaas's recanting of his formerly utopian position on Manhattan, in *Delirious New York* [Oxford, 1978], is a key moment of the book; his celebration of authoritarian China, where he is building the striking CCTV office in Beijing, is another.)

I mention all this simply to note how unfashionable old-fashioned, which is to say early-twentieth-century, utopianism has become to the architectural practice of today. The formalist urges and grand ideological constructs have surrendered to various forms of small-bore theoretical intricacy and bearish pro-business collaborationism. Even the anti-utopian 'realism' of Jane Jacobs in *The Death and Life of Great American*

Cities (Random House, 1961) imposes, from this perspective, far too many controversial teleological burdens, all the worse for being hidden behind her celebrated naturalism. And yet, as our discussions proved over and over, the basic utopian urge, the desire to build with a view to program that is somehow 'improving' or 'uplifting,' whatever those words might be taken to mean, never entirely deserts the imagination of a designing mind. Once a crucial shift in scale is accepted – from architecture as grand social planning to architecture as a virtuous contribution to what Hannah Arendt called 'the space of appearances' – one could even say that, all protests to the contrary (and sometimes despite heated objection from the creators), every good building is inevitably utopian.

Which brings us back to the issue of Daniel Libeskind's Royal Ontario Museum renovation. At the time I am writing this (autumn 2005), the outer structure of the much-discussed 'crystal' is complete and the structural concrete floors almost entirely laid and poured. Cladding will begin soon, at which point passersby will no longer be able to see the fantastic mass of angled beams and riveted florets that gather all the pieces into this multi-planed silhouette. Stories have circulated that the engineer charged with the design, whose firm had never attempted anything so complex, was kept awake night after night by uneasy reveries of the project refusing to come into physical space, of pieces not fitting as they were laboriously modelled – a kind of reverse design dream, you might say: not the imaginative vision of the architectural seer but the mechanical result therefrom, the nightmare of translation from picture (or napkin sketch) to place.

The project still has a beauty of complexity that is the source of my admiration as described below. Like many people, I suppose I remain skeptical about the origin of the design, the validity of Libeskind's intellectual gestures and the resulting transformation of Bloor Street and the museum. I think it a shame that the cladding will cover up what is perhaps the best part of this design: the rusted Erector Set beauty of its steel frame. It has been a peculiar gift to watch it take shape, to grow and colonize its architectural host. Recently I was told by someone tracking the project for a documentary that the workers assembling the structure had given names to the various nodes and buttons that gather five, seven, sometimes nine separate beams into a corner of the jumbled crystal shape. The world of architecture will certainly forget these individuals, just as it has forgotten the brave toppers and rivet catchers who built the Empire State Building or the Sears Tower or Jin Mao, just as the generations who painfully forged the cathedrals of medieval Europe are forgotten, souls saved but names gone; but I bet they will never forget what the museum's new frontal looked like naked, underneath the bright aluminum that will soon enough enclose it, and us, for good.

One day, walking by, I saw a construction worker standing there, apparently alone, on the site. There was a pile of beams, of various lengths, at his feet. His hard hat was cockily backwards. Dressed in flannels and jeans, good-looking, thin, he might have been twenty-five. In his hand, a sheet of paper. He was looking hard at the paper, and frowning in thought.

His thought made mine clear: he was looking at the plan, the diagram, the two-dimensional abstraction, a priori and ideal, of what he was standing there trying to build, to make physical. Like the badly translated instructions for some cut-rate Korean scale-model kit, I thought, he was trying to figure out which piece attaches where in a language at once obscure, precise and intricate. A man lost in concentration, lost in thought, working to make the next move, the right move, to make a building happen.

That, I thought – that right there – is how dreams become reality.

The first seven of these sketches were written as diary entries over a period of about four weeks during the spring of 2005 as part of the ongoing web project Reading Toronto (www.readingtoronto.com). The last was written in fall 2005.

Lorraine Johnson
Roots to roofs: the greening of Toronto

Chicago, with its official motto *Urbs in Hortus* (City in a Garden), gets all the good press as a green city. Toronto is relegated to poor-cousin status, lagging far behind on the greening front. Certainly, budgets contribute to the disparity: Chicago devotes significant financial resources to horticultural beautification projects, such as making the Magnificent Mile (the upscale shopping district along North Michigan Avenue) bloom magnificently, with colourful botanical displays planted along the broad streetscape.

But it's more than money that makes the difference. Toronto could throw thousands at the annual flower plantings up and down University Avenue (as it started to do in the summer of 2005, with cascading foliage spilling over concrete planting boxes, courtesy of Mayor David Miller's Clean and Beautiful City initiative), and we still wouldn't *be* a 'garden in a city.' For that, we need a gardening ethos that seeps not just into thumbs but into minds, leading us away from stodgy conformity (the lawn-and-order aesthetic that surrounds us) and towards brash acts of botanical abandon.

For guidance, we could look to the growing signs that creative stewards on a greening mission are lurking in Toronto's gardening fringes: The proliferation of front-yard plots full of personality and not an inch of inch-high (water-guzzling, fertilizer-hungry) lawn grass. Green roofs in surprising places, like the John Street Pumping Station. Vegetables planted outside stores in concrete boxes on Bloor Street. School grounds where kids can actually touch soil – less asphalt, more cup plants. Community centres where people grow tomatoes so the food bank is stocked with something almost alive. Housing co-ops where residents take charge of their courtyards, planting and maintaining their gardens communally. Parks where neighbours tend crops in allotment plots, and the dynamics of crowded living get negotiated over the shared hose instead of the private fence. Groups like the Toronto Public Space Committee's guerrilla gardening squad, which attract crowds to late-night alley plantings.

The growing signs are out there, but the symbols are lacking. Consider this: Wisconsin has an official state soil. Toronto doesn't even have an official floral emblem. Ontario's got the trillium, the Canadian flag has the taxonomically challenged maple leaf (is it a red maple, a sugar maple or a sport of nature not found in the field guides?), and Etobicoke has a species of politically incorrect common milkweed (probably the only floral emblem anywhere that's included in a legislated noxious weed list and, hence, mandated for eradication).

If one looks to City Hall, though, for symbolic green guidance, it *can* be found – in an unlikely place: on the roof. Here, in 2000, municipal headquarters was crowned with a fuzzy horticultural cap in the form of a green roof, intended as both inspiration and experiment.

With eight different demonstration garden beds, each one focusing on a specific habitat model, Toronto City Hall's green roof was hooked up to gadgets that measure the amount of rainfall captured by the soil (and hence saved from the storm sewers) and read the temperature at various points on the roof. The researchers who are compiling and analyzing the stats hope to contribute hard data to the growing scientific literature on green-roof benefits – adding much-needed substance to the anecdotally persuasive assertion that growing plants everywhere we can – even on rooftops – is a good thing. Sort of like hair on your head – feels cooler, less run-off.

The City Hall green roof is now a bit of an orphan, not particularly championed or nurtured by any department or group, and that too is symbolic. Though Toronto has moved far beyond its uptight days when gardeners incurred municipal wrath (and cease-and-desist orders) for growing vegetables in their front yards, some city departments and politicians are still vestigially hostile to anything that deviates from the rigid code of our collective conformity: the lawn. Thus, a gardener on Davenport Road, on the steeply sloped glacial Lake Iroquois shoreline, could be ordered in the spring of 2005 to trim back the foliage spilling over the erosion-preventing retaining wall. Apparently, stroller-pushing parents and babes in prams would be assaulted by this unruly growth, this sidewalk traffic hazard, according to the city's property standards department.

Likewise, a couple of boulevard gardeners at two different properties in Etobicoke were ordered to remove their plantings on strips of land between the sidewalk and the street: illegal encroachments, according to the city, though homeowners are legally obliged to maintain these strips – but only with lawn grass, it seems.

Vancouver, on the other hand, takes a different approach. The Green Streets Program actually *encourages* people to garden the boulevards, and green-thumb enthusiasts fan out through the city with trowels and watering cans, claiming sidewalk strips and traffic circle medians as their own fugitive plots. What would be considered rogue activity according to Toronto's rules is sanctioned in Vancouver – the city even gives volunteers snappy orange vests, which lend a quaint air of worker-chic to the whole enterprise.

Annual flowers in boulevard planters along University Avenue might make Toronto look a bit better (especially when one is driving by at sixty kilometres an hour), but meaningful change isn't annual, withering and fading like petunias and pansies. It's deep rooted and perennial, just like the enduring change that Toronto's growing band of rogue gardeners is digging in and planting.

Dedicated to Dagmar Baur and Zora Ignatovic, and with thanks to Andrew Leyerle.

Howard Akler
Home improvement:
in appreciation of innovative houses

Take a stroll down Coxwell Avenue. See the monotonous reign of Victorian homes and cheap storefronts and then – surprise! Smack in the middle of this bland east-end stretch is the most distinctive house in the city: 157 Coxwell is built on stilts. And it's clad in squares of coloured plywood, a fanciful collage that remains strangely faithful to the surroundings. The leafy greens, flat reds and twilight blues all come from the southern Ontario landscape;

the house is a holistic fit even though the topography suggests a financial sinkhole. The site sits on a former creek bed. Trees and plant life grow like crazy, but only one developer was nuts enough to buy it. Rohan Walters, an independent building designer with an eye for marginalized land, ponied up $50,000 back in 2001.

'We're not growing land in this city,' he argues. 'We need to make better use of our resources.'

So he built a house on stilts. Helical piles, forty-seven feet deep, provide secure footing in the soft, marshy ground east of Coxwell. A cedar catwalk connects the sidewalk to the front door and also discreetly carries phone, electricity and cable lines. Walters clad the house in resin-impregnated plywood, less expensive than brick or vinyl siding, but equally tough. The three-storey, 800-square-foot

house cost $138,000 and still receives visits from curious neighbours and impressed architects. 'There's this feeling of quiet admiration,' he says. 'Because I had the balls to put my money into something so sketchy.'

Sketchy maybe, but the challenge is certainly clear: Toronto grows by 100,000 people each year. The city, already short on space and suffering an annual summer energy crisis, has countered with twin mantras of increased density and energy efficiency. In other words, we need fresh ideas.

Walters has plenty of ideas. His first major project started with an odd, triangular lot at College and Lansdowne. The owner, Mediacom, had plopped a billboard in the middle of the location, and no conventional builder was willing to meet the $86,000 asking price. Walters scooped it up for $17,000 and rose above the problematic space, building a house on stilts. A garden and parking pad sit underneath the 700-square-foot home.

And the tab? Only $80,000, a price that's even more attractive when the operating costs are added on: one hundred dollars a month, because the house is far less reliant on conventional heating and cooling methods than other homes. Large south-facing, triple-glazed windows make maximum use of solar energy and minimize heat loss. Sunlight is collected through the windows and absorbed by the thermal mass of concrete walls, which retain and slowly release warmth during cooler nighttimes. A radiant heat system pipes warm water beneath the light concrete floors. In summer, window shading helps keep the heat out so the concrete floors stay cool. A well-planned air flow hustles out excess heat. No matter the weather, the house stays comfy at half the cost of a standard, similarly sized home.

Despite these savings, however, progressive home design is still slow to catch on. Why? Walters shakes his head. 'Archaic ideas drive me nuts.'

He's not alone. In 1999, architects Peter Duckworth-Pilkington and Suzanne Cheng paid $50,000 for an unserviced laneway lot near Gerrard and Jones. 'We started with a perfectly rational idea,' says Duckworth-Pilkington. 'We wanted to build a sustainable house. But there's an entire bureaucracy that seems designed to prevent that.' First, the couple had to haggle over a zoning law that makes laneway homes illegal. Then neighbours, resistant to the idea, appealed to the Ontario Municipal Board. The couple won but soon waded into a sea of hassles big and small: garbage pickup, mail delivery. The house was too far from the nearest fire hydrant so they had to dish out $5,000 for a sprinkler system. They hoped to go off the grid with water collection and sewer treatment; the house's entire water supply would have come from rain and snow collected on the roof, and the water purified and stored in an underground cistern. Waste water, normally dumped into the sewer, was to have been treated in a home system using aerobic micro-organisms to duplicate the natural filtration process of soil. 'The technology is there,' says Duckworth-Pilkington. 'But the building codes don't allow it.' One and a half years and seven zoning variances after first applying to build their house, the couple finally started construction.

This is the great irony in our city: the official plan of 2002 stresses density and sustainability, but bureaucratic entanglements tend to counter any sense of innovation.

'There hasn't always been a sense of cause and effect in Toronto,' says Martin Kohn of Kohn Shnier Architects. In 2004, his firm asked for minor zoning variances to build a laneway house on Croft Street. They got a major headache. A four-month detour through the Committee of Adjustment resulted in a rejected proposal. Overdevelopment on the site, they were told. 'We were under the allowable floor area,' Kohn responds. They rejigged the plan and, in June 2004, completed a striking, 600-square-foot, two-storey house. 'They don't make it easy for you,' he sighs.

That might finally be changing. Linda McDonald, a downtown city planner, says there is interest in building laneway homes behind old working-class streets like Harbord, Niagara and Roncesvalles. Although laneway construction is still technically illegal, the city is trying to streamline the rezoning process with a checklist of favourable conditions, such as width of the lane, emergency access and parking. 'We're all for this type of intensification,' says McDonald.

Imagine: a city that doesn't simply sprawl or rise, where planners, builders and home buyers all agree on smart, sustainable growth and where reclaimed derelict sites add millions of dollars to the municipal tax base. 'It's time to make better use of what we have,' says Walters. 'Not just laneways but railway lands and valley lands.' He speaks with infectious enthusiasm; it spreads. 'Solutions sometimes scream for something original.'

Dylan Reid
The St. George campus takes shape

The University of Toronto's downtown St. George Campus was the York University of nineteenth-century Toronto – a sprawling, pastoral campus on the northern edge of the city, dotted with isolated buildings. As the campus was gradually engulfed by the city, it retained something of its original bucolic character, becoming an oasis of stately calm at the heart of the metropolis.

The university, as a public institution and a major landowner in the heart of Toronto, made a significant contribution to the cityscape, both in high-quality public architecture and in the kind of extended green space that is rarely seen outside public parks. Yet this contribution was lost as the university expanded rapidly in the second half of the twentieth century; extensive new building projects left the campus shapeless and utilitarian. At the end of the twentieth century and the beginning of the twenty-first, however, a new round of building has shown a greater consciousness of the university's role within the city. The campus has developed a new shape: around the borders, the university has defined its institutional identity with imposing buildings and branded gates; in the interior, it has begun to create a new kind of urban oasis, where street-friendly buildings integrate into a gentle green landscape. It is a shape that points to both the dangers and the hopes for Toronto's future.

The first buildings to occupy the campus, for the most part constructed by the various autonomous colleges, were built in imitation of medieval styles as they had been revived in Victorian Britain. Over time, these colleges evolved according to the quadrangle model characteristic of traditional British universities. Based on the medieval monastery or castle, the imposing, closed exterior of a quad (often decorated with castle-like ornaments such as gateways and crenellated towers) surrounds a quiet, green interior open space. Interspersed among these college buildings were the elegant suburban mansions of Toronto's wealthy, which were gradually absorbed by the university.

This traditional style of building persisted well into the twentieth century, but a major shift took place with the rapid expansion of the university to the south and west of the campus in the 1960s and 1970s to accommodate the increase in student numbers prompted by the baby boom. Built in a heady period celebrating modernity and change, the new buildings were aggressively different in style, constructed with modern materials – plate glass and concrete, with little embellishment or variation, often resulting in the harsh look that became commonly referred to as brutalism. They were built in an imposing solid mass, remote from the street, either set well back or fronting it with a solid, uninviting surface. Robarts Library is the most inescapable example of this approach. To accommodate this brave new world, streets were widened, trees cut down, green space paved and old buildings demolished. Much of the campus ended up less green than the surrounding city.

Since the late 1980s, the university and its colleges have embarked on a building program that has filled in almost all of the remaining buildable spaces on campus. During this process, the university became conscious of the fact that the building program could shape the campus as a whole in a coherent way. It developed an architectural review process, campus plans for buildings and landscaping, and a policy of defining the entrances to the university as gateways, all of which influenced this new round of construction. There will be a few more new buildings, renovations and landscapings in the years to come, but essentially the St. George Campus has taken its definitive shape, constituting the university's contribution to central Toronto for the foreseeable future.

Much has been written about the individual buildings that have recently been added to the campus, usually in terms of the architects and their design choices. Less has been written, however, about how recent projects have fit into and remoulded the campus as a whole. Viewed from this perspective, the recent building spree has helped to give a distinctive shape to the campus, creating a contrast between the older northeast quadrant where the old colleges dominate the available land, and the newer western and southern sections, which are chiefly controlled by the university administration. Both parts are influenced by the ideal of the quadrangle, but this ideal has developed in different ways.

In the northeast quadrant (which spills over Queen's Park Crescent as far as Bay Street), each of the colleges has at its heart its own self-contained quadrangle built in the early years of the university in variations of the traditional neo-medieval collegiate style. In essence, they are self-sufficient and inward-looking. In practice, these quadrangles are not complete – they tend to have open spaces within their boundaries, and college buildings spill over across adjoining streets. Furthermore, the college buildings are broken up by non-university buildings such as Queen's Park and the Royal Ontario Museum. The result is that the northeast of the university is porous, mixed into the city itself without clear boundaries. In this mixing, as in its architecture, this corner of the university is closer to the European tradition, in which older universities tend to have their buildings intermingled among city buildings, without a clearly defined campus.

During the 1960s building boom, the three colleges that dominate the northeast of the campus (Trinity, Victoria, St. Michael's) each experimented with conspicuously modern buildings. In more recent times, by contrast, they have looked back to their original architecture for inspiration, interpreted through a modern lens, resulting in subtle buildings that integrate into their surroundings. At St. Michael's College, the elegant Sam Sorbara Hall Student Residence extends the campus almost to Bay Street, appearing to be a long-standing extension of the college's older buildings until you look closely and notice its subtle modern elements. At Victoria College along Charles Street, the Isabel Bader Theatre and the McKinsey and Company building (a partnership with a consulting company) both use the grey stone of the old quad buildings, while Rowell Jackman Hall across the street takes its cue from art deco. Meanwhile, Trinity College's restoration of Devonshire House (which now houses the Munk Centre for International Studies and the Trinity library) blends the old buildings together smoothly. The only recent non-college building in this area, the law school's library, is deliberately unobtrusive, buried into a hillside, ensuring that the primary visual experience of the school remains the dignified pillars of the old Flavelle mansion.

All of these edifices are clearly modern, and yet they blend easily into the older buildings they accompany. They perpetuate the self-contained nature of the old colleges, not imposing much on the outside world. Beyond the northeast quadrant, however, the university's outward appearance changes. No longer as broken up by colleges and outside institutions, the western part of the university presents a consistent and well-defined perimeter of imposing buildings along three major streets – Bloor, Spadina and College. This definition has been reinforced by the recent policy of establishing clearly branded gateways at major entrances to the campus. In effect, rather than the individual, inward-looking quadrangles of the old colleges, the university has itself become a quadrangle, an imposing outer wall separating the outside city from the academic landscape within.

Along the northern frontier at Bloor Street, this border is anchored by two older, castle-like structures: the Admissions Office, with its turret watching over the entrance along Devonshire Place (as if to remind potential students how hard it is to get into the university); and the imposing bulk of University of Toronto Schools at the campus's northwest corner. In between, two new buildings continue the fortress-like feeling, guarding the university's main northern entrance along St. George Street. The non-university Bata Shoe Museum calls to mind a distended bunker, while the narrow windows around the base of the new Woodsworth College Residence look like arrow slits keeping the world at bay from the students finding shelter in the tower above. (The studded metal gateposts marking the entrance at the street level are named after the Perly and Rae families, which means that the University of Toronto can claim to be the home of the Perly Gates.) Add the grey brutalism of the Senator David A. Croll apartments (once home to the experimental Rochdale College) and buildings from several eras combine to create a northern wall for the university.

The western border along Spadina feels like the back end of campus, lonely and ignored. The university buildings look inwards, with their main entrances on side streets inside the campus, turning a cold shoulder to Spadina, while the street itself is so wide that each side is almost a different world. A couple of isolated blocks of rather forlorn houses lead to the forbidding western gate of the university, at Harbord. It is bounded by two thoroughly modern buildings that are, if anything, more medieval in spirit that any of the quaint turreted neo-Gothic buildings in the northeast. On the north side, Graduate House, with its heavy bands of precast coloured concrete and its narrow slit windows, looks like the prison where they will lock up the intellectuals after the coup d'état. It is complemented on the south side by the faceless concrete bunker of 'Fort Jock,' the university's Athletic Centre. The effect is like the entrance to the underworld in a medieval tale, flanked by grim brooding structures, with Graduate House's oversized sign an ominous warning overhead.

The rest of Spadina further perpetuates this feeling of fortress-like alienation. The original New College buildings present an almost blank wall to the street; the recently built residence to the south is more open, but its narrow windows still recall arrow slits. At the south edge lies the Gothic outlying bastion of Spadina Crescent, protected by a moat of traffic that echoes Queen's Park Crescent on the east side of campus. The narrow sidewalks and rushing traffic at the southern end of these two traffic circles are disagreeable for those on foot, leaving these stretches the most deserted parts of the campus's periphery.

The southern border of the campus along, College Street, is reserved and severe. The buildings keep their distance from the street through a consistent setback (the only exception being the forward bastion of the architecture school, its new glass eye keeping a beady lookout over the street below), their ground floors often raised high above street level. The two gates, especially the one at King's College Circle, maintain this sense of polite institutional distance separating town and gown. This southern wall of the university is anchored at its corners by two stern tall towers. The Centre for Addiction and Mental Health to the west is a brutalist array of repetitive glass and concrete, while the new Leslie L. Dan Pharmacy Building of plain and dot-patterned glass looms over the eastern end. Its narrow base keeps the bulk of the structure distant from the street – a modernist ivory tower.

In the interior of the campus, new developments have gone in a different direction from the exterior. Built in a modest and integrative style, they alleviate the effects of baby-boom buildings and create intimacy and comfort. Additions to old buildings have had the counterintuitive effect of softening them, and the adjacent open spaces are being revitalized with a comprehensive landscaping plan. The interior of the campus is being transformed into an pleasant urban oasis.

Most of the brand new buildings inside the campus are on the western side, where there was still open space to fill in. By far the largest is the Bahen Centre for Information Technology at the south end of St. George Street. It is remarkable just how much mass manages to squeeze into this irregular mid-block space in an unobtrusive manner. The low, disjointed front along St. George integrates with the heritage buildings to either side, a house to the north and the Koffler Centre to the south, while the bulk of the building stands modestly behind, varied and pleasing to the eye. The Earth Sciences Centre on Huron Street was designed by the same firm, and shows similarities in its mix of square and round shapes, its warm and balanced materials and its integration of the existing urban fabric (it wraps around a secluded interior street that incorporates pre-existing houses).

One of the most attractive features of the new buildings on campus is a variety of modernist spins on the quadrangle, neglected in the earlier baby-boom buildings. The Earth Sciences building incorporates two quads housing samples of natural local forest (the forestry department is housed in the building), reflecting a modern environmental sensibility. The Bahen Centre harbours an elegant plaza hidden behind the Koffler Centre; the new Woodsworth and New College residences both shelter new courtyards at their rear; Woodsworth College and Devonshire House have created modern cloisters connecting old buildings together; and even Graduate House wraps itself around a barren patio jutting into a dank little pool.

Two other new buildings, the eye-catching mishmash of the Wolfond Jewish Centre and the eclectic building blocks of the Early Learning Centre, are low-rise structures that rely on eccentric inventiveness rather than size to catch the eye. Along St. George north of Harbord, the Innis College Student Residence and Joseph L. Rotman School of Management share a street-friendly urbanism, modest in mass and materials, that balances the massiveness of Robarts Library. Finally, University College, the only old college without a previous experiment in modern styles, is building a tall glass and metal tower for its new residence, but even here there is a certain modesty, with the tower stepping back respectfully at its top and a brick base that blends into the neighbouring buildings.

Most of these new buildings are clad largely in brick, a noticeable change from the concrete of the brutalist era, with neither too much nor too little glass. Their street fronts and entrances are near the sidewalk, not high up or set back as in earlier styles. Their construction often incorporates environmental measures. These buildings point to a sustainable urban architecture for the new century, accommodating and integrating into the city at a human scale while providing a lot of efficient urban density. As such, they have made the western part of the campus warmer, more balanced and more accessible.

Additions to existing buildings, too, have managed to soften their severity while increasing density. The heavy blank walls of the Lash Miller Chemical Laboratories along St. George have been lightened by the addition of variegated new storeys of glass and metal. Just to the north, a series of transformations has opened up the once dull and distant Sidney Smith Hall. Its closed terrace has been broken down into steps to the street, its ground floor opened up with windows to a student lounge and its entrance made beautiful with an additional floor decorated with a stylish metallic frontage. Additions to Woodsworth College, the School of Continuing Studies and the Gerstein Science Information Centre have similarly made fairly nondescript older buildings contribute more to the campus.

The final step in the evolution of the interior of the campus into an urban oasis is the transformation of the landscape. The keystone of this process was the revitalization of St. George Street. By narrowing the street and adding landscaping, it was changed from a barrier through the middle of campus into a bond that ties the new campus to the old. Inspired by the impact of this transformation, the university has developed a master plan to use revitalized open spaces to soften and connect the campus. The plan can already be seen in small touches, such as the conversion of two neglected passageways between St. George Street and King's College Circle into restful intervals of native plants. On a grander scale, the utilitarian asphalt entrance to King's College Road has been transformed, through street narrowing, paving stones, new plantings and places to sit, into a place where people visit and linger; the aloof McLennan Physical Laboratories building is slated to be warmed up by an equally thorough landscaping overhaul.

The most ambitious part of the plan addresses the bridge over the end of Wellesley Street on the east side of campus at Hart House Circle. At the moment, this is the secret entrance to campus, almost a hidden passage under the barrier of traffic created by Queen's Park Crescent. The plan is to level this bridge, creating an intersection instead, so that this lost entrance to the university would become a pastoral opening welcoming the city into the campus, a contrast with the dystopian back end of the campus at Harbord and Spadina.

The interior and exterior of the St. George Campus provide exemplars for two different potential directions for Toronto. The exterior of well-defined, branded boundaries formed by severe, imposing buildings and gates points to a potentially disquieting future. Setting itself apart from the city in this way reflects the university's increasing reliance on private funds and the reduced role of public support. These borders tell the story of a gradual privatization of the institution, self-contained and remote, no longer part of the community. This tendency to make the campus an urban island warns of a future atomization of cities, their public spaces atrophied, their buildings standing separate from and dominating the urban environment rather than integrating into it.

Two of the new buildings on this periphery embody this isolationist model. The Leslie L. Dan Pharmacy Building is a cool tower that stands aloof from its environs; Graduate House's distinct and aggressive appearance and huge branded sign clearly set it apart from the surrounding city. The latter is the only new building that embraces rather than moderates the spirit of brutalism of earlier institutional architecture. Yet the tragedy of Graduate House is that its in-your-face exterior masks some attractive qualities it shares with most of the other new buildings on campus: urbanity in squeezing remarkable density into a relatively modest mass that is open to the street, and whimsicality in its irregular, off-kilter lines. The other new buildings around the exterior, on the other hand, show promise by embracing these qualities without the brutish appearance. The Woodsworth and New College residences, even the Leslie L. Dan Pharmacy Building, and especially the Terrence Donnelly Centre for Cellular and Biomolecular Research behind it, create connections to the street with transparent ground floors and lighten their presence with whimsical touches (checkerboard tower, erratic windows, dangling pods, coloured genetic patterns and suspended winter gardens).

So there is hope even at the borders, and if one penetrates this outer shell, one finds an inspiring vision for the future in the interior. It is developing into an urban oasis, a space of calm, greenery and gentle architecture amid the helter-skelter activity of downtown. New buildings have paradoxically made the interior of the campus more people-friendly, breaking down barriers by integrating with and softening existing structures, and extending the quadrangle tradition to the west side of the campus. Revived open spaces are beginning to interconnect the campus with greenery and pathways, reducing the presence of the automobile, improving walking and cycling amenities, and making full use of one of the largest open spaces in the downtown to create a restful green environment. This developing campus points to a potential image not just for a university but also for cities as a whole in the new century – less traffic and smaller streets, innovative human-scale buildings that are integrated into the cityscape while providing dense work and living space, all linked by attractive, green public spaces filled with people.

The St. George Campus is taking shape as a giant quadrangle, set apart from the city by an institutional border, but open on one side and enclosing an urban oasis within. It is a model both of dangers for Toronto's future and of the potential to create a livable, sustainable city.

Stéphanie Verge
Changing lanes: a conversation with Jeffery Stinson

As Toronto's ranks continue to swell and real-estate prices to soar, two local architects have developed a clever solution to the affordable housing question: look to
the laneways. By publishing a 2003 report on the subject, *A Study of Laneway Housing in Toronto*, Jeffery Stinson and Terence Van Elslander hoped
to make it easier for urbanites to build their homes in the alleys that
criss-cross the city. While the project is now stalled at city hall, interest in
condo alternatives like these is on the rise. And as the happy owner of one
of Toronto's first modern laneway houses – a sunlight-filled, three-storey,
2200-square-foot family house now divided into three separate apartments – Stinson is determined to see such energy-conscious, efficient
and elegant dwellings multiply.

SV How did you first become involved in laneway housing?

JS The story really starts in the early eighties. I had done, for myself
and for other people, alterations and additions to houses on
laneways, so I had some sense of what it was like. Then I acquired
a block of land on a laneway in Kensington Market and began
to think about building myself a new house. The process took
about two years to get from the initial sketches to approval at
city hall. What I discovered was that the bylaws simply don't
help with that sort of thing; I encountered very helpful people
at city hall, but they just didn't know how to deal with it. Several
years later, I noticed that the only houses that were being built in
laneways tended to be architects' own houses. It struck me that
the reason is that the architects can gamble on the drawings and

so on because it's their time and they know their way through the system; they can be persistent. And I thought, this is madness, because what I had discovered in living on the laneway was how pleasant it really was to be away from the main street, to have this little enclave at the back.

Where did you start?

Terence – whom I had known for some years – and I made a submission to the Canadian Mortgage and Housing Corporation, suggesting that we study the business of laneway housing, just to see what the realities were – to make it easier to do so that more people could take advantage of it. We proposed a two-stage operation. The first was essentially research, while, at the second, we would actually try to, with the connivance of the city, build a sample house. Then, as we went through it, we would discover the difficulties and dangers and try to make sense of it. The city was very interested but wasn't very keen on the second part of the process: the building of a prototype. They did their own study on laneway housing, which came out generally saying yes, it's a good idea. One of the drawbacks is that the new Official Plan places a lot of emphasis on maintaining the neighbourhoods and all those sorts of things. The kind of language it's got in there makes it very difficult to deal with things that are not precisely in line with the street-oriented, historic nature of the town.

What are the major hurdles you face when building in laneways?

One of the two main problems is servicing: water, sewage, garbage, things like that.

Mail delivery.

Yes, and there's no solution in sight for that at the moment. Clearly, the city, with its large trucks, is not quite set up for laneways, many of which are narrower. But, in a sense, one has to accept the virtue of trying to do this, and get some experts – in sewage and water and all those things – together and find a way to do this. There is a proposition here, from what our research revealed. We looked closely at the southwest quadrant of the old City of Toronto, and what we found is that about a tenth of the lots in that area had back lane possibilities. Out of five thousand lots, we found five hundred possibilities for laneway housing.

If there are five hundred lots in the southwest quadrant, how many are there in the whole city?

I would say that you could probably triple or quadruple that number. So there are thousands of laneway possibilities.

I'm not really sure how much the city would charge for property taxes, but that would represent –

A lot.

Then why are they dragging their feet on this?

There are difficulties. The first, as I said, is servicing. The second one is public perception. Most of the laneway houses that have been built have had to go through strenuous public meetings. Very often the local people are unhappy about it for a number of reasons, but I think if people felt decent houses could be built in the back lanes that would not impinge on the virtue of the front house, the street house, then it would open up a great opportunity for individual entrepreneurship. You would be able to make a little house for the kids when they grow up or for Granny. They are just worried about what is going to be there. There's not much precedent for them to understand the quality of house that can be built in laneways.

Is there a contingent that is concerned with the unorthodox look of laneway houses?

Fitting in with the neighbourhood has tended to be interpreted everywhere as mock Victorian. What we're saying is that laneways are different. Laneways are not part of the streetscape; they offer more interesting opportunities for architects and more interesting kinds of houses for people to live in. They shouldn't be constrained by mock Victoriana; they should somehow be free of that, as indeed my house was.

It certainly doesn't seem to look like anything else around it.

No, it doesn't. That's an asset of laneway housing. But such housing will be raised as an example by neighbours who say they don't want it because it won't fit in with the neighbourhood. However, Toronto has been building laneway houses from the beginning; it is one of the historic forms of city dwelling.

How many laneway houses currently exist in the city?

Dozens. We went around and took photographs of a great number of laneway houses, but because many of them may have happened slightly illegally, we didn't want to identify them. We didn't want to make people think about where they were or who owned them, just to know that there are dozens of them. Not new ones, like ours, but ones that have been there for a long time.

How long?

There's a semi next to my house that was on the maps in 1894, and I'm sure they had been around before that. After all, mews housing is in all cities, all European cities. It was generally for the servants, maybe above the stable.

But now we use that space mainly for garages.

If you happen to have a twenty-square-foot garage, you can make a very nice apartment on top of that – a single-person apartment. It's not legal at the moment, but you could do it. Clearly, in dealing with laneway housing, we'd have to think about car parking as well. So that's another issue.

Do you have any solutions to that particular problem?

Different places call for different solutions. The laneway just outside my house is only seven feet six inches wide. I had to go through the Ontario Municipal Board (OMB). One of the only things that the OMB asked of me is that I didn't build in one corner, because people wouldn't be able to get in and out with their cars as easily to other lots. There are compromises to be made with car parking and manoeuvring, but I don't think any of these things are insuperable. Nowadays, the city is willing to allow reduced parking ratios. We are no longer pushing for one car per residence, and I think that will be applied to laneway housing. In some of them it will be possible to have cars and in some of them it won't.

What's the average size of the laneway houses you are suggesting?

I don't know if we really have an average size.

But it doesn't go above two storeys generally, because it would obstruct the street house's views, correct?

That's right. You don't want to get in people's faces about the thing. Generally, ours are two storeys, although occasionally there's the possibility of a third floor. With my place, we tried to get the city to consider rooftop gardens and things like that as part of the lot coverage. There's a bylaw about the extent of landscaped area that you have, and one needs to think about that as well. Where does that go if you are fitting it on a tight laneway? Well, maybe it's on the roof. There is, at the moment, a great push, with very good reason, for green roofs in the city, and that may be the way to go.

I've heard of something called a house-behind-a-house bylaw that forbids houses behind houses. Doesn't that make your job –

Impossible? Right. Yes, it does. That bylaw was created in the sixties, I think, for what seemed at the time perfectly reasonable conditions. You couldn't get the fire engine to them, servicing was difficult, they would obscure people's views, you would have overlooking and noise. All of which can be true, but not necessarily so. We think that, in most cases, those things can be got around by good design. It wasn't a bad bylaw at the time, but what it's done is to inhibit absolutely our proposition.

Right now, how much does it cost to build a laneway house?

That's really hard to say. Architects' own houses probably range somewhere from 100 to 250 dollars a square foot. Developer houses are somewhat less, but not a lot. So much depends on the particular location. For example, I had to pay for the sewers and water from the street to my place. It cost me about $35,000. That's virtually on top of everything. If you have a little house and it's going to cost you $35,000 extra to get the plumbing and draining to work, then it's going to push up the price. I know other architects who have had to pay $65,000 to get a house hooked up.

If you were to solve the servicing problems and get around the different bylaws and such, do you think it would be less expensive to build a laneway house than a house on a main street? Isn't the idea, after all, to build affordable housing?

I think that if you understand that they are small and simple, you probably are getting in under the wire from standard stuff on the street. I have always said that if you want to build economically you have to have a combination of convention and invention, because you have to work with the sort of trades that we've got. Otherwise, nobody knows how to do it. And the prices go up if everything is unfamiliar. On the other hand, this is a chance to invent things. For example, I've pushed the ground level of my house right down; because it's a small house, I want to be able to think of the garden as a part of the house. There's that old cliché, the indoor/outdoor thing. It doesn't work if you've got to go down two feet six inches, as many houses do. I wanted to be able to open all these double doors and things in the summertime so that it's like one big room and part of it is outside. In order to do that, in order to have a habitable basement, I put in a sidewalk grille. When you step out of my living room and you walk across that, you can –

See into the basement.

But I get winter light right into the back walls of the basement through that stuff. Another thing that's going on down there at the house, but should be going on a lot more, is sustainability and green building. We do have to do better in that line; that will be looking for some innovation as well.

Ultimately, if it is a green building, that will push the cost down.

Yes, with the heating and all those kinds of things. I'm appalled by how many houses are built with vast glass walls, without any shade whatsoever, facing the sun. On warm days, when it's not even summer yet, people are turning on their air conditioning.

If the cost of building a laneway house is only a little bit cheaper than regular housing, what is the appeal for the average person?

Living in Kensington Market, I could walk to the movies and to other things in the city. I could cycle virtually anywhere. Being in the city is really good, but these days where would you live? You would live in giant high-rises that don't suit everybody, or in old houses that are extraordinarily expensive. This is a new house built to modern standards.

The city's plan calls for densification. Doesn't laneway housing seem like a rational place to go?

We've got all these services. We've got all these streetcars. We've got plumbing and draining in most places and all that sort of thing, and we should be using it more intensely, more densely. The Official Plan is perfectly logical in calling for medium density, which probably means four-storey, five-storey, six-storey small apartment buildings along subway routes and major routes. That has always been a good idea. We just think there are other options out there that would be worthwhile pursuing. It's not to build up a huge clientele or open up a whole new development bag, but just to make things easier so that more people can do it. It doesn't take architects building their own houses to do it. We see laneway housing not as a panacea, or certainly not the only way Toronto should go, but simply as another option. Laneway housing has always been a part of the mix in every great city I know. Why are we having such a problem here?

You've been working on this project pretty steadily since 2002.

It's been a while. It's turned out to be more difficult than we thought. One of the difficulties at city hall since we got mega-citied is that some people from what we used to think of as the suburbs have taken their places on committees and sub-committees and have declared that nobody should have to live in a laneway house – as though it were a sort of slum and we were forcing people into them. I don't know if renting at my house is any indication of the demand, but I've had one person that's been there since I left, in the big part, and in the small part I have a queue of people wanting to get in every time it comes up. It's never been advertised. There have been four or five rentals over the past seven or eight years. An opera singer, a belly dancer, computer experts, and all of them seemed to think it was wonderful. There's a constituency out there. I don't have any doubts on that score. I just have the need to make it more plausible.

You talked about other options with regards to the medium-density issue. Is that something you are working on?

Terence is doing some things, but I'm not doing anything in that area. In fact, I'm doing really small-scale housing in the Philippines, where families live in a house that's five metres by four metres. The cost limits there are absolutely unbelievable, so it's a struggle. It has put a different cast on all of this stuff for me, because I just think how well off we are in this city, where the standards people have come to expect for housing are pretty good. I think it's entirely possible to make quite high-quality living spaces at an economical cost. Let's face it, we're talking tiny little bits of land. Out in the Beaches and other places, the land value is so high now – $300,000 or $400,000 for a lot – that quite a few of the houses are not viable anymore. People are buying up houses and knocking them down to build bigger houses, because the lot deserves the house. It seems a bit mad to me, in terms of what you need to live.

Bigger, better, more.

Yes. One of the goals behind the Philippines project is to promote sustainability, and one of the unfortunate things that we are grappling with there is that the model for housing the world over is the U.S. suburbs. In my experience, that's the dream of most people everywhere. We can't address that dream. We just can't deal with it. That's the worst kind of unsustainable building we know about. It's profligate: wastes resources, wastes space, incurs cars. It's just a horror story, yet that's the image people have in their minds of glory. Even in the Philippines, in the middle-class suburbs, you'll see reflections of that. Strangely enough, laneway housing ties into this. If you think you don't get a decent house unless it's got mock Ionic columns out the front, then you are in trouble with laneway houses. Because we intend to build simple, clear, twenty-first-century houses. And that doesn't give you the same kind of image quality you get when you look at Rosedale. We are trying to say, 'Look, we can offer you something, but it's not that. It has nothing to do with those 5,000-square-foot monsters.'

It's hard to change people's dreams.

I think that's the most difficult thing. I don't know how we can deal with that. I think dreams are often based on preconceptions and partial knowledge. I have taught various courses at U of T, and recently I've had classes in the undergraduate stream where not one student has ever been in a modern house. Modern houses are not common. We should be starting people off in kindergarten. We have to get into the game earlier; it's too late now because their images are already formed. I don't think people have a full range of options. They have one set of options, which keeps getting pushed in front of them.

Why are Torontonians clinging to those same options, the same aesthetics?

A primary issue with people I've had to deal with, really intelligent folks, is resale value. And who are the arbiters of real-estate selling? Agents. And real-estate agents are in a kind of circle. They are selling what's around, therefore they feel that what's around is what needs to sell. They are in many ways fine, upstanding people, but I don't think they should be in charge of how the world looks. Their industry is in charge of the aesthetics of the city, and I think that's bad news. I had a client once and I bought his house in the Beaches. Then he bought what he thought was a posher house in Scarborough. It was what we used to call Scottish baronial, lots of stone stuck on, and I spent the next ten years doing jobs for him trying to make this damn house habitable. Knocking down walls, rebuilding this, rebuilding that, putting stuff in, and he used to always say to me whenever we'd start one of these jobs, 'How is the resale here? Are we talking 20,000 bucks worth?' I finally had to say to him, 'Look, you're driving a car you don't like, you're living in a house you hate. Forget resale, for God's sake! Maybe you'll die tomorrow – live somewhere you really like.'

Philip Evans
Paved impressions

Rooftops, fence, trees, grass, sidewalk, grass, pavement, median, occasionally varied by discarded artifacts of clothing such as the all-too-familiar lone shoe, garbage
of all sorts thrown from car windows and, of course, roadkill: the greater
part of my teenage years was spent staring down at the sidewalk.

Like many Toronto suburbs, Brampton had an isolating quality for a
resentful not-yet-old-enough-to-drive thirteen-year-old whose understanding of relentless housing farms was limited to an endless matrix of
sidewalks. I remember counting 1,023 concrete sidewalk pavers on my way
to school. After cutting through the catwalk at the end of my street, it was
a thirty-minute stroll to school along a four-lane road of commuters. This
was hardly a shared experience. On the way, there was a 7-Eleven where I
could enjoy a moment of perceived freedom while sipping a cream-soda
slurpee and kicking a pop can as long as I could. The community offered
a pedestrian few features beyond these. Most of the time, I stared down
at the sidewalk and drifted into my thoughts.

A revived interest in our public space demonstrates a desire to see new
forms and alternative models of urban design. In the past forty years,
new uses of the traditional form of the square in Toronto represent our
attempts to achieve new public forms. But urban planners and architects
who have tried to interpret the square as part of Toronto's urban fabric
have met with some controversy. If we are to measure how the square
functions in Toronto as an alternative form for public encounter, however, we need to first consider the successful and familiar model of our
past: the sidewalk.

Like many other Torontonians on the way to work or the corner store,
my cone of vision is usually limited, from the hands in my pocket to

1

three feet in front of me. I often have to remind myself to lift my head and appreciate the city around the street canopy and my neighbours. There isn't a single street in Toronto where someone I know hasn't pointed out a friend's old apartment or an ex-lover's flat or a backyard where they'd partied. Take a ghost-walk tour through Kensington Market and note the variety of hexagonal mirrors used to warn off evil spirits. It's not often you'll walk past a locked-up bike and recognize its pink basket, but when you do, you'll be sure to search out the owner. It's much easier to feel a part of your environment when you bump into someone you know. These are unmistakably pure urban moments that have come to tell the form of our city. And they most often take place on sidewalks.

The current condition of Toronto's sidewalks is ripe to tell us much about our public conduct. They are the essential edge condition between our most public and most private of realms. Beyond their functional capacity as walking surfaces for pedestrians, our sidewalks have assumed infinite identities by their users and histories – as seen through the traces of activity that have shaped the form of our constructed urban landscape. The future of Toronto's growth can be seen through its almost three hundred years of decay.

Formal and material transformations of our city's sidewalks reveal much about where our city is headed. I've always enjoyed the messy layers upon layers of brick, concrete and pavement peeling away from each other as their own rates of decay determine. The transformation of our sidewalks is closely related to our built environment but, more interestingly, by our conditioning of it. Their rate of deterioration can easily form a palette of aesthetic decay, specific to sites throughout the city, and it can reveal quite intimate relationships to location and circumstance. Most

2 **3**

are accidental, but all are romantically linked to a continued assessment of the city's purpose.

Impressions

While the concrete is curing, within its temporary wooden frame, it is trowelled and stamped to bear the name and date of its construction crew – a formal record of authorship. This is also the point at which control joints are made in anticipation of inevitable cracking and shifting. Within four hours of the pour, the concrete is hard enough to walk on. It takes about twenty-eight days for the concrete to reach full-strength capacity. But are the formal construction-crew stamps as interesting as accidental or guerrilla-mission carvings made during those first four hours? Just north of College Street on Brunswick Avenue, four sections of cat and dog footprints can be clearly identified. These impressions hold a record of the city.

In 2004, ERA Architects Inc. was asked to prepare an assessment of the Asylum Wall, completed in the 1870s, that surrounds the grounds of the Centre for Addiction and Mental Health on Queen Street. In addition to the general condition and state of the wall, they'd learned much about how the wall had been used and its importance to the community and to the patients of the hospital. The evidence was clear throughout the hundreds of thousands of bricks, mortar and stones that stood as a record of the past 150 years. In addition, they discovered the only remaining evidence of the north segment of the Asylum Wall that had once spanned the entire Queen Street perimeter of the property: the repeating impression of the regularly spaced pilaster had been found along the edge of the sidewalk, encapsulated in the concrete panels poured in 1968.

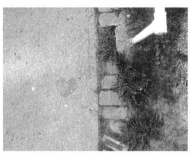

4   5

Disrepair/Repair

Concrete ages. It is a material subject to cracks, shifting, movement from faulty installation, pressure from tree roots and eroding soils below the surface. Independent pavers can be easily replaced without having to affect large areas, but most of the city uses large areas of concrete. With the arrival of spring comes the familiar preparatory spray-painting to flag services below the surface and areas of planned work as instructions. The repair is often a temporary state before its replacement, but an aesthetic has emerged from our temporary repair techniques: materials used to maintain or decelerate the aging process, such as silicone caulking, infill asphalt patching and intentional cuts into the sidewalk to control further cracking, have come closer to articulating a Toronto style than any architectural language.

Surface

Cleanliness is relative. In 1984, a group of Toronto artists selected a single sidewalk panel and cleaned it to an immaculate standard. The artists, dressed in full decontamination gear, were shown on their hands and knees scrubbing and disinfecting the panel as if they would soon eat from it. Though this is an unrealistic standard (which was hardly the point of the installation), it's nice to expect our sidewalks to be free of garbage and somewhat clean. Whether it's the city maintaining regular garbage pickup, street cleaners or the neighbour with the best-swept walkway, sidewalks are exterior surfaces, exposed to the natural elements, so it's understandable that our standards of sanitation should be met with a reasonable level of tolerance. But the natural tone and texture of concrete doesn't satisfy everyone. A personal touch of decor has become a

6

civil right. City Beautiful initiatives have formalized an awareness of the creative potential of our sidewalks. Anonymous interventions like street paintings, trails of hearts throughout Little Italy or a five-year-old's chalk drawing of her family along Concord Avenue continue to inspire our daily walks.

Form

Most of us would assume that sidewalks are designed for us to walk on. This is not true – they're designed for cars. Sidewalks are structurally designed to evenly distribute loads far beyond the expectations that crowds of people could ever apply. Such tolerances designed into sidewalks speak to the level of flexibility for the kinds of things that can happen on them. They offer a form that can easily facilitate the conditions of public encounter. Successful models for urban conditions exist throughout the city, and not just in the obvious places where high numbers of pedestrians are seen, on such streets as King, Queen, Dundas, College and Bloor. Sidewalks serve a variety of uses at any one time. Their flexibility allows citizens to contribute to the identities of a city, a neighbourhood and the individual.

In Toronto, our sidewalks have become ideal public forms. In fact, they've taken on this role far better than what is traditionally the best forum for shared public experience: the square.

Inside the cover of the 1976 album *Dedication* by the Bay City Rollers, there is an astonishing view of Toronto's Nathan Phillips Square. Thousands of teenage fans had swarmed the square for a glimpse of the heartthrob boy band. More peculiar than the dense, crazed crowd of teenage girls held back by police, however, is the rarely seen use of the car ramp

7

that lay at the base of the 1964 design of City Hall. Access to the ramp and the elevated walkways has been off limits since the early eighties. Originally conceived as part of Toronto's PATH system, these year-round exposed public walkways may have presented a threat of potential lawsuits over icy conditions. But as an architectural form, they serve to clearly demarcate routes through the square from areas of gathering. Excluded now from everyday use, their presence has been reduced to nothing more than a formal aesthetic – a polite experiment to introduce the square to Toronto's vocabulary. Without their functional qualities, it's easy instead to see these artifacts as barriers obstructing connections between the square and sidewalk on Queen and Bay Street.

In this respect, Nathan Phillips Square behaves less like a public square open to an endless possibility for encounter and more like an urban forecourt dedicated to the functions of a city hall, biased towards a particular civic expression despite its address within the public realm. In fact, the only direct connection the square makes is to the reception plinth that the flanking towers sit on. The southern and eastern edges of the square's pavers are separated by a grass median, failing to make a necessary connection to the sidewalk. It has ignored standard urban patterns in favour

8

of an over-defined threshold to the square. By trying to frame the ideal conditions of a shared experience through a public square, the design for City Hall has, in fact, ostracized Toronto's most important vessel for that expression: the sidewalk.

Forty years later, the designers of Dundas Square would achieve some success in resolving Toronto's uncertainty as to whether its citizens had developed a palette to appreciate the square's traditional form. The perception of our more mature public understanding was represented by a simple but integral gesture: the divisions between the sidewalk and the square had been blurred. The green-tinted granite of the square carried out to the street edge, completely engulfing the sidewalk, increasing intimacy between the street and the square. The introduction of this blur caused confusion for some Torontonians. The two democratic spaces, each presenting a unique use and role, had fused together, although not without controversy over how the new space should be used.

It's hard to say if using the European model of a square would improve the quality of our public space. It's difficult because we are still developing a palette from which to assess what is good or bad public form. If we're to improve the quality of the public realm, shouldn't we make it easier to facilitate our behaviour in it? A new form would respond to our pride and insecurities, our manners and social practices, all within an existing framework of ideas and place as found in the realm of the sidewalk.

9

1 Large aggregates used on sidewalk panels along Queen Street close to Spadina Avenue
2 Old streetcar tracks rising out of the intersection crossing
  Bay Street along the north side of Bloor Street
3 Sidewalk pavers along Queen Street surrounding a tree close to Bathurst Street
4 Dog and cat prints in a sidewalk panel on Brunswick Avenue just north of College
5 Red painted hearts along Concord Avenue just north of College Street
6 "Love Mom" from child's notebook as found along Concord just south of Bloor Street
7 View looking west along Queen Street on the south side towards
  Dovercourt Road, courtesy of ERA Architects Inc.
8 Impression of north portion of the Asylum Wall as captured in
  the 1968 sidewalk panel, courtesy of ERA Architects Inc.
9 Sidewalk and private brick pathway along Dunn Avenue in Parkdale
10 Intervention: infill of sidewalk cracks along Dunn Avenue in Parkdale

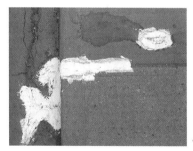

10

Jacob Allderdice
The Toronto Islands: a love story

I love the Toronto Islands. I love the fact that while it's a public park, people live there, in little houses on little 'streets,' without huge fences and without any No Trespassing signs (that I've noticed). I love the fact that in a canoe, which you can rent from a club on Queens Quay, you can paddle your way across the Western Gap (a shipping channel), skirting the buoy-marked no-go zone around the island airport landing strips, and in a half-hour (more or less) find yourself in the still backwaters and lagoons of the island proper, with its bird sanctuary, its long narrow channels and its places to beach your boat and walk around. I love the fact that you can leave your boat there for a while without fear that someone will steal it. I love the ferries too, three of them, that transport people and goods and bicycles back and forth between Toronto's waterfront and Ward's, Centre or Hanlan's ferry docks. For the princely sum of six dollars round trip, it's possible to scoot over to paradise, ride around for an hour or two, find something to eat in a nice *boîte* (or pack a picnic), loll on a beach (nude if you prefer), ride a miniature train, feed a swan or play volleyball. You can stroll the toy-town streets of the residential community, and, if you're lucky enough to have a friend living over there, pay someone a call. Between the little streets on Ward's Island and the slightly wider streets on Algonquin Island, some seven hundred people reside in the car-free park.

While islanders would probably prefer otherwise, the islands have always been in the news, and no more so than in the past few years. First of all, there are the issues surrounding the island airport, which comprises some eighty hectares (two hundred acres) of former residential and commercial land at the westernmost end of the island chain. It's the closest bit to downtown, with the aforementioned Western Gap and five-minute ferry crossing at the bottom of Bathurst Street. Of course, everyone knows something of the struggle to link a road directly across the Western Gap. It's part of the vital history of the islands, with bridges, tunnels and more bridges planned (and even launched) from the start of the motoring age. The most recent incarnation of this struggle had a would-be airline entrepreneur, Robert Deluce, scheming with federal appointees at the Toronto Port Authority to build a $22 million (projected cost) bridge, a plan that led straight to the election of a new mayor, David Miller, who opposed the bridge. The bridge never had the necessary government permits and, until four days before the election of the new city council, didn't have a signed contract. But when the new council voted to stop its construction, the Port Authority, the fledgling airline and the construction company all participated in threatening lawsuits amounting to over half a billion dollars. Next, the federal government paid off the Port Authority with $35 million and a

WISH I COULD LIVE HERE.

request that they shut up about bridges 'forever.' *Globe and Mail* columnist John Barber famously questioned how $22 million to build a bridge becomes $35 million to *not* build it. The bad news is, now the original schemers have money greasing their pocketbooks. It's unlikely we've heard the last of their lot.

But this came in the wake of another mad-eyed scheme, aired in April 2005, to 'investigate' making a bid for the 2015 World's Fair. The proposal, which garnered lukewarm support from the city politicians, would see the airport razed and rebuilt with pavilions, the Western Gap filled and a new ship channel dug to the south, and an underwater tube to run a train back and forth to a secondary fairground at the mouth of the Don River. The razing of the island airport, source of so much grief to the island residents (and others along the waterfront), is the one beacon of hope in the proposal.

Island residents are used to vexing news, and will take a ray of hope where they find it. Their bucolic car-free setting at the edge of Canada's largest city seems to set teeth on edge among those who willingly drive several hours to cottage country. When island residents complain about noise, such as that generated by the airport, the neighbouring Docks nightclub, or the Wakefest festival, they are called NIMBYS or squatters or worse. 'You live in a park,' folks say. 'You deserve the bad with the good.'

The interesting thing about the island residential community is that, while everyone acts as if they resent and envy it, no one makes the obvious leap to say, 'Why not build more of it?' While there is a 500-name waiting list of families who pay a yearly fee to be considered, should the opportunity arise, to buy one of the 362 coveted homes on the island, where is the developer with the vision to contact those five hundred families directly? Why not ask if there might be people eager to live in a similar community that could be built elsewhere and anew? That this developer fails to materialize despite the fact that the list is 'capped' (a yearly lottery is held for the chance to take one of the spaces on it that opens up when people lose hope and drop out) seems utterly without logic.

Back in 2000, the Toronto Society of Architects held a juried public design competition to develop the theme of something called the Fung Report. This report analyzed the entire waterfront of Toronto for opportunities and projects. The competition generated its share of schemes to replace the Gardiner Expressway, to develop a naturalized mouth of the Don River and to place 'gateways' and markers at significant points along the

— 1 —

THIS PROPOSAL places a new URBAN COMMUNITY on the Island Airport PALIMPSEST. It leaves open the former runways, RECYCLING them as BROAD AVENUES on the "Main Streets" model, where people can stroll, bicycle, or ride a tram. The STREET WALLS of the new avenues would be a maximum of 5 storeys, about the highest a fit cliff-dweller should have to climb. IT RECYCLES the existing hangars and airport infrastructure; they can serve as LUMBER DEPOTS during the construction phase of the project; later, they may be turned into TRENDY LOFTS (30' ceilings!), a hospital, a school and a grocery store to serve all the island.

WITHIN THE PRECINCTS of the new avenues, where once brown grass and pesticides mixed in equal measure, new NARROW "STREETS" will grow, lined with HOUSES AND TREES at the same density as WARD'S ISLAND. Corner stores and cafes will abound.

THIS PROPOSAL IS REAL. It is no utopian fantasy. It is based on actual, local models, on Ward's Island, on Queen Street and the Danforth. IT COULD BE BUILT. IT WOULD MAKE A PROFIT. It doesn't call for a phony "Olympics," it doesn't ask us to emulate BARCELONA, it doesn't SHRIEK about a "LAST CHANCE" for Toronto requiring a "MASSIVE FEDERAL INFUSION" of money to fly. IT DOESN'T WANT TO FLY.

What is more, it could well serve as a model, itself, for Mr. Fung's "Portlands" site or other URBAN BROWNFIELDS SITES in Ontario—or anywhere.

— 3 —

REGARDING THE PORTLANDS SITE: far better, in our opinion, would be to LEAVE IT ALONE. You might as well build the ADAM'S MINE DUMP there as put the "Fung Report's" SAME OLD, SAME OLD watered down brand of NEW URBANISM on it. Indeed, putting the dump in our front yard might remind us not to PRODUCE SO MUCH GARBAGE.

But what does REJECT THE STATUS QUO look like, urbanistically? HOW FAR do you have to go to find a place that isn't "cars, cars, cars?"

NOT VERY FAR AT ALL.

TORONTO ISLAND, for example, houses hundreds of families with a WAITING LIST (now capped) of 500 more. PEOPLE PAY MONEY ANNUALLY just to keep their name on the list. It's a cohesive community despite the hardships imposed by its isolation and its ZONED lack of shops and businesses. PEOPLE LIVE THERE WITHOUT CARS. They LIKE IT LIKE THAT.

"BUT," we hear a whine, "Can regular people live like that? How many regular Torontonians could LIVE WITHOUT CARS?"

The answer is, PLENTY. In fact, 52% of "downtown" households, according to a City of Toronto study, have NO ACCESS to a car. That this is possible is testament to the DENSE, MULTILAYERED DESIGN of the old city of Toronto, as well as to the successful Toronto MASS TRANSIT SYSTEM.

— 2 —

THIS PROPOSAL REJECTS out of hand the PHONY NEW URBAN "vision" of both the "FUNG REPORT" and the "TORONTO 2008 OLYMPIC BID."

While, taken in pieces, the notions of NATURALIZING the mouth of the Don, CREATING COMMUNITY on the "Portlands" brownfields site and ENHANCING the "Emerald Necklace" that is the shore of LAKE ONTARIO are laudable, these goals are INCONGRUOUS with schemes that MEEKLY ACCEPT the STATUS QUO.

THIS IS OBVIOUS in the "BIGGER IS BETTER" Olympic Stadium, and its "Bigger is Better" PARKING LOT basking in the heat of the sun just behind. IT'S OBVIOUS when the "Fung Report" calls for 40,000 new housing units without QUESTIONING the 40,000 CARS that come with those units: CARS, with their attendant parking spaces, road allowances, pollution and CRASH STATISTICS, that inevitably SUBURBANIZE even the best-intentioned "new urbanism" schemes.

IN THE WORDS of Mayor Richard M. Daley of Chicago, "YOU CAN'T JUST HAVE CARS, CARS, CARS, 24 HOURS A DAY."

THE STATUS QUO GLARES from behind the artist's rendering, attempting to "GREEN-WASH" the 820-acre AIRPORT SITE. You can't "green-in" that much sun-baked grass and asphalt: THE AIRPORT IS A LUMP OF ASH IN THE EMERALD NECKLACE.

The Island Airport CALLS FOR ACTION.

— 4 —

"BUT," we hear another whine, "You can't take away the Island Airport. People NEED the airport."

WHO NEEDS IT, we answer. It LOSES MILLIONS every year. It's a NOISY HAZARD, it POLLUTES the lake, KILLS BIRDS AND WILDLIFE and it LIMITS URBAN DEVELOPMENT in its flight path. The people who need it are the ones who like their water bottled, their rainbows an oily scum, and their "wilderness" through the window of a car. When the planned TRANSIT LINK TO PEARSON INTERNATIONAL is completed, it will be the final NAIL IN THE COFFIN of the Island Airport. The only sorry ones then will be the MILLIONAIRES hoping to "end run" cottage-bound highway traffic every weekend.

GOOD RIDDANCE, we say.

IT'S A FACT that a bridge to the Island Airport is also planned, but IT CAN NEVER BE BUILT. A fixed link to the Island will only mean one thing: CARS.

CARS WILL KILL THE ISLAND, just like they kill everything else they come near. A fixed link is the THIN EDGE OF THE WEDGE, bringing in its wake "cul de sacs," traffic humps, drive-thru windows and drive-by shootings. In other words, SUBURBIA. This proposal JUST SAYS "NO" to a fixed link. The ferry is (almost) all right. For THIS PROPOSAL, it will need to be more frequent, and run day and night.

"This proposal? Tell me about it."

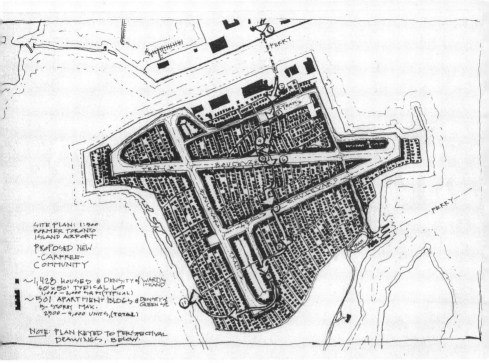

SITE PLAN: 1:500
FORMER TORONTO
ISLAND AIRPORT

PROPOSED NEW
-CARFREE-
COMMUNITY

■ ~1,428 HOUSES @ DENSITY of WARD'S
    40' x 50' TYPICAL LOT   ISLAND
    1,000 - 2,000 SQ FT (TYPICAL)
■ ~501 APARTMENT BLDGS @ DENSITY's
    5-STORY MAX.   QUEEN ST.
    2,900 - 4,000 UNITS, (TOTAL)

NOTE: PLAN KEYED TO PERSPECTIVAL
      DRAWINGS, BELOW.

waterfront. The competition awarded some prizes and some honourable
mentions, and melted away into the night.

I entered this competition too, and while my project won no awards,
it did garner specific mention by the chief juror, architect Rodolphe el-
Khoury (then director of the University of Toronto's Master of Urban
Design program). And John Barber mentioned my scheme in his column.
What I did was look at the Fung Report for what it was pretending *not* to see.
For while it proposed an 'emerald necklace' of green spaces and new civic
programs to ring the harbour, it ignored the lump of coal that is the airport.
On all the maps of the site, there it was, glaring at any who looked at it, an
untouchable blight. I merely asked the obvious question: what will happen when the government carries through on its promise to build a rapid
transit link to Pearson airport, and the island airport dries up and goes
bankrupt? What should happen to the acres and acres of super-hardened
concrete runways, and to the flat hinterland of seagull-fertilized grass that
lies between? What about that waiting list for car-free housing? Why not
redevelop the airport along the model of Ward's and Algonquin?

The model is simple, really. First, there is the grid pattern. There are
two types. One, the Ward's Island model, is a grid of approximately 40- by
50-foot lots, laid out in long rectangular blocks of some twenty houses per

street. House size is limited to 1,200 square feet, often quite a bit smaller. The other, the Algonquin Island type, has 50- by 100-foot lots, with a similar block pattern, and proportionately larger houses (up to 2,400 square feet). Houses are freestanding, usually frame in structure, one or two storeys in height, occasionally with belvederes or widow's walks at roof level. However, the key element is not the architecture or the grid pattern, but rather the narrowness of the 'streets' (at eight to twelve feet) and the fact that they are entirely without cars. In fact, there is no reason why considerably larger houses, in the realm of 4,000 to 5,000 square feet, could not be built there (given large enough lots). There is no reason why there couldn't be apartment buildings, shops and offices. I included in my drawings new 'main streets' of four- to six-storey buildings, with retail at grade and apartments above, lining the former runways. These new avenues would have trolley buses or trams serving as the only permissible motorized transportation. These trolley lines would extend to the Ward's and Algonquin communities, bringing them the opportunity to use the existing ferry at the Western Gap, especially in winter when crossing the harbour can be slow, treacherous and sometimes impossible because of ice.

Today, we have a different situation than at the time of my proposal. First, Bay Street is having the notion of peak oil shoved down its throat. (Peak oil refers to the fact that, at some point, it becomes more expensive to pump existing oil reserves than the profits derived therefrom. This happened in the U.S. around 1970. It's said to be happening to world reserves as I write this.) Earlier this year, General Motors and Ford were demoted to 'junk bond' status in the U.S. (not least because of the falling demand for the gas-slurping 'portable furnaces' the two companies promote so heavily). In addition, the island airport has been kicked in the head by the city, the province and the federal government. The only support it has is from a gang in towns like Ajax and Newmarket, far from downtown Toronto, who write letters to the editor every now and then that refer to the islanders as elitists who should be thanking their lucky stars for the airplanes that circle their homes and belch pollutants into their backyards. The 2015 World's Fair proposal is yet another insult to the airport as, in that proposal, the airport would be razed and rebuilt as a fairground. Meanwhile, the province is making moves to limit sprawl-type development in the farm fields at Toronto's margins. People are moving into the downtown in droves. And that 500-name waiting list for the islands has not shrunk any. The time is more ripe than ever to consider an alternative future for the island airport site.

Should it be an extension of the existing park, as many call for? Should it be an extension of Harbourfront, with condo towers and underground parking lots, wide windy streets and cars everywhere? Or is there something, as I propose, between these two extremes: the runways remaining as palimpsests for new main streets, small houses on small lots in the hinterland, with the possibility of larger houses and larger lots at critical locations, and the whole thing accomplished without cars? Remember, before you answer, that old Toronto Island rallying cry: 'Parks and people belong together!'

Images by Jacob Allderdice, from the Toronto Society of Architects' 2000 waterfront design competition.

BOULEVARD LIFE

BLISS ⑪

Sheila Heti
Dream of the waterfront

The best thing that could happen to the waterfront would surely be caves and coves. And cigarette ladies, the kind in stripes with cigarettes and candy bars dangling from their necks in shiny little trays. And hot-dog boys for the girls. And, of course, cabanas, a little weather beaten but all lined up the way you see them in the movies.

It would be great to have a wooden shack, white, but painted on the sides like an ice-cream truck, and inside they would sell snow cones and cool drinks and french fries in paper cups. Another stand would sell beach umbrellas.

Then we could put in areas of grass and areas of new sand and a very proper boardwalk and a dance hall, like the existing Palais Royale but open to the sky, open all around, and on Sunday nights there could be dances for the young people and the old people, with coloured lights and balloons and some modern-day crooners. Big-band stars. We'd make real heroes out of some of those crooners.

People would dance, and other people would sit on the benches or stand along the walls, waiting to be asked. Until nine o'clock, the boys would be standing on one side and the girls on the other, until the first boy asked a girl, or a flirty girl asked another girl to dance.

This would be summer at the waterfront. I miss Toronto as it appeared in the 1930s. It's how I think of this city when I conjure it in my mind. Hogtown. As long as you looked south, it would be as though nothing had changed since your grandma was a girl.

The lake would ideally be pumped clean, but if that's impossible, we could build little pools, with real lifeguards, and real water wings, and real dads teaching real children to swim while real mothers lay on beach towels reading books they'd never dare read on subways. We'd all be happy a day at a time. We might even devise a new lingo. People might start winking more.

In the winter, it would be barren, and sad people could go down alone and mourn their lost childhoods and throw cherries into the snow. It would be so quiet there in the winter, and it would truly seem like the corruption of spring. The whole city doesn't have to be buzzing and productive year-round.

In the winter it would be desolate, but the bathrooms would stay open, and people who wanted to could meet other nice people there, very late at night. And the fella who ran the concession stand would be employed by the city year-round, and in ten minutes he could fix you up a burger or a shake.

As for the caves and coves, some would be majestic and some would be small. A certain percentage of them could be given over to squatters, and some could be rented out cheap to people who always wanted to live in a cave or a cove. Others would be given over to the amusement of children who could explore and get lost and finally, after several days, find their way back, stumbling out, spooked and smudge-faced and sick with stories of the bones they found inside.

Within days, their tale of terror would turn into a tale of bravery, and that's how word of the coves would spread to the good people of Toronto:

the boasting of the little boys and little girls who escaped by the hairs of their noses.

The important thing is that there should be no new buildings. There should be no greater utility to the development of the waterfront than that of providing some old-fashioned pleasure to exhausted modern city folk. People would be allowed to bring little radios to the beach but no Walkmans. No cellphones. No sunglasses with the Internet inside.

There would be no billboards, no ads in the washroom stalls, no blimps flying overhead. The waterfront would be an oasis of calm at the base of the city, and the city dwellers who'd venture down to the waterfront would do it to leave the work-a-day behind.

Or we could pave over Lake Ontario and set up a troop of thousands of granite Indians, like an army poised to destroy the whole of downtown.

This article originally appeared in the *National Post*.

TOIL

Sally McKay
Fly on Queen Street

When I first came to Toronto, I felt relieved, revelling in big-city anonymity after the curtain-twitching claustrophobia of my youth in rural southwestern Ontario. Now, fifteen years later, I can't leave the house without running into someone I know. Ex-boyfriends, co-conspirators, friends, enemies and acquaintances whose names I can't remember lurk in every beer- and bookstore. No matter how big your city, if you live long enough you will put down roots.

Torontonians operate in microcosms. Physical neighbourhoods and social networks overlap and intertwine. When I moved to town in 1990, my roots sought nourishment in the niche of Queen Street West. I remember meeting an older friend at Future Bakery. He'd lived on Queen throughout the eighties, when the zone was characterized by drugs and bands and seedy, fascinating glam. 'Oh, this street is all yuppified now,' he said. 'It's soooo depressing.' To me, it was vibrant and exciting, full of artistic people leading alternative lifestyles. I was discovering a big world full of quirky endeavours. There was a one-woman restaurant, the Night Kitchen, where cats were allowed on the tables; there was a big sprawling bar, the Squeeze Club, owned by a rock star. At Future Bakery, you could sit and people-watch all day on a single cup of coffee. I drank and dined regularly at the infamous aggro Tex-Mex hole-in-the-wall La Hacienda, where the staff were so self-empowered as to intentionally scare customers away. La Hacienda still feeds me once a week, but the place has mellowed considerably, and the staff now literally own the place. I'm older, and so is the street. Tea shops abound, along with oyster bars and boutiques selling all the bits and bobs you need for yoga, baby and home decor. Nowadays, as the urban demographic inevitably shifts around me, I'm the one whining about change. But my nostalgia is misplaced.

As an active participant in the local culture, I have played my own small part in the upscaling of Queen Street West. All this makes me crabby, complicit and confused.

The relationship between art and ambition is complex, and 'mid-career,' like 'middle age,' is a dreadful phrase. An 'emerging' artist is welcomed, ribald irreverence being a refreshing kick at the old order. An 'established' artist (of which there are considerably fewer) is both loathed and revered, conceded a position in society that is rarely very lucrative but invariably acknowledged as carrying cultural weight. The 'mid-career' artist simply stumbles along, devoted to work, wrestling with demons, trying to keep body and soul together and bravely hoping that these efforts are meaningful to somebody somewhere. In such circumstances, a shifting niche can feel like betrayal. As Queen West, a sort of 'mid-career' strip itself, is increasingly characterized by its high-brow nightlife, it's no wonder that local community-minded artists are feeling a little lost. Which is why the tiny Fly Gallery is a flagship of inspiration.

Fly is a small window gallery that has been operating on Queen Street for about five years. Scott Carruthers and Tanya Read are two remarkably grounded artists who live in the storefront apartment and run the gallery as an offering to passersby. They do not sell the art on view, and they don't take a commission or charge rent. As Scott explains, 'There's no capitalist concept at play here – it's just about displaying art.' Sandwiched between the upscale 'boutique' Drake Hotel and the not-quite-so-upscale Gladstone Hotel, the Fly charts its own cultural path through the high-brow/low-brow maelstrom, a genuine labour of love.

The Fly gallerists fell in love thirteen years ago in Florence. They first met as students at the Ontario College of Art and Design. Scott complains to Tanya, 'You thought I was a bum for a whole year. You didn't want anything to do with me. I remember back then you were making decorative paintings with lots of animal figures. I asked if you were influenced by Native art and you just walked away. That was my best pickup line!'

Tanya smiles. 'Yeah, but what you didn't know was that I went and got a book on Native art right after that. I was thinking, hmmm, good idea that guy had ... '

Both attended an eight-month school program in Italy. Florence provided the right circumstance for romance, as well as for art collaboration, and the bond has remained firm ever since. After school, the couple joined other artists to form a collective, Impure, which showed regularly in Toronto for five years.

The move to Queen Street happened in 1997. 'When we first got here,' says Tanya, 'there wasn't anything going on. You could park on the street for free. There was a tattoo shop, some appliance stores, people living in storefronts. We took this apartment because we wanted to have a window gallery, but it was a couple of years before we got off our butts to make it happen.'

Today, I count twenty-two art galleries between Shaw and Gladstone. Tanya thinks back, counting on her fingers. 'There weren't as many galleries in the area back then. Tableau Vivant and Angell Gallery were a little further east. Zsa Zsa [which closed shop in August 2005] opened up pretty early on, and Propeller Gallery was around. And, of course, Katharine Mulherin's BUS Gallery was in its first location, west of Dufferin. When Mercer Union [an artist-run centre with an international reputation] moved to Lisgar Street, we realized we'd better start doing our thing,' Tanya laughs. 'It was time to get the plants out of the window!'

Over the past five years, Queen Street pedestrians have been exposed to the work of over fifty artists in Fly's window. When I ask if their mandate has changed over the years, Scott says, 'We don't show as much painting now, because of all the painting-based galleries in the neighbourhood.'

Tanya adds, 'It's also important that we don't look anything like a boutique.'

'In the beginning, we really wanted to show work that hadn't been shown before,' says Scott. 'The real mandate now is to show what we like.'

The beauty of a storefront window is that the art reaches a broader audience than it would tucked away inside a gallery. Most of Scott and Tanya's best memories are of people's reactions. 'Remember that time the pipe burst in the basement?' asks Scott. 'The landlord called the fire department, and instead of rushing inside, they were all standing around on the sidewalk analyzing the art!'

One of the most popular works was Kathleen Hearn's simple video of herself jumping on the spot for over an hour, which, according to Tanya, everybody loved.

'This was before there were a lot of art-goers in the neighbourhood, but the video really worked for all kinds of people. I remember this one particular down-and-out guy who was jumping along with it.'

Some artworks are a challenge to live with. 'The most annoying piece so far was by Eldon Garnet,' says Scott. 'It was a loud rattlesnake tail on a mechanical arm that shook whenever anyone walked by. The sound was so unpredictable, it startled us every time.'

When I ask why they do it, the Fly gallerists display obvious pride in the project. 'It's a way to keep in touch and be involved,' says Tanya. 'We contribute something.'

Have they ever considered charging artists rent? Tanya says, 'Hmmm ... maybe if our rent went up drastically, or if the administration became too difficult – we've talked about this a lot.'

'I'd rather close down than charge,' says Scott. 'This way we can have a liquid mandate and show what we want.'

'It's true,' adds Tanya. 'When you enter into a paid relationship, people expect a lot more from you. This way we can keep the time commitment down as well. Our selection process can be really chaotic. We connect with the artists informally, through word of mouth or written submissions. Sometimes people drop submissions in our mailbox. Once we even got a poem delivered – an ode to Fly Gallery!'

Keeping the time commitment down is important. These two are busy. Scott's art practice is a frenetic, prolific whirlwind. He is always drawing; even as we talk, he is doodling on a tin can with a permanent marker. I went to a solo show of his in Hamilton. Drawings filled three and a half walls floor to ceiling: a pair of dismembered forearms typed on a computer, giant eggs dropped from the sky to destroy a city, a chained werewolf read the newspaper, a baby with a five o'clock shadow floated like a balloon on the end of his umbilical cord, and on and on, an overwhelming mass of iconic images jammed up against each other, each of the small scenes as strange and compelling as every other.

'I started doing this in Italy,' says Scott. 'I had no money and I had to squeeze as many drawings into one sketchbook as possible, so I drew in

Scott Carruthers, 'All at Once' (detail). Black marker on transparent mylar, dimensions variable, 2004

these little boxes. I started liking the way it looked. I was mostly making paintings back then, really tactile and thick.'

'You had to pull the paintings out of his hands,' says Tanya, ''cause otherwise he'd just cover over them. He had layers and layers all on top of each other.'

Scott laughs, 'I couldn't wait for the paint to dry to change the idea. That's partly why I moved to drawing. It's more fresh.' Even during our interview, he is working furiously, completing work for another solo show coming up soon in Calgary.

Tanya is busy too, working towards a solo show at Katharine Mulherin Gallery. Her ongoing project revolves around Mr. Nobody, an everyman character based on the work of thirties cartoonists like Max Fleischer and George Harriman. Through Super8 films, sculptures, paintings, T-shirts and buttons, the narrative around Mr. Nobody is ever deepening, while the protagonist himself stays the same. In a short essay for Tanya's 2004 show at Truck in Calgary, I wrote, 'I've seen [Mr. Nobody] lose his arms and lose his head, fall off a flight of stairs, materialize in three dimensions to travel around town, hang out with visiting art mascots from other lands and morph into a gigantic empty-headed, sphinx-like cardboard robot. All the while he remains implacable, too naive to register that his adventures are in any way remarkable.'

I ask Tanya what her favourite moments with Mr. Nobody have been. 'I really liked the giant robot version of Mr. Nobody [shown at BUS Gallery in 2002]. It had such presence. I made it in our apartment, and we had to crawl underneath it to get to the front door. The first film I ever did was really special too. When I actually got it to work, it was a eureka moment. My heart started beating fast. I worked so hard on that little film ... then at the opening it caught on fire!'

'But then you drew on the wall,' says Scott. 'It turned out great.'

'This was the Impure collective's big Karaoke show in 1998,' says Tanya. 'Someone came running up to me, saying, 'Tanya, your film's on fire.' When I got to the projector, the film was shredded. I had to do something, so I just drew Mr. Nobody on the wall in the square of white light from the projector. I remember all these people kept saying the piece was genius, but I was just trying to salvage something.'

Typically, Tanya downplays her own acute intelligence. She and Scott, both brilliant and both fervently dedicated to the pursuit of their ideas, are philosophical about defining success. 'I'm in this for the long haul,' says Tanya. 'I'm an artist – it's what I do, and I'm always going to be doing it.'

'My day job requires a lot of energy,' says Scott, who is a bike courier. 'I don't have a lot left over every day for other things. But it pays the rent, and it allows me to do exactly what I want. I don't have to make art to sell – it's never a concern. Remember what Gully Jimson said in *The Horse's Mouth* by Joyce Cary? Being an artist is a privilege. In what other calling do you get to express yourself like this? You just can't complain!'

Tanya, who works at a desk in St. Joseph's Hospital, explains. 'I'm really lucky in my job. It's part time, and I don't have to bring it home with me. But still it's not enough money to live and make art. Unfortunately, I didn't get either of the grants I applied for this year, and that is going to affect how I make work.'

Queen Street has been changing fast around Fly. Scott sighs. 'At root, what I despise about the Drakification of the area is that these people come in with an agenda to change the neighbourhood into something they think is more desirable. You're not even allowed into the Drake if you come in a streetcar – you have to arrive in a cab or a stretch Hummer.'

'The traffic has definitely gotten worse,' says Tanya. 'When I ride my bike home, I fear for my life. Those cabs zip right in front of you and cut you off.'

'Artists move into a cheap neighbourhood and integrate themselves,' says Scott, 'but then gentrification comes and they have to leave.'

What would it take for Fly Gallery to leave Queen Street? 'Well,' says Tanya, 'if the rent gets prohibitive or if a really loud bar moves in next door.'

Scott scoffs, 'We've already tolerated a loud karaoke bar next door, and before that it was a smoky pool hall with no windows. We used to choke in here, but we stayed.'

As urban demographics shift, so too does the public perception of the artist's life. A condo dweller purchasing an 'authentic artist's loft' near Bloor and Lansdowne may not realize that scant months earlier a bunch of artists living in the building were kicked out to make way for the development. Since art is invoked as a selling point in classy joints—from real estate to nightclubs—those culture consumers who aren't directly involved with art may be forgiven for thinking that artists themselves also exist as a financial elite, when in fact most are scraping by. But this discrepancy also leads to misperceptions about the role of art itself, and the common perception that artists are pulling a fast one, getting rich on esoteric abstractions that that 'any six-year-old could make.' In reality, of course, Queen Street's burgeoning gallery scene is primarily showing artists who work at day jobs to support their careers. While money is always needed and appreciated, the offering of art itself is more frequently  gratified by responses from engaged viewers than by financial gain. In this respect, the tiny Fly is exemplary, displaying art for the simple reason that art should be seen, in the midst of the ever-intensifying 'culture-tainment' glam that has descended on the microcosm of these few blocks on Queen Street West.

Tanya Read, *Nexus*, digital video, 2005

Mr. Nobody joins the line in front of the Drake Hotel, barred entrance
by a simple velvet rope. A flurry of activity surrounds this Queen West
hot spot. Patrons gather, talk on cellphones, show their ID, gain entrance
with a handshake from the bouncers. A steady rhythm of a college
marching band drum corps echoes the hurried procession into the bar.
Mr. Nobody keeps his stoic stance at the front of the line, only to be
denied access again and again.

Misha Glouberman
No place like Kensington

In the summer of 2004, a group of business owners and activists launched PS Kensington, a weekly pedestrian street fair in Kensington Market. Many of the organizers saw it as a first step towards a fully car-free Market, a plan that had been floating around in various circles for some time. It was a big idea, generated by people who recognized a very real problem in the world (in this case, over-reliance on cars) and saw a plan for a better future. PS Kensington was a little bit of utopia right in Kensington Market.

As soon as I walked into Pedestrian Sunday in the Market, though, I felt uncomfortable. I didn't like it. And I didn't like not liking it. There were musicians and there were performers and there were, at least in my memory of it, children laughing and dancing in the streets. Who is opposed to that? I felt like a curmudgeon. But much as I love a street fair, I love a great neighbourhood more. And Kensington, possibly more than any other place in the city, is a great neighbourhood, famous in Toronto and elsewhere, the kind of neighbourhood people write about when they write about remarkable urban places. I loved it while I lived there, which I got to do for seven years, until the Harris government's cynically named Tenant Protection Act failed to protect me and I had to move. I still love it there. It remains the first place I bring visitors from out of town, the neighbourhood that most makes me proud to live in Toronto.

What makes Kensington great is the mix of all different sorts of people going about their lives. It's a fantastic bustle of people of tremendously varied ages, classes and ethnicities, all engaged in the day-to-day business of real life. Festival Sundays replaced that real life with rock bands, sidewalk DJs, huge crowds and street performers.

The plans for pedestrianization reminded me of Prince Arthur Street in Montreal, where I grew up. I remember when it was a mixed neighbourhood very much like Kensington, a lively place where lots of immigrant groups lived and worked alongside a smattering of young people and artists, in an area with residences and a mix of different businesses. Prince Arthur was partially pedestrianized in 1981, fully in 1983, and very quickly became a monocultural strip of touristy restaurants.

Still, I felt uncomfortable objecting to the idea of car-free days in the Market. I tried to find out more. I talked for hours with the program organizers. I called city hall. I met with academics, neighbourhood activists, local merchants and residents. I read up on cities and pedestrianization. I talked it over with friends and found that a lot of them felt the same emotional mix I initially did: they disliked what they saw, but they also felt as if they weren't supposed to feel this way and so they kept their opinions quiet. Part of the force of a utopian idea is that it can make you feel ashamed to disagree. It's unpleasant, in the face of enthusiasm, to feel like a naysayer. But after everything I learned, I couldn't help it.

Our society's reliance on automobiles is a huge problem. And so it's tempting to make broad assumptions like 'car-free = good' and 'motorist = bad.' Of course it's not so simple. It's not clear whether cordoning off pedestrians into a special festival zone is better for the cause of pedestrianism than having everyday neighbourhoods like Kensington, where it's easy to get around by foot, where accident rates are low and where cars routinely cede the way to cyclists and pedestrians who rule the road.

It's easy, too, to imagine motorists as anonymous yuppies driving SUVs. But the merchants I spoke to told me that the car drivers in Kensington are their delivery people and, more important, their customers. They're working-class people who need to bring carloads of food to their families, to their restaurants or to their homes in parts of town where rents are lower and living car-free isn't an option. (I get around exclusively by bike and on foot, and I wish more people in the city were able to. For the fact that I can, I count myself lucky.) The utopian vision of the Market imagined a population of healthy young people with the kinds of lives that don't require cars, lives like my own and like those of the festival organizers. This vision excluded the realities of many of the people who had used the Market for decades.

In the summer of 2004, Pedestrian Sundays attracted more than 10,000 visitors each week, but these people were looking for a party, not for groceries. If you ran a sidewalk bistro or a cappuccino bar, the car-free days were great for business. But according to the food merchants I spoke to, whose businesses form the backbone of what has traditionally defined the Market, the effects of Pedestrian Sunday on grocery sales were disastrous. The punk bands and erotic spoken-word performers weren't exactly a great enticement for their mostly older, mostly immigrant customer base. But more important, for the fish stores and spice shops and butchers, the ban on cars was logistically miserable. Their customers needed to transport big orders and so were doing their Sunday shopping elsewhere, where they could drive.

The festival organizers tried to listen to the concerns of these businesses, but they mostly seemed confused as to why these people were standing in the way of progress and wished they wouldn't be so negative. The pedestrian crew told the merchants not to worry, that it would be okay, that the organizers would come up with solutions to the problems that they themselves had created. They made it clear that they did not intend to run the fish stores and spice shops out of business. But if there's one lesson of urban planning, it's that good intentions routinely go awry. When Prince Arthur Street was closed to traffic, organizers said they were certain it wouldn't become an 'artificial' neighbourhood. But it did, and the full transformation took just a couple of years. Kensington organizers said it wouldn't be like Prince Arthur. (Utopian thinking isn't interested in the lessons of history. The planners, for instance, would jokingly ask whether their opponents worried that Kensington might turn into, say,

Yorkville, as if such a prospect were too absurd to even consider. It was unclear whether they forgot or simply never knew that, not so long ago, Yorkville was a low-rent neighbourhood where European immigrants ran coffee shops that attracted an ever-growing population of young bohemians. It was, like Kensington, precisely the sort of neighbourhood that no one could ever imagine turning into what Yorkville is today.) The organizers said a pedestrian Kensington wouldn't be like Sparks Street or the Granville Mall or the Distillery District either, or any of dozens of other pedestrian-only areas that are more tourist attraction than real neighbourhood. They promised that what they were doing would avoid the mistakes of the past. It would be something entirely new.

Kensington still has a broad diversity of businesses, but every year a couple more grocery stores and spice shops close, and someone opens another upscale restaurant or café or skateboard store. There's a real danger of the old marketplace being fully transformed into a boho entertainment district.

The fact that Kensington is so wonderful is what makes people want to 'improve' it. When Martin Zimmerman, a businessman who had lived and worked in the Market for decades, announced plans to open a small supermarket, it drew howls of protests for being too 'corporate.' Reverend Billy, a New York performance artist, led a group of protestors to the site to pray for the Market. No such prayer was deemed necessary at the new trendy nightclub, or the new upscale vegetarian restaurant, or the expensive French bistro, or the new art gallery or the hip new skateboard store. In an odd inversion, it was not these businesses but the supermarket that was viewed as a tool of 'gentrification,' even though the supermarket is one of very few new businesses in Kensington that is owned by a long-time resident and that serves the needs of local working families. There is plenty of room in Utopia for performance art but not for people who would like to buy canned foods and toilet paper.

It may be true that in a perfect world there would be no smog-belching cars or soulless chain stores. But in the real world, trying to ban cars and supermarkets may not be the answer. Utopianism at its worst can mean letting Good Ideas supplant what is actually there, even when what is actually there is wonderful and worth preserving. Thinking about big-picture principles can lead to overlooking the importance of historical accident, of mess and of specificity, and trying instead to clean everything up. It's easy to get caught up in ideas about making everything special and to forget the importance of the everyday: that buying groceries is as much a part of life as having parties, and that the ordinary needs of working families define the life of a city just as much as the activities of energetically cultured young people do.

The word *utopia* was coined with an intentional double meaning. It doesn't just mean 'good place'; it also means 'no place.' There's a real chance that Kensington will become not just a 'good place' with no cars but also a 'no place,' indistinguishable from the rest of Toronto's supply of medium-hip clublands. Some argue that to oppose this change is to oppose what's natural. They forget that Kensington Market's character isn't the outcome of passive evolution but the result of decades of active and often fierce resistance against people who have tried to force their ideas of progress upon it. Some claim that it's inevitable for Kensington to change and become more like the rest of the city. But if the dissolution of one of our greatest neighbourhoods really is inevitable (and it's far from clear that it is), why not try to slow that change rather than take steps that will actively accelerate it? There may still be hope for Kensington Market. What's needed most is a lot less utopia.

A version of this piece origiginally appeared as 'Cars over Happy Children?' in *Eye Weekly* (August 5, 2004).

John Lorinc
Stripping away stereotypes: Toronto's retail plazas

Cities need old buildings so badly it is probably impossible for vigorous streets and
districts to grow without them. By old buildings I mean not museum-piece old buildings,
    not old buildings in an excellent and expensive state of rehabilitation ...
    but also a lot of plain, ordinary, low-value old buildings, including some
    run-down old buildings.
    – Jane Jacobs, *The Death and Life of Great American Cities* (1961)

Mordechai Sorek, known as Motti around his shop, is wedged into a tight
basement space between a pair of industrial-sized freezers, a shelving unit
with a closed-circuit security TV and large plastic tubs filled with grain.
This is his office. The morning I met him, he was smoking du Mauriers,
keeping a watchful eye on the monitor, and cheerfully extolling the virtues of old-fashioned baking, as it was taught to him twenty-one years ago,
when, as a young Israeli émigré, he bought the Haymishe Bagel Shop.
    'You can make a bread,' shrugs the barrel-chested fifty-six-year-old,
'and you can make a *bread*. As my old baker says, "If you want to sell good
baked goods, you have to suffer." We continue to do it the old way, with
the experience of forty years.'
    Customers come in expectantly and leave with fragrant buns, bagels,
loaves of various shapes and sizes, desserts. On the wall is a sign singing
the praises of spelt. The counter ladies fuss. Sorek brims with a merchant's
pride, that sense of satisfaction culled from the combination of profit
and the knowledge that he's selling products his customers can't get just
anywhere: 'I'm not afraid to say it: if the customer wants something with
quality, he has to pay for it.' And they do, year after year after year.
    If you think you know how Toronto's retail sector works, you might
assume that Sorek's independent business is located on one of the city's

bustling, vibrant main streets: the Danforth, Bloor out near High Park, College Street, Queen, Yonge north of Davisville. These retail strips – serving high-density urban neighbourhoods – have proven over the years to be exceptionally fertile commercial soil for independent stores. Where the newest suburbs, with their big-box power centres, have succeeded in killing off traditional street-level retailing, downtowners still lovingly support indie businesses.

But Sorek's shop is actually located in an inauspicious suburban strip plaza on Bathurst Street, near Lawrence – a part of Toronto that was developed in the 1950s and 1960s. It's a standard-issue post-war retail development: two storeys, a bit shabby, resolutely utilitarian in design, with a cracked sidewalk and a skinny row of angled parking spaces out front. Sorek's neighbours include a meat shop, a fishmonger, two frame galleries, a cleaner and a green grocer. Not more than a hundred metres away, however, is a large, all-purpose chain-store shopping mall anchored by a twenty-four-hour Dominion. The supermarket has sat on his front step for fifteen years, and the mall's been there even longer. The little plaza thrived anyway, and not because it's a thing of beauty.

In any taxonomy of urban retail establishments, the strip plazas around Toronto's inner suburbs enjoy the status of a weed species. They obviously aren't in the same league as high-end regional malls, with their pricey shops, indoor features and pension-fund landlords. They don't have the utility of local shopping plazas, the ones wrapped around a large parking lot and tenanted by a supermarket, a bank, a drugstore and a video rental outlet. Nor do they have the vitality and aesthetic appeal of the down-town retail strips. Urbanists indict them for crimes against the pedestrian realm because they are separated from sidewalk by those narrow, unattractive parking lots (not to be confused with the genuinely barrier-like blacktop moats surrounding large malls). Yet they are qualitatively different commercial creatures than the endlessly blah stretches of stand-alone drive-through fast food and auto-body outlets that have had such a profoundly deadening impact on suburban arterials, rendering one indistinguishable from the next.

Toronto planners, nevertheless, have come to view these low-slung structures as development fodder. Why? Because they under-use commercial land that can support denser mixed-use buildings. In fact, the City of Toronto's Official Plan (an otherwise urban-minded vision that was originally adopted by council in 2002 and subsequently tweaked to deal with concerns about overdevelopment) effectively declared war on nondescript post-war strip plazas. Many suburban arterials have been redesignated 'avenues,' where landowners will be given carte blanche to develop buildings that are as high as the street is wide, provided they hug the sidewalk and keep the parking out of view. The goal is lofty and urban-minded, at least in theory. Such revitalization schemes, city planners have said, would situate five- and six-storey housing along transit routes and create aesthetically pleasing street walls with a European flavour.

The truth is that these older strip plazas facing onto busy arterial roads have played a vital public role in the urbanization of the post-war suburbs. Indeed, they've become as important, in an urban sense, to their communities as the old warehouse and market districts have been to the inner city. We demolish them at our peril.

Though it seems counterintuitive, there are parts of Toronto's suburbs that can be considered, if not exactly old, then definitely well into advanced middle age. And these areas, now in the middle of the GTA, have deteriorating buildings. In some suburban neighbourhoods, homeowners snapped up the pokey post-war bungalows and replaced them with monster homes. But suburban commercial zones for the most part are showing their age, especially in contrast to the gleaming new mega-developments in the 905.

Nearly forty-five years ago, Jane Jacobs taught us to look at old urban buildings in new ways – not as historical artifacts or monuments, but as a kind of rich social and economic soil. 'Time,' she writes, 'makes the high building costs of one generation the bargains of a following generation.' Mortgages have been paid off, original tenants have died or moved on, landlords have declared bankruptcy, rents have dropped. A certain shabbiness sets in. In the old factories downtown, such conditions proved to be perfect for the artists who, in the late 1980s, began to rent warehouse loft space on the sly, setting off an extraordinary renaissance in many post-industrial downtown neighbourhoods.

Out in the suburbs, there's been a fascinating variation on this reclamation of neglected commercial space, but one that gets a lot less adulation in the media. In the past two decades, Toronto's inner ring suburbs – i.e., the former municipalities of Etobicoke, North York, Scarborough and East York – have become ever more multicultural, long ago shedding the Don Mills–era stereotype of bedroom communities filled with white nuclear families. As large-scale suburban development pressed outward, the 1950s and 1960s strip malls fell victim to the centrifugal forces of sprawl.

Bit by bit, however, immigrant entrepreneurs began renting space in these low-rent plazas, setting up the very ordinary businesses that one sees along most commercial retail strips: hair and nail salons, ethnic restaurants, cleaners, food stores, travel agencies, electronics outlets and so on. For most, it's a matter of pure economics. 'If I had to start today, I'd go broke,' says Armand Moyal, who's run the framing gallery a few doors down from Sorek's bagel shop for thirty-three years. 'You go somewhere else and you're working for the landlord. You can't survive.'

The offices above these stores were rented by professionals, a great many of whom are also new Canadians: tax preparation firms, doctors, alternative health clinics, realtors, as well as offices for all sorts of indescribably exotic businesses. Unlike stand-alone chain outlets, strip plazas aren't purpose-built; their no-nonsense design allows new businesses to move in without the need for substantial renovations. The cumulative result is strip plazas that reflect the teeming ethnic diversity of the inner suburbs – dozens of small-scale Kensington Markets sprinkled around North York, Scarborough, Etobicoke and East York.

Some slightly larger strip plazas have an anchor at one end. Once upon a time, these stores may have been occupied by a Dominion or a Rexall Drugs. Today, they are 'supermarkets' serving local ethnic communities: Vietnamese in one strip plaza, Middle Eastern in another, Italian in a third. An older plaza at Lawrence and Warden, in Scarborough, is home to Nasr Foods, the city's largest halal supermarket. Go inside and you can buy Oreos and junky cereal in one aisle; in the next, hookah pipes, ornate chess sets with ivory inlay, and sticky Middle Eastern desserts.

A few doors along, in the Wexford Plaza, there's a venerable Greek diner that's well known in the city's east end as a must-go stop for Scarborough politicians who want to get the pulse of the neighbourhood. The walls are festooned with newspaper articles and hockey paraphernalia, the enamel-melting coffee comes in bottomless cups, and the owner will proffer a meaty hand to visiting dignitaries. The rest of the stores in the Wexford Plaza are always rented, but there are no chains. In fact, the plaza has become the focal point of one of Toronto's first suburban 'business improvement areas,' formed by rookie councillor Michael Thompson shortly after he was elected in 2003. Levies paid by the 400-plus businesses that belong to this BIA are going towards streetscaping features – benches, trees, flower beds – to doll up the parking lot and the sidewalk. In 2004, the plaza became the staging ground for A Taste of Lawrence, a summer street festival with music, kids' activities, and tasting stations set up by the local restaurateurs. Not exactly the hackneyed image one has of a deserted suburban arterial. But, as Thompson says, the Wexford Plaza has played an critical role in allowing a diverse working-class neighbourhood – made up of Greeks, West Indians, Lebanese and other immigrant groups – get acquainted with itself, in much the same way that this socialization process occurs in and around downtown retail strips.

It's not the only plaza that's become a kind of destination unto itself. In the barrens of northern Etobicoke, you drive along and suddenly find yourself staring at a lively conglomeration of East Asian restaurants and sweet shops arrayed in a single plaza at Islington and Albion Road. At night, these vividly lit eateries buzz with the sort of activity downtowners associate with Little India on Gerrard Street.

From a social perspective, these small ethnic businesses produce jobs and income for the members of their own communities, while the owners become local leaders. The managers import and sell goods that simply aren't available in mainstream retail establishments. And, as has always been the case with local retailers, these stores serve as landmarks for immigrants trying to carve out their own space in an alien urban landscape.

This intimate connection to surrounding community is no accident. Such retail developments have an organic, self-correcting tenant mix that's typical of retail streets but very uncommon in commercial shopping centres. Why? Because in many such plazas, the individual units have different landlords – sometimes the merchant, in other cases offshore investors. They tend not to be owned by the huge institutions and real-estate investment trusts that control large malls. In shopping centres, the mall officials closely manage the assortment of tenants, focusing on high-end chains and imposing their owners' investment expectations on a commercial environment. Malls don't typically rent to small independent businesses, not because they don't attract customers but because these firms don't produce chain-store returns. (The bustling indoor Chinese malls in Markham and north Scarborough are the exception, and that's because they are organized on a condominium model: individual merchants buy and sell their stalls, and pay fees to a management company responsible for maintaining the premises.) Nor are they public spaces. Mega-malls are not 'free markets.' Strip plazas are.

After I left Haymishe, I headed up Bathurst, which is lined with little plazas dominated by businesses serving the heavily Jewish population in that part of the city. At the Bathurst-Wilson intersection, I found one wrapped around the northwest corner. It revealed more of the shifting texture of the area: there were some businesses catering to Jamaicans, others to Jews. An Eastern medicine clinic and a Korean accountant had offices upstairs. There was also an Internet café, open until midnight, and a new Starbucks, packed with young mothers and babies in strollers. Though it wouldn't win any urban design prizes, the corner was bustling with life.

There were rows of strip plazas along Wilson heading west. Some of them had the familiar mish-mash of little shops, while others seemed seedy even by strip plaza standards. Nick Lattanzio, owner of a sleepy-looking travel agency, didn't seem especially happy. He'd been at that location since the late 1960s, when the area was new and prosperous. There was a well-protected gun store next door. 'The environment has changed completely,' he complained. 'We've become a ghetto.' He rhymed off his gripes about taxes, garbage collection, unfair competition from businesses run out of homes a few blocks down, and the empty stores next door. Yet for all that, he wasn't planning to move because his customers were 'used to that location.'

A bit farther north and west, I pulled into the Finch-Weston Centre, another L-shaped strip plaza. Unlike those on Wilson, it was busy and prosperous, especially in contrast to the windswept abandoned mall on the other side of Weston Road, which had been shuttered for years. In effect, it couldn't compete with the Finch Weston Centre, which has, among other tenants, an electronics shop, a Vietnamese restaurant, an Italian jeweller, a KFC, a cheque-cashing outlet and a store curiously calling itself Cleptomania Shoes. There was a medical clinic in a stand-alone building in the parking lot. Two doctors, Balwinder Bansal and Surender Rath, had their practices above the drugstore.

I wandered into an Argentine bakery, a tiny store with a few tables. At first glance, it looked like any small coffee shop. But the owner also sold Argentine baking products and magazines, and she'd meticulously displayed the business cards of several Argentine businesses – a realtor, a dental surgeon, tango schools – on the counter next to the cash register. In halting English, the owner told me she'd been in this location for seven years. When she couldn't understand my other questions, she turned for help to Franca Cicco, a middle-aged woman whose cellphone kept ringing as she waited to place her order. Cicco, a regular customer, lives in Woodbridge, a fifteen-minute drive north on 400, where she and her husband run an Italian restaurant. But she herself is Argentine, and drives down to this bakery because 'it's the only Spanish store in the area.' In its own way, this modest shop is the nexus of a network of Latin American immigrants living in the northwest corner of Toronto, serving the same role as the Hungarian eateries on Bloor Street did in the 1960s for their patrons.

Next door was a family-run jewellery store, an elegant, hushed place with a buzzer on the door and bars in the windows. Andre Lijou, one of the owners, told me the business had been there for thirty-three years. Over the years, he had opened two more shops, up in Woodbridge, to make sure his customers weren't leaving him behind. It's a nice story, because he'd succeeded in building a prosperous independent business in a suburban environment where huge malls suck in customers and their cash like industrial-strength vacuum cleaners.

My sense was that Lijou may have begun to think about packing up and relocating the business entirely to Woodbridge. 'We have to take it as it comes,' he shrugged. Yet there were no empty stores in the Finch-Weston Centre, and his space would likely be filled immediately with a local entrepreneur who, like Lijou three decades earlier, has a very precise fix on what his friends and neighbours need in their lives.

Back at the bagel shop, Sorek was similarly philosophical. The owner of his store, he'd been approached many times over the years to expand or to move into better commercial premises. He'd always refused. But, as he knows, eager developers have been erecting luxury condos all along Bathurst, and their appetite for desirable locations, like his, are unlikely to be sated any time soon. 'If I could see the future, I maybe would not be a baker. I like the business, you understand. If it happens, it happens. We cross that bridge when we come to it.'

But if those modest 1950s strip plazas begin to disappear in the name of suburban intensification, a critical piece of what built Toronto's peaceful diversity will go with them. After all, the luxury condo developers won't be leasing their ground floor stores to tiny Argentine bakeries. They simply couldn't afford the rent.

Or perhaps there's an alternative future, one which can grow out of a renewed appreciation of *places* like Wexford Plaza and their evolving role as surprisingly spontaneous community hubs. Because the fact is that they have become 'places' in their own right, in the way that the commercial districts centred around the Danforth, College Street and Kensington Market transcended their retail function and gave rise to true urban communities. In our vision for a transit-friendly, compact city, let's not lose sight of the fact that in these unassuming corners of suburbia, there's already a there, there.

Infiltration of Toronto in progress

The following stories are taken from infiltration.org, a companion website to *Infiltration*, the zine about going places you're not supposed to go. Ninjalicious created the

website in 1996 as a place to chronicle his many adventures throughout the urban landscape. His book, *Access All Areas: a user's guide to the art of urban exploration*, was released in 2005, shortly before his death from cancer.

Gooderham and Worts

Toronto's ginormous Gooderham and Worts distillery contains forty-five separate structures, the oldest of which dates back to 1859 and has sat abandoned and neglected since 1990. Recently, developers have begun work on the site, which they plan to refurbish into – guesses? anyone? – condos. Gilligan from the Cave Clan, a society of drain explorers in Australia, was in town and eager to visit some local abandoned breweries, so we decided to try our luck at the old Victorian industrial complex, though we knew that it was in the midst of renovations and actively patrolled by on-site security.

When we arrived that night, however, we found that access wasn't really a problem. We strolled through an open and unwatched gate and headed to the largest nearby building. We slid under a flimsy sheet of transparent plastic held in place

by a wooden skid and emerged into a large well-lit room. Eager to get away from
the light and the windows, we pushed aside a sheet of wood that was blocking our

way up into the rest of the building. Hopping up into the room beyond, we could clearly hear the sound of a hammer hitting steel, so after a quickly whispered consultation, we headed up an old wooden staircase nearby. As we came out onto the unlit second storey, it became necessary to turn on our flashlights; since we didn't have any fancy red filters or gels to dim our lights, we made do by smearing a packet of ketchup on the lenses of our flashlights.

We felt far from safe as we crept around on the thin, dusty floorboards in the dim, ketchuppy light, particularly since the hammering noise sounded so close. Retreating from the hammering, we headed off to another, better-lit section of the same complex. Taking concrete and metal catwalks running two storeys above the ground to the far end of the complex, we stumbled upon stairs and ladders leading up to some large metal vats, which Gilligan eagerly climbed into.

After trying and failing to take a suspended hallway into another building, we headed back to the area with the hammering and quickly climbed the stairs to the fifth and final floor. From here, we had a good view of the city, and of the various bits of bizarre Victorian-age machinery left around the building, as well as down into some huge empty grain bins. We felt very frustrated that we weren't able to take any flash photographs

of anything near the various windows and skylights; we were also disappointed that we weren't able to find any way out onto the roof.

Heading down a few storeys, however, we did find a way out to a lower-level rooftop covered in ice and gravel, which provided several opportunities to get to other parts of the complex. There was a large pipe here billowing steam into the frigid February air. Gilligan idly mused, 'I wonder where all this steam is coming from,' and did an odd bit of detective work by putting his hand directly in front of the steam. 'Oh SHIT!' he cried out, grabbing his hand in pain. After making sure he was okay (and probably already dreaming about the 'Biggest Mistake' Clannie Award he had coming to him), I headed towards the far edge of the roof. Gilligan warned me to look out and pointed to show me that flashlight beams were scanning up and down the walls of the building across from us. We decided to head back inside before those beams found us.

Venturing through a suspended hallway to a neighbouring building, we stared out through a window at the rest of the complex. Gilligan spotted a guard walking the perimeter of the grounds with a flashlight, as well as a pickup truck slowly driving around the side of another part of the complex. It was obvious they were guards looking for trespassers, but were they looking for us? We figured they probably weren't, but decided to stick to the large, unlit buildings we were already in, just in case.

We headed back to the ground floor, passing by some brightly lit construction areas and leaving the large gas blowers well alone. We then descended some stone steps into a tunnel set in the back corner of one of the rooms, which took us back to near where we'd first come in.

There was only one section of our complex that we hadn't accessed yet: the well-lit area from which the hammering noise was emanating. The only unlocked entrance to this area we could find was through a small circular hole about ten feet up the wall. There was a mechanical lift platform near this hole, so we climbed up to take a peek. Standing up on the rails at the sides of the platform, we could see a large, brightly lit engineering room on the other side, but it looked like it would be tough to climb up through the hole. It was at this point that Gilligan informed me that he was actually licensed to operate mechanical platforms like the one we were on. I laughed nervously. 'That would be awfully noisy, wouldn't it?' I asked. 'Maybe,' Gilligan replied, flicking the machine on and attempting to move it closer to the hole.

Unfortunately, we couldn't get it any closer than it already was, but by now our resolve to go through the hole had strengthened. Gilligan stood up on the top rail, grabbed at the hole in the wall and pulled himself up and through, moving out of the way so I could scamper up behind him. We looked down upon a large, brightly lit mechanical room with an entire wall of windows. Immediately beside us was some sort of large boiler that was obviously the source of the loud hammering noise that had haunted us all night. There appeared to be no easy way down from our perch at the top of the room, though Gilligan did climb up a little farther and find a ladder leading down into an apparently flooded basement. But the lights

were too bright, and our position was too precarious. Further investigations would have to be put off.

We carefully hopped back down to the mechanical platform, making as little noise as possible, and started to head back the way we'd come in. There was only one problem: while we'd been inside, someone had closed and locked the gate behind us. 'Do we look for another way out?' Gilligan asked. I told him I didn't want to risk running into anyone, so after looking around to make sure no one was watching, we scaled the fence, jumped down and took off.

OCAD

Whether you prefer to think of it as the ugliest building in the world or merely the weirdest, Will Alsop's new expansion to the Ontario College of Art and Design makes a strong impression. The dramatic part of the project, officially called the Sharp Centre for Design but more commonly called the Tabletop, is a nine-storey structure that has forsaken storeys one through seven in favour of large, colourful crayons and empty space. Personally, I find it creative and playful and like it a lot, but I think the architect and I are about the only two people in the world who feel that way.

After doing some initial scouting trips of the bizarre project, Avatar and I were determined to find a way up for a sneak preview – Av doing so in spite of his immense distaste for the building. Usually, exploring a construction site is a simple matter of hopping the fence and finding a way in, but since this project began seven storeys in the air, it required a less direct approach, through the old building and up into the new. Sneaking past an inattentive guard into the older part of OCAD one night, we began to scour the building for possible routes into the under-construction part of the building, but at first we encountered nothing but an endless series of locks and chains. The old building was empty aside from security guards, but we encountered three of these in our first ten minutes, so we didn't feel too lonely.

After trying many doors on many levels, we eventually found a complex route into the big white empty hall in the middle. Knowing that two of the guards we'd stumbled upon earlier were watching the hall from above, Av and I moved about very slowly, quietly and carefully in search of a route up. After failing to get past a locked door in the stairwell, we decided to take a risk and see if, by any chance, the elevator was in work-

ing order. We hit the button for the elevator and hid – a moment later, an empty construction elevator appeared with a mercifully quiet ding. We quietly hopped in and pressed the button for the top floor (nine storeys up, but labelled Level Six because of the missing levels).

We were inside the half-built tabletop now, but we didn't have it to ourselves. Some voices down the corridor sounded as if they were coming towards us, so Av and I scurried off into a small dark room to wait for them to leave. Instead, the voices grew louder and louder until I realized with dread that they were coming into the same tiny room that we were in. There was nothing to hide behind, so Avatar and I turned away and pressed ourselves into a dark corner, where we watched the workers fumbling with some supplies through a reflection in the glass. They were only about five feet away from us but, amazingly, they didn't see us. Afterwards, one fellow went to work in the hallway immediately outside the room we were in, so Av and I ran out past him when his back was turned and took the elevator from the sixth floor down to the fifth.

We had the fifth floor to ourselves, and we took our time to explore and photograph it thoroughly, paying special attention to the incomplete outside walls and the half-finished metal staircase. When we were done, we found another staircase and took it up and out to the roof, where we left a huge mess of footprints in the thick snow while we circled the roof and took pictures of the gorgeous view. Afterwards, we headed down the stairs and played around in the scaffolding jungle on the fourth floor for a bit before heading out. We were surprised to find the door we'd come through to get into the construction area had locked behind us, but fortunately it wasn't too difficult to navigate our way out by a different route. The guard at the front door scarcely glanced at us as we left.

James Bow
Where have all the subways gone?

On Friday, January 27, 1978, the Toronto Transit Commission celebrated the open-ing of the Spadina subway, a ten-kilometre, $212-million line stretching from the University of Toronto to the city's northern suburbs. Many dignitaries came to listen to speeches and watch Premier Bill Davis cut the ceremo-nial ribbon.

The act had symbolism. It was Davis who'd cancelled construction of the Spadina Expressway, a roadway that would have paralleled the subway south of Eglinton Avenue. The expressway raised a firestorm of opposi-tion among Toronto residents, and its cancellation was a sharp turn from traditional car-oriented urban development. Davis himself said, upon cancelling the expressway, 'If we are building a transportation system to serve the automobile, the Spadina Expressway would be a good place to start. But if we are building a transportation system to serve the people, the Spadina Expressway would be a good place to stop.'

The Toronto Transit Commission was on a high. Nineteen consecu-tive years of subway construction had produced a fifty-kilometre-plus network extending deep into the suburbs. The commission was hailed as the safest system in North America, an example beleaguered American systems struggled to emulate. With Davis's support and Metropolitan Toronto explicitly charting a pro-transit future, it seemed nothing was going to stop these good years.

The day after the ribbon cutting, the Spadina subway opened to the public. It would be the last new subway line built in Toronto for twenty-four years.

In 2000, transit fan N. Q. Duong, indulging his own fancy, designed a plan to extend Toronto's subway network through all corners of the city. He placed this on a website, the centrepiece of which was a map that aped the style of the maps seen above the doors of Toronto's subway cars. Duong called for subways to the Port Lands and Sherway Gardens, a subway running the length of Eglinton Avenue, and an extension of the Sheppard subway into northern Etobicoke and the Scarborough Town Centre. Had his vision been reality, there would be few places in Toronto more than two kilometres from a subway stop.

Duong's website soon vanished, but his map lived on, popping up on a number of Toronto-related blogs. It came loose from Duong's name, as if it were a creation of the transit community's collective dreams. The map achieved the status of a minor urban legend, and the *Globe and Mail* reprinted it in the Saturday, March 15, 2005 edition, quoting TTC commissioner Howard Moscoe, who claimed that the proposed system would cost $50 billion to build.

But neither Moscoe nor the blog authors seemed to recall how close the TTC came to adopting just such a plan. In 1984, as Toronto celebrated its sesquicentennial, Metropolitan Toronto debated what was called the Network 2011 plan. The plan called for $2.7 billion to be spent over the following thirty years. Construction would have started in 1989 and gone in the following phases:

1. Construction of a Sheppard subway between Yonge Street and Victoria Park, opening 1993.

2. Construction of a downtown relief line, taking pressure off the Bloor-Yonge interchange, running from Donlands station south to Eastern Avenue then west along the railway tracks, past Union station, to Spadina Avenue, opening 1998.

3. Construction of an Eglinton West busway, fully separated from street traffic, running from the Spadina subway to the Mississauga border, connecting to a Mississauga busway along Highway 403, opening 2003.

4. The extension of the Sheppard subway east and west, so that the line would run from the Scarborough Town Centre to an extension of the Spadina subway (what is today Downsview station), opening 2009.

5. Conversion of the Eglinton West busway into a full-fledged subway, opening 2014.

When originally conceived, Network 2011 was supposed to be a blueprint for Metropolitan Toronto's subway development through to 2011. By the time Metropolitan Toronto was ready to approve the plan, and the Toronto Transit Commission promoted its particulars in a special supplement in the *Toronto Star* in May 1985, the proposed completion date had been pushed back to 2014.

At the time, Metropolitan Toronto was divided into six lower-tier municipalities: the City of Toronto proper, the Borough of East York and the suburban cities of York, North York, Etobicoke and Scarborough. The Network 2011 plan was an attempt to extend subway service to the outer suburbs, fostering the development of satellite downtowns, and to balance the aspirations of the various cities on Metro Council. The three lines travelled through five of the six municipalities (only tiny East York was left out). But even with the subway plums evenly distributed, politicians complained about pecking order. York mayor Alan Tonks said, 'The plan is on the right track, but has the wrong routes priorized.'[1] Another factor was the debate over the type of technology to be used on these lines.

1 Mike Smith, 'Network 2011: The battle over who gets what,' *Toronto Star*, February 8, 1986.

When the TTC opened a two-station extension to the Bloor-Danforth subway on November 22, 1980, twenty-one consecutive years of subway construction drew to a close, with no prospect for expansion in the near future. Through the 1960s and the 1970s, the low-density development of the suburbs increasingly hurt the TTC's ability to provide service. New services had to travel farther to serve fewer people, and the TTC was unable to match the convenience of car travel. The commission lost money and market share. Municipal and provincial subsidies, which were almost unheard of before 1954, became commonplace.

As subway construction continued into the seventies, the dense areas of the city most amenable to subway service got served. The high cost of subway construction and its diminishing rate of return could not be ignored. However, vast areas of Metropolitan Toronto were far from any subway line. The TTC and Metropolitan Toronto, encouraged by the Davis government, looked for a vehicle that could bridge the intermediate capacity gap between the highest feasible levels of bus and streetcar service and the lowest economically feasible ridership of a subway line.

The TTC looked to streetcars, proposing in 1974 to link the Scarborough Town Centre to the end of the Bloor-Danforth subway line with high-speed streetcars running on a private right-of-way. The technology was proven and inexpensive. The line between the town centre and the subway would have been the trunk route of a new streetcar network stretching deep into the northeastern suburbs.

The province, however, turned to high tech. To encourage the development of transit in his province, Premier Bill Davis created a Crown corporation, called the Urban Transportation Development Corporation (UTDC), to build the TTC's next generation of streetcars, and to market technology around the world.

At Davis's urging, UTDC began development of a magnetic levitation vehicle for urban transportation. UTDC partnered with Krauss-Maffei of West Germany to build an experimental test line, known as GO-Urban, in the Canadian National Exhibition. The project got as far as building pillars to support the guideway when Krauss-Maffei pulled out. Undaunted, UTDC pursued the technology, now known as ICTS (for Intermediate Capacity Transit System), producing a linear-induction motor that used electro-magnets to drive a vehicle along traditional rails.

With the prototype created, the province wanted a test system that could be used to showcase the technology. Turning to Toronto, the province asked the city to redesign the Scarborough rapid transit line to accept the new technology. They offered to pay for all cost overruns, and the TTC agreed. The Scarborough RT line opened in March 1985, three years late, and more than $100 million over budget.

Even by 1985, it was clear that the province's ICTS technology was insufficient to serve the lines proposed under the Network 2011 plan. It had the capacity of a streetcar, with the price tag of a subway. Thus, traditional subways were back in vogue.

The revised plan approved by Metro Council in 1985 had survived political infighting and the investigation of experimental technology. It was presented to the provincial government – just in time for Premier Bill Davis's resignation.

With Davis's departure, Ontarians lost one of the most transit-friendly politicians of the age. Afterwards, Davis's Conservative successors back-pedalled on his major transportation initiatives. Then, in 1985, the Conservative dynasty fell and the new premier, Liberal David Petersen, looked at Network 2011's rising price tag and balked. It wasn't until 1989 that the Ontario Liberals brought forward rapid transit proposals of their own.

The Liberal plan of 1989 was an attempt to get around the cost of Network 2011. The downtown relief line was expensive and did not have the political return of extending subways into vote-rich suburbs. To handle overcrowding at the Bloor-Yonge interchange, a multi-million-dollar renovation was proposed: to install a third platform between the tracks to speed up loading and unloading. By speeding up the crowds using the station, more trains could be scheduled per hour. To get around the delays experienced at the terminals, Petersen proposed closing the loop between the northern ends of the Yonge and Spadina subway lines, creating a gigantic belt loop.

Petersen also proposed extending the Bloor-Danforth subway to Sherway Gardens and allowed the first phase of the Sheppard subway to proceed, provided North York mayor Mel Lastman could secure private funding for the line.

Debates stalled the approval process even more. As the proposal to extend the Spadina subway from Wilson Avenue to Sheppard was common to both plans, Metro Toronto and the province approved construction of the extension, even though it was described as a link 'from nowhere to nowhere.' Work on extending the subway network resumed for the first time in a decade, and the first subway extension to open since 1980 opened to the public on March 30, 1996.

Whatever the merits of Peterson's proposals, they were out the window after his loss to Bob Rae in September 1990. The newly elected N D P government, facing a $10-billion deficit and the onset of a major recession, set about reviewing the T T C's expansion plans. Finally, late in 1994, the Rae government unveiled a four-line extension proposal as a jobs-creation project. They called for a Sheppard line, operating between Yonge Street and Don Mills (two stations shy of the originally planned terminus at Victoria Park), as well as an Eglinton line, using subway technology from the start, operating between the Spadina subway and Black Creek Drive. The proposals also called for an extension of the Spadina subway to York University and the Scarborough R T to the Sheppard/Markham Road intersection.

Concerns over Metro's ability to fund its portion of the four lines caused approvals of the York University and Scarborough RT extensions to be delayed. Work commenced on the Eglinton West and Sheppard subways in 1995, only to be halted when the Conservatives returned to power, led by the fiscally frugal Mike Harris. In his bid to cut government costs and pay for a thirty-percent reduction in income taxes, Harris cancelled the Eglinton West subway immediately and then sought to pull the province out of public-transit funding altogether.

And if these struggles weren't enough, the TTC's reputation as one of the safest transportation agencies in North America took a hit when, on August 11, 1995, a subway train heading southbound towards Dupont station passed three stop signals and plowed into the rear of another train stopped in the tunnel, killing three people and shutting down the Spadina line for a week.

The results of the coroner's report into the Russell Hill train crash, and the Harris government's decision to pull out of public transit funding, changed the focus of transit funding in Metro. The loss of provincial operating subsidies resulted in the most severe round of service cuts in the TTC's history, and every penny that the TTC received from the city was diverted towards maintenance to ensure the system entered 'a state of good repair.'

As suburban development bloomed and provincial funding dried up, system ridership dropped twenty percent. The TTC and the City of Toronto lost a decade for a confluence of reasons: political infighting and a lack of political will, a vision that strayed too far from common sense, and a lack of vision when the time came to commit to funding. Worst of all, a complacency that allowed planners and politicians to focus on expansion and ignore the maintenance of the rest of the system had resulted in people dying. By 1996, the TTC's struggles mirrored that of Toronto: underfunded, ignored by the province, barely able to handle the pressures of today and unable to plan for tomorrow's growth.

Under the leadership of David Gunn and his successor Rick Ducharme, the TTC pulled itself back from the brink. The management structure was streamlined, with a greater emphasis on improving the maintenance of the current system. Broken and underperforming equipment was replaced, driver training improved and the signal system modernized. New subway cars were purchased, and the TTC was able to expand service on the lines again, with service times of, at worst, five minutes on all routes.

The Spadina streetcar line opened in 1997 – a legacy of the late 1980s, when the province and Toronto were more interested in spending money to expand the system. But that same year, the TTC took a different approach to expanding its network. A report entitled *Opportunities for New Streetcar Routes* examined ways to use a number of streetcars rendered surplus by service cuts. It identified a 'missing link' on Queens Quay between Spadina and Bathurst, where no streetcars could go, and recommended that it be bridged. Three years later, for $13.25 million, the TTC opened the 509 Harbourfront streetcar route between Union Station and the Canadian National Exhibition, a bargain compared with the $67 million originally proposed for an LRT spanning a similar distance. The new line serves a developing residential area and carries up to 11,000 passengers per day.

A cautious optimism took hold in the City of Toronto in the late 1990s, enough to bid on the 2008 Olympics, and enough to agree to a new Official Plan. This plan calls for the city to grow to a population of three million over the next twenty-five years, primarily through increasing the density of housing around underused arterials throughout the city. Mirroring this, the TTC stabilized its ridership through a system that became more reliable through improved maintenance and piecemeal expansion of the streetcar network. For all of its faults, the TTC cut the ribbon on the 6.4-kilometre first phase of the Sheppard subway in 2002, which increased transit use along the Sheppard corridor and spurred a boom of urban development in the area.

Reflecting this piecemeal, baby-steps approach, the TTC unveiled its Ridership Growth Strategy in 2003, laying down what it would need to increase its ridership beyond 500 million passengers per year. It speaks of adding more buses to crowded routes, expanding the streetcar network and installing private rights-of-way. This past August, work began to convert the St. Clair streetcar route to such a right-of-way, a project that started when the TTC realized that regular track maintenance scheduled for the line in 2005 and 2006 could be augmented for just $7 million more. A similar project is being considered for Fleet Street between Bathurst and Strachan.

The Ridership Growth Strategy also talks about subway expansion, but rather than grand plans for lines spanning the city, the TTC suggests expanding the current network at a steady rate of $175 million per year. This baby-steps approach would be enough to open one kilometre of new line each year, allowing for a massive system approaching Duong's fantasy after thirty years.

Fantasy is not just in the form of maps imagining what could be. Dreams and visions don't just concern systems; they concern attitudes and political will. Duong's dreams weren't the first this city has seen. They existed twenty years ago and they failed, primarily because politicians fought too long before agreeing to a vision, or chased great fantasies rather than focusing on more achievable goals that could accomplish the same results. They ignored proven technology in favour of flashier projects, and they forgot to protect the system that was in place while focusing on expansions they could ill afford.

Torontonians are coming to understand that their region is being backed against a wall. Sprawl is pushing unmanageable suburbs far from the city core. Traffic congestion is putting the city under great pressure. The same political will that brought David Miller to the mayor's office is backing support for urban redevelopment of the Port Lands and intensifying development around Toronto's arterials. Although the St. Clair private right-of-way project was controversial, it had support from such community activists as SCRIPT (St. Clair Right of Way Initiative for Public Transit). And Torontonians, as evidenced by the bloggers who linked to Duong's map, all admit that it has been too long since serious subway expansion has been considered.

Twenty years before the TTC started to go off the rails, enough political will and clarity of vision existed to build it into a remarkable system. It's only a matter of recapturing some of that sensibility, the art of what's possible, before fantasy can be turned into reality twenty years hence.

There is hope for Duong's dream yet.

REFERENCES

Howell, Peter. 'NDP puts transit expansion on hold.' *Toronto Star,* October 13, 1990.

Laver, Ross. 'Rapid Transit: an issue so hot that politicians are putting it on ice.' *The Globe and Mail*, September 7, 1982.

Toronto Transit Commission, *Network 2011: A Rapid Transit Plan for Metropolitan Toronto,* Toronto: Toronto Transit Commission, May 1985.

Heather McLean
Go west, young hipster:
the gentrification of Queen Street West

When the Beaconsfield, a slick, urbane new bar that replaced an old appliance shop, applied for a 120-person patio to be open until 2:30 each morning, the residents in the adjacent apartment building and in nearby houses decided that it was time to mobilize. With bar after bar opening, they were worried that, before they knew it, their neighbourhood – Queen Street West from Dovercourt to Dufferin – would be transformed into another entertainment district. According to one resident in the apartment adjacent to the Beaconsfield, a few pubs dotting the Queen Street strip was fine, but to have an influx of entertainment and drinking venues just outside your window was too much for the nurses, pastry chefs and actors – working people who need to be able to sleep in their own homes. Thus the Queen-Beaconsfield Residents Association was born.

According to QBRA representatives, an application for a new bar called Unit at 1198 Queen Street West will be the seventh bar within the 125-square-metre corner of Queen and Beaconsfield and the fifth bar to open or reopen since 2004. QBRA organizer Misha Glouberman points out that this concentration of bars exceeds the legal limit for bar densities in many other cities, including New York. This lack of diversity in planning is puzzling for Glouberman: 'In a city that celebrates mixed use and Jane Jacobs–type urban planning, why should neighbourhoods be overrun with bars as a single use?' he asks. The QBRA has discovered various studies arguing that this type of geographically specific bar concentration can be problematic for people who make the transformed neighbourhood their home. A high number of bars fosters an exponential growth of people coming to the neighbourhood to party, which inevitably increases noise and crowds. Once a whole strip of bars is developed, people don't just go for a drink at one place; they go from one bar to the next, and two martinis becomes six, then eight martinis. This concentration of bars has been a serious concern in Toronto's 'entertainment district,' the area bounded by Queen, Front, Simcoe and Spadina, currently a destination for as many as 60,000 people a weekend. With 2,500 new condos, the neighbourhood is becoming a contested terrain as people try to live, work and party in close proximity.

Along with the crowds, QBRA residents say, come the motorcycles, the taxis, the stretch SUVs and the recycling trucks picking up empties in the mornings. One QBRA resident comments, 'The people who open up these bars liked to think they "cleaned up" a dismal neighbourhood with appliance shops and prostitutes. The prostitutes weren't as obnoxious as packs of hipsters standing around in groups below my window when all I want to do is go to sleep at night.'

The transformation of a traditionally working-class neighbourhood into a 'hip' entertainment hub is typical of many complexities and contradictions of the gentrification process – a spatial transformation driven by the imperative of economic growth and development. This process has come to mean changing neighbourhoods through an increase in housing prices, an accentuation of socio-economic polarization, the change in local retail structure, land-use speculation and a shift towards accessibility for people with higher incomes.

While urban transformations are not new, various theorists explain how gentrification expresses larger global shifts: national and regional economies have moved their priorities towards recreation and consumption and a global hierarchy of world, national and regional cities has emerged. Encouraging hip, urban livability has become the goal as municipal governments and private-sector initiatives throughout the world try to attract new economy workers and the 'creative' classes to purchase condominiums, eat in posh cafés and shop in boutiques. Toronto's latest Official Plan (the guiding policy and planning vision for how the city will grow in the next thirty years) uses the city's arts, music and cultural communities as a selling feature to attract investment and real-estate development. As urban-planning researcher Susannah Bunce notes, rather than promote a bland King and Bay Street image of the city, local arts communities are highlighted to attract potential investors and residents. While this type of promotion might help sustain an interest by levels of government in supporting arts and culture, it also encourages gentrification and the inevitable displacement of working- and artist-class inhabitants as higher-income earners move to buy their way into what is packaged and promoted as a hip lifestyle. In this process, neighbourhoods like Queen-Beaconsfield and Parkdale become a new frontier for redevelopment.

Geographer Neil Smith's writing on the gentrification of New York's Lower East Side in the late 1980s talks about the emergence of the 'frontier' myth in the politics of gentrification. Entire neighbourhoods where people lived and worked, Smith notes, when viewed through a colonial lens, were ripe for so-called 'revitalization.' New York newspapers, for instance, celebrated the 'courage' of urban homesteaders and brave pioneers moving into non-white, lower-income neighbourhoods. Smith's writing exposes how one couple was quoted in the *New Yorker* as saying, 'Ludlow Street. No one we know would think of living here. No one we know has ever heard of Ludlow Street. Maybe someday this neighbourhood will be the way the Village was before we knew anything about New York.'

Twelve years after Smith's writing, Drake Hotel owner Jeff Stober uses the same frontier language to describe his goal of 'revitalizing' the corner of Queen and Beaconsfield. 'Four years ago, if you had said this area would be described as a chic walkway, people would have said you were nuts. It was the wild wild west,' Stober stated in the *Toronto Star*. According to Stober, this neighbourhood was a blank slate, a frontier just waiting for investment and redevelopment to bring it to life.

Bars and other establishments love to employ this constructed urban 'authenticity' to attract trendy partiers. In this process, long-time homeowners and renters, seniors, new immigrants and people experiencing social exclusion, addiction and mental-health issues, and poverty are rendered 'edgy' for people attempting to create a bohemian experience for pubgoers and second-hand-clothes shoppers. This is articulated in a new pub on this strip called the Social, with its intentionally rough decor and the word 'welfare' painted across one of the walls.

These narratives are further perpetuated by the media. Like a mesh ball cap or seventy-dollar used sweater, some of the neighbourhood's residents serve to accessorize the hip experience of consuming martinis and cultural activities. One pub is described as being 'conveniently located steps from the Queen West Mental Health and Addiction Centre and a hop, skip and a jump from Toronto Western's detox centre.' Another notes 'media types pound single malts while checking out colourful Parkdale street life.' This lack of political self-reflection and the commodification of space contribute to the transformation of working-class and politically active neighbourhoods into what sociologist Christopher Mele calls 'bourgeois bohemia.' A place where, Susannah Bunce notes, a neighbourhood's supposedly authentic and quirky character is used to sell ten-dollar brunches and martinis.

Artists requiring affordable places to live and work are also adversely affected by the process of gentrification. Bunce points out that working artists often seek out neighbourhoods like Parkdale because the rent is cheaper; ironically, these people who contribute to making the neighbourhood culturally appealing in the first place are at risk of being displaced by higher-income earners and the services and amenities that aim to serve them. This is evident in the Queen-Beaconsfield neighbourhood; Sis Boom Bah, Luft, Burston and Brackett galleries have already had to close due to increased rents. That there are fewer buyers and more art tourists has also been cited as a reason for closing. One gallery owner mentioned that although she has not had to move, the building owner has refused to keep up with anything beyond basic maintenance. While he insists that he cannot afford upkeep because of increases in property tax and insurance, he seems to be waiting for tenants to leave so he can charge double the rent for the space. There is a rumour that another landlord in the area is looking to open a franchise like Starbucks in a former gallery space.

Another regular feature of the colonial process in gentrification, Smith points out, is that developers and gentrifiers often dismiss local residents in the development process. Because the area is defined as a frontier – a place with all this potential where nobody of importance thought of living before – local residents are often rendered invisible and are excluded from planning processes and decisions. QBRA residents are bewildered at how little they have been included in the planning processs for the large late-night patio at the corner of their street. 'They had this sense of entitlement,' commented one resident. 'It was like we never existed in the first place.'

The lack of community involvement in the changes to Queen West highlights pro-business, anti-community involvement trends in planning processes. Stefan Kipfer and Roger Keil of York University illustrate how the attempts by the City of Toronto to open up its neighbourhoods for investment coincide with the scaling back of participatory planning processes where residents have input in their neighbourhood goals. For example, they argue that municipal-level planning departments have eliminated or drastically reduced development charges on new buildings in an attempt to streamline the approval process and foster rapid development while, at the same time, reducing public participation in the development approvals process.

The QBRA has seen first-hand that there is little opportunity to intervene in local planning discourse and that the processes that are available are so bizarrely tangled as to be nearly useless. When they contacted councillor Adam Giambrone's office, the QBRA learned that the bar-licensing process is under the jurisdiction of a provincial body called the AGCO (Alcohol and Gaming Commission of Ontario). However, the AGCO laws state specifically that a bar cannot open if the municipal council says that a bar is not in the interest of the community. The residents' group has learned that its only hope to slow down the proliferation of bars and to have a say in how late the patios are open is to raise this issue with its councillor – who has a wide range of other community issues to contend with at the same time. QBRA has been persistent in contacting the councillor's office, but the provincial AGCO will not give the group information on plans for future bars opening in the area, so it is difficult to forecast where development is going. This lack of clear access raises the issues of who is included and excluded when community members try to act as stakeholders in their own neighbourhood's affairs. 'What is troubling is that we are a pretty privileged group – there are lawyers, academics, writers in our group researching these processes, and we are having trouble making sense of how we can access information and challenge the planning processes,' says Glouberman. 'Imagine if you speak English as a second language or your work and commuting don't enable you to have time to take this kind of research and commitment on.'

The transformation of the Queen-Beaconsfield neighbourhood highlights the tensions that evolve as residential and commercial uses are mixed and areas become sites of both living and recreation. This so-called mixed use is nothing new in cities around the world – a fact that QBRA residents are well aware of. One resident states, 'It's not like I am against bars, it's just that it is so commercial – there is no organic process of growth, no community involvement. I used to live in France, where there were neighbourhood pubs and restaurants – but they weren't just dumped suddenly on the neighbourhood. I think it was a more gradual process.' This resident's frustrations stem mainly from the fact that the planning process has lacked resident involvement and favoured wealthy hipster developers wanting to turn the neighbourhood into an edgy, urban party destination. 'All of a sudden, boom, you are a wacky, hip neighbourhood and the people living there aren't really part of any process to shape the future of your neighbourhood.'

Another resident is quick to explain that the problem is not that bars have opened but that *just* bars have opened – so many, so quickly. The problem is a lack of diversity. 'I participate in arts events, go to indie-rock shows, go to the Drake sometimes and consume culture, whatever that means – I'm just worried that the neighbourhood is changing too quickly. I don't necessarily want to live somewhere where everyone is from the same age and demographic range and reflects the same lifestyle choices.'

It could be argued that the QBRA is another example of NIMBYists (Not In My Backyard) out to protect their own interests. Maybe they are first- and second-wave gentrifiers who moved to the area for its 'quirkiness' and affordability and are now trying to hold back the third and fourth waves that seem inevitable in a city where neighbourhoods are commodified and consumed? But the QBRA is raising some important concerns about the lack of mix and diversity in planning processes – which are closely linked to diversity and social inclusion in the neighbourhood. These are especially important issues for low-income residents and people who might require affordable units close to work downtown or to the services at the Centre for Addiction and Mental Health facilities. Diversity in planning also means access to amenities and services to buy average things like milk, cornflakes or a toothbrush – not only martinis, knitting supplies and pricey used clothes. 'In terms of income, Beaconsfield is a pretty mixed street, and a lot of people are not necessarily at risk of being displaced,' states one QBRA member. 'But I do feel really bad for people who are pushed out by these changes; rents are going up pretty quickly around here, and the area is changing pretty rapidly.'

Interestingly, QBRA's work is very timely, because the neighbourhood is about to participate in a multi-stakeholder study that links community-based agencies like St. Christopher House with various community groups and activists in the neighbourhood. Through research and a community engagement process, they will explore ways of ensuring that growth does not alienate local businesses, low-income families and aging homeowners in the neighbourhood. University of Toronto professor

David Hulchanski explains, 'Right now, people are talking about the importance of cities, especially in the global economy – but life happens at the neighbourhood level. That is where we live, work and shop and where our sense of identity and responsibility to each other begins.' Community development workers in the Queen West neighbourhood are increasingly having to negotiate tensions between the expectations and concerns of new condominium, home and business owners interested in 'cleaning up' and 'revitalizing' the area and residents on the verge of being pushed out by rent increases and the loss of affordable housing stock. QBRA and other neighbourhood groups in this area have the potential to challenge gentrification by asserting resident concerns in planning processes that favour commercial development.

The Queen West neighbourhood has been framed as derelict and in need of improvement, but a wide range of people call it home. And the fact that some of those people have volunteered so much of their time and energy battling bureaucracy to keep it livable is cause for hope. Issues of affordability and accessibility have deeper underlying causes, of course, and are broader than the QBRA can possibly take on. But the sense of responsibility they are fostering towards the planning process is crucial. We need more groups like QBRA to initiate dialogue about how neighbourhoods are developing, who is included and who is excluded in planning goals, and how commercial and business developers and city planners can be more accountable to resident needs; it's great to have a city to play in, but we need one to live in too.

REFERENCES

Bigge, Ryan. 'Flipping a Flophouse into a Hip Hotel,' *Toronto Star*, March 2004.

Bunce, Susannah. 'The Rising Cost of Urban Space,' *Wavelength Music Series and Zine*, May 2004.

Kipfer, Stefan and Roger Keil. 'Still Planning to Be Different? Toronto at the Turn of the Millennium,' http://www.yorku.ca/rkeil/kipferkeil.htm.

Mele, Christopher. *Selling the Lower East Side: Culture, Real Estate and Resistance in New York City.* Minnesota: University of Minnesota Press, 2002.

Smith, Neil. *The New Urban Frontier: Gentrification and the Revanchist City.* London: Routledge, 1996.

Social Sciences and Humanities Research Council of Canada Newswire. 'Urban development threatens inner-city diversity,' February 2005.

Darren O'Donnell
Toronto the teenager:
why we need a Children's Council

Wikipedia tells us that there are ten alpha cities, cities that have specific attributes, including participation in international events, advanced transportation systems, advanced communications infrastructure and world-renowned cultural institutions. Wikipedia lists London, New York City, Paris, Tokyo, Chicago, Frankfurt, Hong Kong, Los Angeles, Milan and Singapore. Toronto doesn't make the cut. It's listed as a beta city, with many but not all of the relevant qualities. As a beta city, Toronto isn't quite in the loop – it tends to overhear conversations more than participate in them. At meals, it oscillates between the adults' and the kids' table, feeling at home at both and neither. Toronto is a teenager and, as a teenager, Toronto understands the indignities of youth, the untenable position of being able to understand the situation but do nothing about it. And this visceral understanding of disenfranchisement makes it the ideal seat for a rigorous challenge to the legal status of youth with respect to democratic participation.

If you're searching for utopia, you need look no further than the kids. The beautiful thing about focusing on youth is that while we may not be kids now, we all were once. And we carry the somatic memory of those days into almost every encounter; we all share, to some degree or other, a visceral understanding of powerlessness. Barring children from full political participation not only makes no sense when we consider the rights of the child, but also when we take into account the greater good. Excluding a huge segment of the population – a segment in the midst of forming views and attitudes that shape their behaviour for the rest of their lives – is a narrow-minded act that can only serve to limit our own possibilities as adults. So, while this proposal is for the children, it's truly for the benefit of who those children become, for the adults who have to deal with the results of eighteen years of their own political disenfranchisement.

The movement to lower the voting age is active, relatively strong but experiencing continued resistance. Early in the 2005, Liberal MP Mark Holland teamed up with then Conservative Belinda Stronach, Stéphane Bergeron from the Bloc and Nathan Cullen from the NDP to introduce a private member's bill to amend the elections act to lower the age to sixteen. In June 2005, Parliament voted it down. In January 2005, a couple of teenagers from Edmonton, Eryn Fitzgerald and Christine Jairamsingh, attempted, unsuccessfully, to get their views on the issue heard by the Supreme Court, but the Supremes refused to even consider it. New York City councillor Gale Brewer introduced a bill on June 8, 2005, which has yet to be voted on, that would also see the voting age dropped to sixteen. And in Britain, the recently initiated Votes at 16 campaign has strong support and membership from a wide variety of groups representing youth and the youth wings of many of the political parties, including the ruling Labour Party.

In the June 2005 House of Commons debate, Conservative Pierre Poilievre, at twenty-five the youngest Member of Parliament, articulated a mainstream nervouness by mistakenly pointing out that 'the responsibility ... to pay taxes usually arrives around the age of eighteen' – forgetting, of course, that everyone pays GST and most pay PST. He goes on: 'Values such as thrift, responsibility and hard work are most exemplified in the years that follow, having reached the age of majority.' Even assuming this statement is true, what do thrift, responsibility and hard work have to do with anything? If I want to laze around and spend all my money on pot and porn, I shouldn't be barred from voting; the consumption of pot and porn keeps the economy rolling.

Around the world, a number of countries and municipalities welcome the participation of young people: Iran lets the kids vote at fifteen, and Brazil, the Philippines and many municipalities in Germany at sixteen. The logic employed by youth and their advocates is that if you're allowed to screw, drive a Hummer and be taxed on your chocolate bars, then you have every right to participate. In Canada, we have a contradiction: you can join a political party at fourteen and vote to choose the leader of that party – and potentially the whole country – but are barred from further participation.

The drive to lower the voting age can, in some ways, be seen as a response to the stretching of youth upwards into our thirties. This youth drift encourages the luxury of not taking life too seriously, of being okay with working crappy, low-paying, precarious jobs, of happily deferring full civic engagement to later years. As we left behind Fordist modernity, where adulthood is tied to working 'real' jobs, we have seen living with parents, contemplating video games as the next big narrative form, playing in bands and other facets of youth culture jump in to fill the employment gap and make it all seem a little less onerous. Art and culture get involved in this dynamic by providing distraction and the lotto-like hope that fame and fortune will come our way. This whole situation is supported by myriad print and electronic media, all providing a variation on Warhol's fifteen minutes, where the avenues and portals of notoriety have proliferated to such a degree that fame is thinly spread into an electronic eternity of self-Googling. The youthful thirty-year-old finds no avenues for civic engagement or political enfranchisement in today's electrometropolis but does find a semblance of community and the illusion of interactivity. And, worse, as we drift into our forties, we suddenly find that these many playful passions have morphed – if we've had any success at all – into a low-paying career where the opportunity to work intrudes into almost all moments.

By nudging youth inexorably upwards and keeping children sheltered from the responsibility of full citizenship, we ensure that childhood is a time when civic irresponsibility is a given, when not too much is expected of us: childhood as halcyon innocence. But childhood has never been innocent. There have always been drugs, sex, dirty uncles and dirty thoughts. We kid ourselves precisely to the degree that we inculcate our children into states of passivity and, in turn, our adulthoods into years of servitude.

And there's another thing: at the same time as youth pulls itself into the thirties, we have the zombie-walk of consumerism down past youth and now fully into childhood. The child becomes the consumer while the adult becomes the youth. We learn how to be consumers first, and only much much later do we have the opportunity to become engaged citizens. If we feel it's okay to allow the complete consumerization of the children, then we must insist on their complete political enfranchisement.

Let's leave aside the very important discussion of whether there's any worth in voting *at all* – after all, when it's always a case of the lesser of two evils, it's hard to whip up any enthusiasm. Municipal elections hold a little more interest, but until cities are granted the right to govern themselves, what's happening provincially and nationally will always be more relevant. Cites are the children of the provinces – a fact that can be seen with full clarity in the Municipal Elections Act, a piece of provincial legislation in which the complete contours of how a city must run its elections are laid out – including, of course, voter eligibility at age eighteen. That the province dictates who can engage in constituting the city is a democratic deficit of the first order. As cities continue to grow, becoming home to a greater percentage of the population, the struggle to gain more power and autonomy can also be expected to flourish. And with this flourishing will come an opportunity for cities – with their diverse and relatively progressive populations – to demonstrate creativity when it comes to policy. This, in turn, has the potential to hold some interest for voters – with specific opportunities for civic engagement from more and more of the youth population. Designing a system where full engagement is the norm rather than the exception should be the goal.

Already existing avenues for youthful political participation are most prevalent at the level of municipalities. Some cities have youth advocates who, while claiming to represent concerns of young people, still determine their own agendas. Toronto, Edmonton and Montreal, for example, have gone as far as inviting youth to participate in the process via youth councils. But the process has some deficiencies. Edmonton and Montreal assign youth of their liking, so from the start there's good reason to be suspicious. In Edmonton the exercise starts to look a lot like school with the hard line they take on attendance: 'If a member misses two consecutive meetings without prior notification, he/she will be asked to resign from the Council. Event attendance is mandatory.' Imagine laying those rules on our professional politicians. In Toronto, the politicians do not choose the reps; the Youth Cabinet is open to anyone between the ages of thirteen and twenty-six. This sounds good on paper, but like most activities of this nature, it attracts people inclined to view civic engagement as not only desirable but possible. This, it seems, would rule out a lot of youth – as can be seen by the fact that only about two hundred have decided to take the leap and join.

Imagine a polity comprised of representatives of all age groups, a polity where the practical concerns and political opinions of the six-year-old are considered as valid as those of the sixty-year-old. It's safe to say that for most of us there's a knee-jerk recoiling from such a bizarre idea. But in this age of so-called human rights, what could be more bizarre than structuring a society so that the individual is deprived of basic political participation for the first quarter of her life? That seems more ludicrous than the incredible proliferations of playgrounds we could expect if six-year-olds were elected to office.

The Toronto Children's Council I'm proposing would provide an opportunity for direct participation in the political process. For our purposes, I'll define a youth as anyone who does not have a legal right to vote – so, at this time, anyone under eighteen. Using the municipal ward system, every school in a given ward would elect a couple of representatives to a ward council. The ward council, in turn, would elect a couple of representatives to sit on the Toronto Youth Council, which is permitted one vote on city council with respect to any policy at all. The time spent selecting representatives, discussing issues and participating as representatives would be incorporated into the curriculum as a distinct course of study. The exact number of representatives per school would have to be adjusted for difference in size. Youth who are not attending school would participate through organizations serving youth, composing their own caucus within the council.

How the Children's Council would work, what they would do, how they might try to influence policy, are questions that would need to be addressed in the doing. One form might be to have different wards focus their attention on different aspects of government, with all students participating in any debates about global issues such as budget. The children could essentially form a shadow council, with representatives syncing their participation with the councillors in their ward. So, if their local councillor has specific responsibilities – say, involvement with the police services board – the curriculum in the corresponding schools would also focus on policing. The fear that these kinds of discussions may be beyond the comprehension of some of the lower grades is unfounded. It simply becomes a matter of developing a curriculum that takes the kids as far as their interest is sustained. More important, it comes down to courage on the part of the teachers to communicate to the students some of the harsher realities – there's little doubt a child can understand the implications of, say, the police association spying on politicians – but will the teachers have the courage to work with this material? Some will and some won't.

But beyond utopian visions, there are practical avenues for bringing this kind of headspace into fruition. Those who work with boards of directors, whether it's within a community organization, a not-for-profit or a money-making concern, can recruit youth to serve and participate in a decision-making capacity. Develop some structure that protects the kid from fiduciary responsibility – not that it will be needed; if anybody sues you, they won't be coming after the kid but the richest fool on the board. If you think the matters of the board are too complex for a kid to understand, you're probably kidding yourself, but, in the event they are, you should figure out how to capture the kid's interest. It will probably benefit the work you do, forcing meetings to stay on point, with enough distillation of information to keep the attention of a fourteen-year-old. Most organizations already have a few members with more compromised attention spans than that, so this tactic could be a way to improve the functioning and commitment of the organization as a whole.

Serving on boards could also be included in the education curriculum and would count towards credits. But again, and most important, kids would be serving on the boards because their contribution will make the world a better place – if only for the duration of the meeting where they will force a brevity and focus into the proceedings. Keeping in mind that a kid needs to be kept in the loop will focus the meeting on the essentials. If this means that the organization has to change the pace at which its work gets accomplished, then so be it. Throughout history, people have always had their citizenship rights suppressed in the name of expediency; giving women and blacks the vote was supposed to cause chaos.

Chatting with some kids on the street the other day, I asked them what they would change if they were mayor of the world. Eradicating both poverty and biting were two of the first responses. There was debate among them about the value of taxation, but everybody deferred to the thirteen-year-old girl when she pointed out that taxes were important to make sure that obvious stuff like schools and traffic lights would run. As you might expect, they were concerned about war and world poverty. They wanted more community centres, more places to engage their minds and their bodies on their own schedule. Kids get it. It's that simple. They are capable of being as fully informed as it takes to engage responsibility in the civic sphere.

But, ultimately, the burden doesn't have to be on children and their advocates to prove the worth of allowing kids full civic participation. We don't have to demonstrate the various healthy benefits for the city and its citizenry. The benefits of allowing all citizens full participation are intrinsic to the gesture itself; there's no need to prove social benefit beyond the full enfranchisement of every single citizen. We don't even need to speculate on what the effect may be, but since it's an interesting exercise, let's give it a whirl.

What would a city governed – in part – by children look like? What new rights would need enshrinement?

▣ *The Right to Candy.* All children would have the right to reasonable access to candy. For the less privileged, a candy allowance would be provided by the state. This form of welfare acknowledges that children do not have the means to provide for themselves and that their parents' fiscal situation should in no way interfere with free and easy access. Candy is one of joys of childhood, and fair and equitable access should be a given. The children acknowledge that this right brings with it a concomitant responsibility to brush their teeth.

▣ *The Right to Play Doctor.* Playing Doctor and its many variations would not be prohibited in any way. The prohibition of Playing Doctor is only effective in getting the game banished to dank, clandestine basements, garages and hidden corners. It would be an offence to interfere with any reasonable expression of sexuality.

▣ *The Right to Toys.* It will be expected that companies involved in the creation of play technology will supply less advantaged youth with state-of-the-art toys. These companies would engage in this redistribution of wealth with the confidence that plenty of compensation would be generated once the kid had the purchasing power to invest in her own toys. It would be acknowledged as an investment in future consumers; thus, no state funding would be required.

▣ *The Right to Public Nudity.* There is the tacit understanding that naked infants do not pose a social risk. This needs to be enshrined in law. An exact identification of the age at which public nudity becomes an offence is required, however; ambiguity on this issue lets shame creep into the formula. It should be clear: on a particular birthday, one dons underwear, never to remove it unless in the privacy of one's own home or at Hanlan's Point.

▣ *The Right to Take Physical Risks.* Doing so-called dangerous stuff like skateboarding, riding cushions down the stairs and running on the pool deck would be permitted on a need-to-do basis, with full acknowledgement by the child that a risk is being taken. If repeated injuries are sustained, the child would agree to attend Tai Chi classes (or a range of other designated modalities) in order to gain a greater awareness of his body in space, build stamina, strength and balance.

▣ *The Right to Talk to Strangers.* There would be the acknowledgment that the public sphere is a relatively safe place, certainly safer than the comfort of the home, where one is far more likely to be molested or beaten. This is not to deny that pedophiles lurk but that the prohibition against chatting with strange adults is irrational and tends to generate a fearfulness that is carried well into adulthood, in turn creating a profound atomization in the social sphere. There would be a limited right to talk to strangers but an acknowledgement that accompanying an unknown adult to another locale is strictly verboten.

▣ *The Right to Be Hugged by Teachers and Caregivers.* The prohibition against physical contact does nothing to reduce incidence of abuse but does interfere with the natural need for physical contact. Navigating this particular realm would have to involve a soulful exploration of the culture's hysteria and denial around childhood sexuality.

The Toronto Children's Council would have to be merely a stop-gap in a drive to abolish any remaining limits on democratic participation, opening the process up to anyone who has the will to vote. There is no reason to fear. Concerns about a kid's ignorance of the issues are unfounded. It's a delusion to believe that children can't assemble informed opinions about general policy issues; their interest in human rights, animal rights and the environment can be clearly witnessed on any given Earth Day. And who will forget the kids booing Mike Harris into silence to the astonishment of Nelson Mandela? If only we had the courage to let the little brats vote. And the argument that they will either be strong-armed into voting for their parents' choice or, in childish rebellion, cast a dissenting ballot, is based on the false assumption that most adults are somehow behaving differently.

As Toronto the teenager knows, youth is a frustrating state. We want to be a player. Who doesn't? Everyone desires agency. But alpha status will always be difficult for Toronto to achieve, particularly with our proximity to the U.S. and relatively low population concentration. Rather, Toronto and, in turn, Canada (a teenage country if ever there was one) are in a good position to enjoy the benefits of our youthful understanding to promote progressive, utopian agendas. The contours of this are already in evidence with gay marriage and our slightly more liberal attitude towards marijuana. The urban arena, with its diverse and generally more progressive populations, is a great place to push further and push harder.

TOols & TOys

Conan Tobias interviews Alfred Holden
Streetcars, street lights and street smarts

The following discussion on public transit, city streets, architecture and heritage took place on a northeastern balcony of 190 St. George Street, on April 10, 2005, between Conan Tobias and Alfred Holden – writers, editors and city enthusiasts, both. It has been heavily edited.

CT I'm sure we could talk for days about Toronto revitalization, but space is limited, so let's discuss a few of the major topics that make cities, and this city in particular, livable.

Funding issues aside, it's seemed over the past several years, since maybe the mid-nineties, that the public has lost its love affair with the Toronto Transit Commission. Taking the subway or the streetcar doesn't seem to conjure up the warm feelings it once did. I have to think a big part of that is marketing. If you look at London, for example, it markets the hell out of its subway system with route-map posters and all kinds of merchandise featuring the Underground logo. The TTC can be – and has been – just as iconic, especially to the people who live here and use it every day. But recently it's seemed like the public has done more to promote the TTC than the TTC has. You've got people making up buttons and dream subway maps and accessibility guides – I don't think the TTC even has a gift shop anymore. It doesn't seem to be doing such a good job of selling itself. The most recent bit of marketing that comes to mind is that campaign about transit cops.

AH I know. Sometimes those posters are right by the ticket wicket – angry bold-faced posters that are obviously targeted directly at thieves or fare evaders. The number of fare evaders is a small percentage of riders, but everyone gets assaulted with this thing every single time they get on. It doesn't make you feel good about your transit system.

If the TTC marketed itself better, would people look at it a little more the way they used to in 'the glory days'? Do you think it would affect anything?

The glory days in Toronto weren't that long ago. In the United States, it's about seventy years ago. But here, I think most living souls remember why they liked the TTC, because the system seemed energetic. You walked to the streetcar stop and there was always a car in sight. It's always hazardous to talk about golden ages, but if a Canadian city ever had a golden age, it was Toronto in the 1970s. Things started to go downhill in the eighties. I think it was apparent when the trolley bus system was in danger. The TTC would complain about the cost of maintaining basic infrastructure: wiring and repairing buses. The telltale sign is when they don't want to buy new ones; you know the system is in danger.

Is there a connection here? Obviously, the TTC can do only so much to prevent funding cuts, but could it try to bolster its reputation in other ways so funding cuts aren't all you hear about?

The TTC can probably do more to improve the public's perception of its service than it can do to get more money. You can do something about public perception on a relatively modest budget – a bit of advertising and some posters. And then, if you can create a feeling that the system is valuable, over time you'll probably get more funding. Transit in Europe kind of works that way, and it did here in the golden age. I think funding for transit came as a result of people feeling that it was worthwhile.

Why did the golden age end? Is it the TTC's fault?

I think it's a symptom of a much broader North American public apathy towards public transportation. That's pretty hard to do something about. Toronto managed for a time, but I think things just kind of caught up with us. That said, the whole idea of promoting the transit system in subtle ways that build appreciation of it, or even just build a warm, fuzzy feeling, is invaluable. I say 'warm, fuzzy feeling' and people might dismiss that, but how does Madison Avenue do advertising? You create a sense that the system is invaluable or interesting or simply quite able and capable and a great alternative. They need to do two things: they have to get people to understand the system, how it works and how easy it is to use; and they have to create a pleasant aura around it, which can be done.

London is perhaps the poster boy, literally, of transit promotion because it has this ongoing, subtle campaign to create a sense that the transit system is yours, it goes anywhere, you'll enjoy using it. The poster art in the London subway is amazing. The posters are so interesting that they sell them at London's Transport Museum, which is, of course, another thing we should have. They should have made the Wychwood yards into Toronto's transit museum. Cost-wise, it's a drop in the bucket, but it creates a focus and would help with publicity. You have to get kids interested, teenagers interested; you want to keep adults interested. I think, overall, the publicity strategy for the TTC has been very amateur. That's a pretty brutal summary, but remember the Our Riders Write campaign? I suppose it had its cleverness, but it was also insulting.

How do you think it was insulting?

Well, it's like the fare evaders. The rider's being told, 'You, you're bad. It's you who's causing these problems.'

I can remember only two of them: one about people taking up seats with backpacks and one about people putting their feet up against poles. I don't recall them adding to the campaign at all from about the mid-eighties until they finally took them all down, around the mid-nineties.

The only one I remember that wasn't an insult to the rider was one about why streetcars short turn, but it wasn't a very good explanation, so it kind of fell flat. 'Ride the Rocket' – I guess that sort of came back. They keep bringing back old, memorable slogans. 'The Better Way' is okay, but over time some slogans become clichés that people laugh at, that mean the opposite of what you want them to.

Let's say the T T C did do some good campaigns and did do merchandising and did give everyone that warm, fuzzy feeling about the transit system – how would that improve things in the end?

A marketing person could give you a very padded answer, but I would say the goal of any organization trying to market something is to build a brand, and build a brand based on a number of levers that you can pull to create either a pleasant feeling in someone who might be inclined to like transit as a means of getting around, or do the missionary job, which is to say, 'Look, this works for you. Use it.' You want to draw riders, but also to create public support for the system so the tax-paying public feels represented.

The transit system needs to have the same support as the road system. I've pointed this out many times, but the road system, Highway 407 aside, is virtually free to use. The road system is an entirely public investment. And the transit system ought to be seen in the same light. But for a number of historical reasons, it's not. In the early days of transit, people thought the five-cent fare was about right, and they didn't want to pay more than that. But inflation came along, and when the transit companies raised fares, they were accused of gouging. Soon enough, cars came along and people had an alternative, the perception being that it was free because they just got in their car and drove off. But, of course, it wasn't free because all this infrastructure had to be provided for it. Meanwhile, the perception was that the transit company was a business, and you didn't like that business because it was taking your money. The motorist thinks he's competing with transit, but he's not. They actually work great together and people have to be convinced of that. How could you say that in a T T C promotion? You kind of hope for the occasional transit strike, because that's when the usefulness of the system becomes apparent. So much of the gloss is off the golden era that it's hard to say whether a nice, slick campaign could bring it back.

Like I said, I think it's got a lot to work with in terms of iconography: the TTC logo, the streetcars. I think it's interesting that the current streetcars seem to have become as classic as the old red and yellow Presidents' Conference Committee cars.

Even those of us who have lived here for years pinch ourselves that we have this excellent system.

I know you've always had a fear that they're going to be gone someday. I was just reading in the *Globe and Mail* about the plans for a new generation of Toronto streetcar. You must see that as a good sign.

My scenario always was that some financial crisis would come along at a time when the streetcar infrastructure was starting to age, some crisis like amalgamation. When the electric trolley bus system was starting to go, that's exactly what happened. The infrastructure had aged, the buses had aged, and all of a sudden service was stopped. There was a brief reprieve, when they brought in buses from Edmonton. It was very weird. I remember that those of us who were advocating for the trolleys to be saved hoped the reprieve would be a foot back in the door, but it wasn't. They'd become old and decrepit and very problematic. A lot of people have this perception about streetcars, but a lot of the problem with streetcars is insufficient service. The streetcar system is prone to certain kinds of delays, but it does a lot of good. You can throw it all away and say, 'Just get rid of that,' but then you realize that the streetcar system supports so much else in the city that's of value.

I still believe the TTC has been so bad at marketing itself that it has squandered a lot of goodwill it could have capitalized on. In most ways, the system is still quite viable. You mentioned how other people pick up on what's interesting about the TTC – CBC Radio will often use the doors-closing subway chime to mark a transition. 'Up to the news: do-do-do!' Why is it they do that?

Because it's Toronto.

Exactly.

We've talked a bit about roadways, but let's talk about streets – the pedestrian version of roads. You and I often discuss the city's small details: the design of street signs, manhole covers, mailboxes, street lighting, sidewalks. Personally, I think they're all very important things. They give a city its character. When they're radically altered, as we're now seeing with the street-name signs, I find it seriously alters a city's look. So obviously, if they're altered in a bad way, which I think is what's happened with the street signs, it makes the city a bit less pleasant. Unfortunately, I think a lot of people just don't care about such things.

I think they do, subliminally. I think that's one of the reasons Toronto's successful: it has neighbourhoods. People want to be in it. It's not a beautiful city, let's face it. When I come back from a trip to Paris or Brussels, there's something dumpy about North America. However, there's affection people have that can be tapped. These things that you're talking about are symbols. They're symbols of both the city and their neighbourhoods. People care about their neighbourhoods. The loss of the old street-name signs is unfortunate. They were traditional and iconic.

I really don't think people care.

They do if things are framed so that they can understand there's an issue. It happened with street lighting. Street lighting is pretty abstract. You wouldn't think we could mobilize a city to care about street lighting. What is it? But somehow several generations of Torontonians have noticed street lighting and have had precise things to say about it. Street lighting should enhance a neighbourhood. You want to walk down the street at night and think, 'This is a nice place, let's keep going.' The last time this topic came up was in the nineties, and I got involved. I had just been studying historic preservation at the University of Vermont, and I wrote a paper on street lighting while learning some amazing things about it. Toronto had long had soft incandescent street lighting – white light – which is the Edison type of light with the little filament. It's very expensive and inefficient by today's standards, and the original idea was to switch to high-pressure sodium, a pukey orange-coloured light, which is the standard everywhere in North America. Most people don't think about the effect of light, but Toronto had kept the old system for so long that when you walked around the city you could really see the difference between the two in areas that had both.

City Council appointed a committee, which I was part of, to study the matter and make recommendations. It was a fairly lengthy process, taking a couple of years. The goal was to provide nice light for the city while also saving energy. The committee looked into all the latest technologies and found a few that were promising. By the time the day came to make a decision, one of the big lamp companies was willing to go out on a limb and warrantee their product. The technology of metal halide provided a very nicely balanced white light and is now in widespread use. Council didn't know how remarkable it was to adopt a new technology, and even put in fixtures that were very beautiful – re-engineered versions of the ones that had served the city for years.

Residents' recent fight to keep the Palmerston lampposts was about more than lighting: it was also about design. Rosedale had lost its cast-iron lamps not long before.

Both cases show how preservation battles are often re-fought. When our committee made its recommendations, in 1993, all these historical lights were grandfathered in and the idea was that these were permanent amenities to be preserved for all time for the enjoyment of Torontonians. People forgot about that and the issue sort of circled back. That's what happened in Rosedale. They were very beautiful lamps. And, particularly when the city was still incandescent, the effect was magic. They replaced the lampposts and globes with facsimiles, and the effect was lost. You can't even see the posts at night now because the light itself is so bright. The globe doesn't diffuse it.

On Palmerston, they got wind of the possibility they might lose their lights too. Citizens lobbied their city councillor, Joe Pantalone, who tends to be fairly responsive to such things, and the lamps were saved. Sometimes people will say, 'Keep these things because it's the past and we value our past.' I never say that. It's not an easy sell with engineers. You have to argue that things are valuable. Not because of the past but because of the future. This is great and this is beautiful and it works. I doubt you can go to some lamp shop today and buy a post that's going to be there a hundred years from now.

Another small detail of the city I love is the row of brick trim along the edge of most streets, between the road and the sidewalk. A lot of the bricks tend to get paved over these days, which is a shame.

I'm told they help the roadway expand and contract in the cold weather, so I guess it doesn't matter if they're exposed or not, except that they look nice, especially from a few storeys up.

When I lived on Bernard Avenue, at the corner of St. George, we could go up on the roof and look down at the intersection and see those bricks from above. They're attractive. You know in your heart there's a reason for them. They lift the street.

Is there a loss over time if these little details go?

Over time, if you take away all this stuff, some of which is very nice, you devalue everything. Unfortunately, when the city is having so much trouble paying its bills, these small things get cut. There are great details in Toronto. Like manhole covers. There's a mention of a photographer and draftsman named Arthur Goss in Michael Ondaatje's *In the Skin of a Lion*. He was a real person who was written into this book of fiction. Every time you walk across a manhole cover of a certain design – and there are thousands of them around – you see the work of the real Arthur Goss. He designed Toronto's standard manhole cover, which looks like a waffle iron. There's one dated 1910 down at the University of Toronto, east of the medical building. Knowing stories like this helps people love their neighbourhood and respect their city. There's a tangible result. People start to care. So there is support for white light and keeping streetcars.

I think this is a good lead-in to the topic of preservation. You and I both have problems with the weakness of Toronto's preservation laws. We've seen a lot of good buildings fall – a lot of art deco buildings, the Uptown, the Eglinton to an extent. We have our own reasons why we want these buildings to remain, but what do you tell other people? Why preserve?

This is a very difficult and fundamental question, and I think a lot of it involves the fact that these things are of more value to the greater community. These are iconic, valuable artifacts that the public identifies with that have helped build the prosperous communities around them. If you look way, way ahead, they're kind of like a diamond ring or some great investment. The Uptown was this superbly functional giant theatre. The funny thing is, it was an eighty-year-old theatre, but it had just about everything that everyone wanted and liked: big screen, comfortable. And if that one was the classic giant theatre, the

Eglinton was the classic iconic, gorgeous art deco theatre. The Eglinton evoked feelings, and that's extremely valuable. And okay, maybe in 2003 it was kind of hard to fill all those seats, but the argument to preserve it is a big-picture argument – what's it really worth? Not what's it worth on my ledger today, but what it's really worth to this big city over time. That's a tough one to calculate. But to answer your question, preserving builds a community – a city that's vibrant, economically diverse and exciting. This is very marketable, and Toronto's a very marketable city, despite all the destruction that's taken place, partly because it has preserved one thing really well, and that's neighbourhoods – infrastructure, streetcars and tree-lined streets.

Is saving the facade of a building enough?

If that's the only alternative, then fine. But you know, buildings are like so many other things: you want more than packaging. The Eglinton was a great art deco theatre. You can destroy it now because it's not going to be that valuable for the next two years, but if you keep it, it'll be valuable for all time because it's so wonderful. And that's marketable.

What about something like the Gladstone Hotel? I'm glad something's being done with it so it doesn't become beyond repair, but wouldn't it have been great if they'd restored it as it was instead of just renovating and modernizing it?

Jane Jacobs would argue that these minutiae don't matter – she's bigger on infrastructure of the systems, and she would say it's not so important that the wall of the hotel is painted the original green. That said, there is one culture on earth that assigns great value in accurate restoration of landmark buildings, and that's the United States. Maybe it has to do with patriotism and nationalism, but Americans are better at preserving buildings in their entirety and in detail. I realize that it's not always feasible. For example, the hotels on Queen Street, the Drake and the Gladstone. In order to do what they're doing, they have to cater to a certain kind of hipness. They've inserted a modern aesthetic into these hotels – in a fairly intelligent way. The 401 Richmond building is a commercial venture that was handled that way, and it's been very successful. But the Eglinton should not have been 'renovated.' It should have been accurately restored to be a showcase forevermore. Details matter.

Keeping the city running – and I'm not just talking about city hall here, but the private sector as well – is obviously a very important thing. The city will save a few dollars on street signs by making the knobs on top flat. It will pave over the brick trim to save a few more dollars. Famous Players tore down the Uptown because it favours multiplexes. We'll probably never see anything like an art deco building built again because no one wants to pay for it. Developers will just build utilitarian buildings that, more often than not, I'd argue, aren't very attractive. Obviously times have changed, but should we really just have a utilitarian city? There is a point to everything that we're talking about, isn't there? What's the upside to maybe spending a little more time and a little more money?

The city you're describing – with everything stripped away – exists. It's most cities in North America now, most places where people live. It's Mississauga. Toronto is an extremely successful city not because of one thing, but because of many things. All the things you've mentioned are part of it: street lights, streetcars. I would argue that even the manhole covers are in there somewhere. They're good infrastructure, effective infrastructure that works, and that's good for business. And that's good for people. A lot of the things you've described create an environment where people want to be. You get what you pay for, and it's easy to let things run down because you don't want to pay for it.

What really sets Toronto apart from other cities? Not the domed stadium, but clean streets, good transit and livable neighbourhoods. There's great hope for Toronto. Because so much of it's still here. You're not starting from wreckage. The federal government has to understand that Toronto is vitally important to Confederation, as are other large cities in the country. It has to have the means to maintain itself. I think ultimately the hope for Toronto lies in getting a taxation system that supports – as it once did, handily – the city's infrastructure and its different needs. I think that's the basic thought. A good future for Toronto lies in organizing the tax system so it allows the city to tap the prosperity of its residents and supply infrastructure. At the same time, we have to be mindful of what we do to the city and try to keep iconic and beautiful things, and some that aren't so beautiful, just because. Just because ... And in the long run, 'just because' becomes Paris.

Dale Duncan
I ♥ infrastructure

I'm hiking through the woods of Algonquin Park with my nature-loving small-town friend Beth. Beth is one of those people who are always overflowing with curiosity, and here in Canada's largest provincial park, she's like a little kid at the Science Centre. Beth's interest in quirky details is one of her most endearing qualities; she once took me gallivanting through an arboretum to net butterflies, stopping to categorize and record each specimen in her butterfly journal before setting it free.

Beth spent a summer working at Algonquin, and as we hike along a familiar trail, she tells me about Moth Boy, famous throughout the park for his love of everything to do with moths. The seventeen-year-old had snagged a good job working in the park as a naturalist that year due to his obsession with the natural environment; moths in particular were his passion. According to Beth, a one-hour walk with Moth Boy turned into two hours because, well, 'he just loved to identify moths.'

Nature often inspires such behaviour; there's always the cousin who stops to collect different rocks, the little boy who searches for snakes, or the aunt who points out various birds. It's hard, in fact, to find people who don't like nature, or, at least, those who admit to it. Everything's connected to nature. There's so much diversity, so much complexity. You can't hate nature. It's pure and innocent, tainted only by the hands of humans. To Beth, the city is cold and empty in comparison. It's representative of the follies of the human race: depressing, sterile and uninviting.

Regardless, there was something eerily similar in Beth's description of walking through the forest with Moth Boy to my experience walking around Toronto with my friend Matt Blackett. Sustaining a conversation while walking with Matt was becoming increasingly difficult. He, too, was focused on the details around him, his eyes ever fixed on the pavement below his feet. And then it hit me: Matt was a city version of Moth Boy. He had become Sidewalk Stamp Boy, obsessed with the age of the sidewalks across Toronto, the companies that had built them, the styles of the stamps that marked their completion.

It was a cute obsession, but I didn't quite get it. Finding the oldest sidewalk and impressing others with your discovery may be kind of fun, but really, what's the big deal? What kind of impact do these stamps have on us? I suppose one could argue that moths aren't really all that important either. But in biology class we learn that, in nature, everything is linked to everything else; studying small details, like moths, can lead to important discoveries that affect us all. When we learn about cities, if we learn about them at all, we focus on how their structure functions to help us through our daily tasks; the city exists to provide us with a place to work, to entertain us with its nightlife and to make money from tourists with its flashy attractions. Break down the city into its details – roads, sidewalks, lampposts and streetcar tracks – and all you're left with is a bunch of pavement and metal.

Pavement may be the antithesis of nature, but the more I thought about it, the more I realized: Matt and Moth Boy are not really all that different. In fact, more and more people seem to be walking through the city as if they are walking through the forest, not necessarily to get anywhere, but to take note of the details around them. I soon discovered that urban Moth Boys and Girls are everywhere in Toronto, taking notes in their notebooks, bragging about their discoveries, annoying their friends and snapping hundreds of photos.

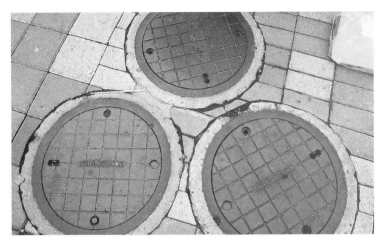

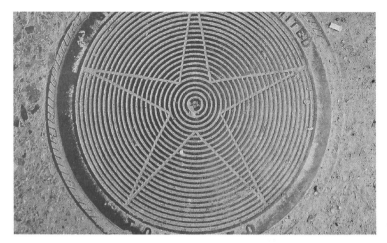

Manhole Cover Girl (a.k.a. Suzan Krepostman) got into the habit of identifying different utility covers while living in Hoboken, New Jersey, and New York City. She now documents Toronto's own sewer-maintenance-hole covers with the same zeal that Beth documents her butterflies. Suzan points out, and a quick search on the web confirms, that this is a widely practised activity, with dozens of websites, art books and historical societies cataloguing the creative covers found on streets and sidewalks around the world.

At first, it almost seems comical that anyone would give much attention to the appearance of the covers marking the entrances to our sewers. City sewers are supposed to be smelly and rat infested. They're supposed to be inconspicuous and practical, never mind the fact that they are often hidden under moving vehicles. Nevertheless, many cities, including Toronto, have gone to lengths to create covers with designs that get noticed. One of Toronto's most common maintenance-cover designs looks like a giant snowflake, but at Baldwin and McCaul you can find one sporting a fish. At Church and Shuter, Suzan found one stamped with a star overlaying concentric circles.

'Utility-hole covers are interesting precisely because you expect them not to be,' says Suzan. 'An artistic utility cover is so unusual and unexpected that it makes people smile and wonder what else they've been missing about their city as they trudge through their day.'

Though Toronto's utility-hole covers may not be as noteworthy as those in other cities, like Vancouver, where they hold design competitions, the promise of finding hidden works of art where you least expect them keeps Suzan looking, camera and notebook in hand.

But it's not just the pretty things in the city that get noticed. Matt's interest in sidewalk stamps, I later learned, goes beyond simple dates and designs. To Matt, they are like 'I was here' stamps, providing tangible proof that people travelled, stood or worked on that spot at a particular point in time. Standing over a sidewalk constructed in 1964, for example, one can't help but wonder how things have since changed, while the cement, now cracked and weathered, has remained the same. What was the streetscape like? What kind of people lived and worked there? How was life in the city different?

'There's something about standing in the oldest spot in the city,' says Matt. 'I've begun to think of our history as all these ghosts. I think of all these people who have experienced different moments at these intersections, and how I've experienced something where they've experienced something.'

Our stories, it seems, are tied to these details. Manhole covers encourage us to explore the city and develop new experiences. Dates stamped into our walkways tempt us to imagine what came before. Sidewalk stamps are not just sidewalk stamps in the same way that moths are not just moths.

'When I first went to England, and I came back, I didn't like Toronto, because it felt like there was no history here,' says Matt, recalling a trip he made in 1999. 'But I later came to realize that Toronto is full of history; it's just more hidden.'

Examine the right clues, and you'll find there's a story hidden behind many of the details we often take for granted. Ever notice the thick concrete curbs that used to run along the sidewalks by Crawford Street as it cuts through Trinity Bellwoods Park? These were the remains of a bridge built in 1915 over a ravine once home to Garrison Creek. In the 1960s, city officials decided to fill the ravine with the displaced debris and soil from the construction of the new Bloor-Danforth subway line, burying the bridge in the same way they had buried the river. Most pedestrians crossing Crawford Street during a stroll through Trinity Bellwoods Park probably never knew they were walking atop a once handsome bridge supported by three dramatic arches. That is until recently, when the invisible structure began to crumble after years of use, forcing the city to fence it off, dig it up and narrow the street in an attempt to once again make it safe. Between the long-forgotten river and bridge, there are likely hundreds of stories to be told.

'Unless you pay attention to the details, history gets forgotten.' Wise words from one of the biggest urban Moth Boys of them all, self-described transit geek James Bow. James is the editor of Transit Toronto (www.transit.toronto.on.ca), a website devoted to everything and anything to do with Toronto's subways, streetcars and buses. Apart from the topic, the website is in no way tied to the Toronto Transit Commission. And James has never been a TTC employee himself, although he probably knows just as much, if not more, about Toronto's public transit than most of its employees. The website is such a wealth of information that it would be impossible to read it in one day. It's updated regularly with current info on 'The Better Way' and is overflowing with articles and photos documenting transit history and infrastructure. Working on this website, discovering forgotten stories about the TTC and sharing his knowledge with other transit enthusiasts (there are a lot of them out there) is just one of the things James enjoys doing in his spare time.

Like Moth Boy, who no doubt played with bugs as a child, James the Transit Geek was obsessed with another popular boyhood passion: trains.

Growing up in Toronto in the eighties, the TTC was an integral part of his life, and the fond memories he developed only helped to fuel his childhood interest. In the nineties, he joined Aaron Adel, who had already started the Toronto subway web page. Aaron's passion was the subway; James loved streetcars. It was a perfect partnership.

Like Matt, James enjoys searching for the ghosts of Toronto's history: old defunct streetcar tracks peeking out from under paved surfaces on streets like Mount Pleasant (which saw its last streetcar in 1976), or seemingly useless metal poles that once supported overhead wiring for streetcars and trolley buses, like those along Harbord, Ossington and Davenport.

James tells me the story of the disappearance of a moving sidewalk ramp with almost as much urgency as Moth Boy would likely talk about an endangered species of moths. When the Bloor-Danforth subway line first opened in 1966, he explains, it ran between Woodbine and Keele stations only. Travellers wanting to go farther west at Keele had to transfer to a streetcar, and a pedestrian tunnel with a moving sidewalk ramp was built to take them there. When the new modern sidewalk opened, the TTC went out of its way to celebrate it, but in 1968, a mere two years later, when the subway was extended to Islington, the moving walkway was shut down and the pedestrian tunnel closed off. A mysterious indent in the wall at Keele station, where the entrance to the walkway once stood, is all that remains.

'Hundreds of thousands of people were taking these tunnels every day, but in a matter of years, no one even knew they existed,' says James.

Talking to James, I realize that while Toronto's built environment is inextricably tied to the collective history of the city, in many ways it is connected to our own personal stories and recent memories as well. Case in point: whenever my dad goes for a hike in 'the great outdoors,' he picks up a small rock along the way to remind him of his journey. James, on the other hand, collects his subway transfers.

'Transfers are souvenirs of the trips you've taken,' he says. 'You can collect them as if they are hockey cards.'

On the Transit Toronto website, James has put together a gallery displaying transfers from between 1944 and 1955. Most betray routes that no longer exist. They are an interesting window to years long past, but I can't help but wonder if they contain more significance to those who actually used these different transfers through the years. Like a particular scent, or an old song, could the sight of these transfers bring back long-forgotten memories?

It happens unconsciously, perhaps, but the city's infrastructure, which at first seems important only because it helps things to run smoothly, becomes connected to our memories and finds its way into our fondest stories about ourselves. Every time we pass by or come in contact with one of these details, we develop an association. Transfers are not just transfers.

'What are you wearing that pin for?' an older man once asked me when he noticed the Christie subway station button I wear on my coat. 'Does it have something to do with that riot?' He was referring, no doubt, to the riot that took place between members of the Jewish community and anti-Semitic groups after a city baseball game back in 1933. My reasons for choosing Christie, however, were not nearly so serious. I wear it for the pickup soccer and basketball games at the park, the perfect meeting place in the small square outside the station where I often run into people I know, and the yummy, inexpensive Korean restaurants I frequent when I'm too lazy to cook. Christie subway station – its font, its tiles and its escalators – is tied to my memories of the English students I have taught, the people I've met playing sports in the park and the many parties, gatherings and conversations I've had with close friends nearby.

There's a sense that Torontonians tend to search elsewhere for their stories, looking to New York, London or Tokyo for the real legends of urban life. But perhaps, like our history, they're just more difficult to find. If these urban Moth Boys and Girls are any indication, it seems that Toronto is now beginning to identify with and embrace its symbols, in the same way that New Yorkers identify with their yellow cabs or Londoners embrace their Underground. People love these symbols, not because they look cool, but because they've been mythologized through their connections to different people and events – they are the backdrops and settings to the stories that play out in our everyday life.

I've come to realize that the more we uncover the layers of the city, the more the way we see and experience the city changes. It's when we sense these stories and seek out the details of our history that our city becomes an interesting place to live. Perhaps that's why Moth Boy is so into moths; it's not so much how they function that makes them fascinating, but rather the mysteries and stories they reveal.

Toronto is home to more than four million people. It has as much diversity, albeit a much different kind, as all the forests and lakes of Algonquin. And the exciting thing is, even if you spent your whole life studying it, it would be impossible to discover all there is to know.

Deborah Cowen, Ute Lehrer & Andrea Winkler for Planning Action
The secret lives of toilets:
a public discourse on 'private' space in the city

Public washrooms are more than just places to piss. They are places where bodily needs meet social desires. They are political spaces, where all sorts of activities, both obvious and unanticipated, can take place. Public washrooms are places of refuge, of nourishment and of contemplation. They are makeshift spaces for cleaning, cuddling, feeding, medicating, laundering, breast-feeding, shaving, debating, fucking and crying.

In the privatized spaces of competitive and capitalist Toronto, where every bit of land is turned into property, the needs of the body are rarely a 'planning priority.' In fact, they are hardly provided for at all. At the turn of the nineteenth century, public washrooms were part of the strategy for modernizing cities, but today's public washrooms are no longer celebrated as one of the achievements of urbanism. Instead they are being shut down, demolished and replaced with private bathrooms in spaces of consumption: coffee places, restaurants and shopping malls.

What used to be designated as the 'public sphere' is increasingly becoming a string of spaces of consumption. The right of the citizen to dwell in the very space of the city is concealed by the rights of the consumer to shop, eat, shop, shop, buy and spend. Since consumers need to shit and pee, bathrooms are the logical extension of places of consumption. In this context, it is interesting to note that the 'real' public washrooms are disappearing, those where you can go no matter what you look like or how much money you have, and being replaced by those you can frequent only when you buy a cup of coffee or a muffin. This also means that the kind of activity that is welcome in public space is specific and exclusive – the consumer has become the figure for which 'public space' is produced, designed, marketed and maintained.

Public washrooms, then, become crucial spaces where all manner of things that are policed out of so-called public spaces can find some sort of refuge. The physical, emotional, political and cultural necessities of everyday life that are evicted from other public places end up flooding public washroom spaces. But where do these people and practices go when public washrooms are closed?

The City of Toronto does not provide adequate public facilities. Instead, it provides public washrooms in areas and during times that offer use for a specific segment of the public – for tourists, shoppers and businesses. For example, security guards monitor the public washroom in the newly built Dundas Square; the hours of operation coincide with shopping and business hours. In other words, the washroom facilitates are not for people who need to use them outside of shopping hours.

When public washrooms in the City of Toronto were closed, the rationale was that they were dangerous places where homeless people sleep and wash themselves, where drug addicts shoot up, where teenagers vandalize, where people have sex – all elements of a supposed 'moral terror.' The city says that in order to have public washroom facilities, they need to have security guards to maintain public safety.[1] Currently, a 'feasibility study' is underway that will look at Automated Public Toilets (APT), which are cost-per-use, self-cleaning, self-timed and, on top of all this, privately owned.

Fifteen years ago, when APTS were introduced in Europe, one of the main rationales was the possibility for increased social control. Older public toilets were closed down and replaced by APTS. Dropped like UFOS

[1] Toronto City Council, Dec. 4, 5 and 6, 2001, *Community Services Committee Report* No. 13, Clause No. 14: Report is referring to Expanding Hours of Operation for External Washrooms at City Hall and Metro Hall (pg. 6) – which states 24-hour washrooms are not possible due to lack of financing for security.

in the middle of a plaza or on a sidewalk, these new toilets give access only to those who have money to pay. With a timer on, they also make it impossible to spend more than twenty minutes inside without being flushed by cleaning fluids. These toilets are prominently placed in the public eye so that everybody who goes in is exposed to the surveillance of passersby.

In North American cities, where we can foresee the appearance of these automated, self-cleaning, privately run toilets, there is a

close link between private need and business interests. In return for installing APTs, the private owner usually gets to advertise on them. In other words, what used to be a public amenity, a sign of progress and a symbol of modernity in cities throughout the world has now become a privatized commodity. And having private enterprises responsible for providing APTs allows the city to shift its responsibility for a public service onto the private sector. What are supposed to be public amenities become corporate spaces.

The Flushing of Spaces?

Planning Action is investigating the built form of public washrooms in order to launch a discussion of the body in public and of 'rights to the city' in the increasingly corporate and privatized spaces of Toronto.

The Public Washroom Project uses humour, design, fictional and biographical stories, and historical and political analyses, and it addresses the *lack of public space in the city* for the body and its complexity of needs, functions and expressions. This discourse on the private lives of toilets sits on a commitment to *public space and peoples' rights to the city*: by taking over public washroom space, bringing activities into this semi-private sphere, we are making known our bodies in the city. Images are shot on location, and this manifesto is written in these spaces, *linking research with action*, engaging the public.

Proclamation:

1. Public washrooms are a basis for *rethinking and rebuilding* a radically democratic and socially just urban citizenship and urban politics.
2. Public washrooms provide a platform for raising questions about the entwined micro-political geographies of *belonging, bodies and built form*.

3. The design, access and availability of public washrooms tell us about which *activities* are *collectively valued in the city* and built into public space. This space needs to provide for the manifold needs of the body, including hygiene and health. In addition to basic shelter, this could include facilities to wash the body, clothes for the body, amenities to address addictions and medicinal needs.

4. *At this moment*, agencies feel they need to compensate for the failure and withdrawal of government in providing the most basic services such as public washrooms for the general public. Community groups say that lack of public washrooms should be viewed as a serious public-health issue for the homeless and the general population.

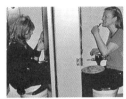

The *definition of 'public' becomes exclusive.* Public resources are provided for those who can pay and who locate themselves in economic centres of the city, while those who need public amenities the most are restricted spatially and encounter problems of health, restrictive hours of operation and stigmatization.

The Public Washroom Project prioritizes our embodiment in all its complexity and diversity in our built form as a starting point for a new, open and democratic practice of public space.

Out of Place?

We have said that public space is built around the needs and desires of a very specific figure: the middle-class shopper who occasionally needs a pee. We've also said that public washrooms, where they exist, become makeshift spaces for all kinds of activities that transcend the stale and fixed categories of public/private (Is brushing your teeth public or private? What about pumping breast milk? Or shaving your

armpits? Washing your socks? Making love? Who decides?) What would 'public' (toilet) space be like if it were understood to support such a range of practices? How can we make sense of the fact that there is no place to go in Toronto when you need to do such basic and necessary things?

Cleaning

Where do you wash your socks if you have no home and no cash? What about your body, or your dishes? The majority of people in Toronto have private homes in which to wash, but those homes aren't portable. Where do you go to scrub a stain that landed on your shirt at lunch? Who hasn't needed to dry their socks on occasion, especially in a city like Toronto, where we are snowed on and wet for most of the year? Hand dryers make for makeshift laundromats, and if one happens to have clothesline and pins, then maybe a stall would do. Public toilets are public places for cleaning our clothes, our dishes and our selves.

Breastfeeding

'I spent many days in a bathroom stall at York U pumping milk crouched on the lid of the toilet seat. (With no private office space to relax and pump milk in, the bathroom stall was my only solace – ah, the life of a student as new mom!) When I used to exit the stall after pumping (which has a particular sound that some might equate with a sexual-stimulation product), other people in the bathroom would always give me the same curious look! Still, to this day, I wonder what they thought I was doing in there ... ' – Sue

Cuddling

As semi-private spaces of the public realm, *public toilets are places of intimacy*. Toilets are where people go to have a good cry when they are in the public spaces of the city, where people compose themselves after an argument or bad news. Public toilets are also places where people go to meet for sex. In a public toilet, you can get away from the public gaze, for a short while.

Feeding

We bathe where we piss and shit. We keep our garbage where we wash dishes. It's not a stretch to say that a public washroom is a good place for a time-out, a place to enjoy a good meal with a stranger or two. Sinks are provided for clean-up afterwards. For those who don't have a kitchen or money to sit in a restaurant, public spaces can become the dining room.

Partying

The public toilet is a community centre. Public toilets are often used as places to hang out with friends, to share gossip, to take a break from work or bad weather. For youth who don't have access to many spaces, washrooms can work as important social spaces for meeting and hanging out.

'I can't tell you the number of times that a public bathroom has been used because of how it affords some measure of privacy in times of public distress – whether it's someone sitting in the stall bawling their eyes out, or talking to themselves trying to summon up the courage to face the public world again, or cleaning off their raccoon-eyed mascara and breaking out the Visine, or a couple of girls, one comforting the other, out by the sinks.' – Elise

Medicating

People take their meds in public toilets.

'I know that this sort of activity can be a bloody nuisance. I remember years ago, when I lived in Vancouver, trying to wash my face at the Carnegie Centre washroom and getting spattered with blood when some user of injectable narcotics botched the procedure and burst a vein. But the cost of managing the problems of impoverishment and social dislocation must be paid. We should not tolerate a city that is under siege because of a refusal to deal with social realities. In places like Kensington Market, where people gather and spend time, there should be public washrooms.' - Tim

Debating

Public toilets are political spaces. Their walls are host to debates and discussions that rarely happen in the same way anywhere else.

'Back in high school (ca. 1991?), abortion was a hot topic in the news. In the second stall on the second-floor washroom by the geography hallway, someone started a debate on this. It became known as 'the abortion wall.' Girls would line up to get into that stall even if the other stall was free, just to read the wall and add their comments. You'd try to check it out every day for new postings. People would talk about it in the hallways: "Did you read the abortion wall today? What did you think about what they said?" It was such a big topic of hallway conversation that some boys stayed around after hours to sneak in and read the wall (they didn't seem to think it was a big deal). It felt like it lasted for months but was probably closer to two or three weeks before the caretakers washed it all off. It was reincarnated once or twice after that but was never quite the same.' – Karen

Spatial justice? Towards an embodied right to the city

If we take the word 'public,' as in *public washrooms,* seriously, and if we are engaged in practices of justice, we need to demand not only more public washrooms but also washrooms that are spaces with multiple public social functions. One of these functions is the political realm that washrooms give to us. A lot of voices scrawled on the walls of the toilet stall grab your attention for a moment and maybe even provoke you to respond. These traces are a way for people to communicate with others anonymously – latrinalia, or graffiti. It is a record of users, it is a record of the public. Many people have tested their political voice in these spaces for the first time. However, this form of communication is silenced, removed regularly with fresh coats of paint. There are even specially designed metal walls being installed in washroom spaces that prevent the possibility of these minute marks of democracy altogether. Instead of public debates about abortion, sexuality or the identity of local sex offenders, the walls of washrooms are now adorned with Viacom boxes for corporate advertisements for military recruitment, solutions for yeast infections and an endless variety of cosmetics. Besides the most obvious reality that this creates, namely the commodification of a place of primary bodily functions, it also reveals how the attempt to control the space of public washrooms is simultaneously an effort to control the politics in and of those spaces. Therefore, we need to address this in any efforts to build a progressive future for Toronto. Democratic and inclusive politics can only take shape through democratic and inclusive spaces.

It is possible to reclaim space. Many people have already begun to rescue the spaces of public discourse in public washrooms from this corporate invasion. People have begun to scratch their thoughts, ideas and outrage into the metal frames of the Viacom boxes, or onto the plastic shields that protect the corporate ads. Ad boxes have been vandalized and ads removed – replaced instead with political stickers and graffiti. These are spaces that are, can and should be spaces of democratic exercise. The reclamation of these spaces is part of a larger process of reclaiming space in the city for the public.

We can conclude that public washrooms are more than just toilets; they are social spaces, where all kinds of activities take place. This brings us back to the question at the heart of the Public Washroom Project: what would Toronto be like if we actually prioritized our

embodiment in all its complexity and diversity in our built form? That is not for us to answer, but for us all to work towards. This is a politics built around the right to the city. It is a politics built on the right to meet bodily needs and desires in the spaces of the city. It is a politics of openness, embodiment, materiality, inclusivity and radical democracy.

Chris Hardwicke
Velo-city

Cycle tracks will abound in Utopia.
– H. G. Wells, *A Modern Utopia*

It's Monday morning. You get your gear on and strap your bag onto your bike. It is cold and raining today, but after just five minutes of riding you can see a glazed on-ramp in the distance. A quick lane change and you pump your way up the ramp. Switching into the slow lane, you can already feel the draft pulling you forward as cyclists in the fast lanes blur past you and into the distance. Once you get your rhythm, your shoulders relax as you let down your defences. No more cars breathing down your neck.

It's strangely quiet as you ride along, looking through the raindrops on the glazing out to the panorama of the urban landscape. In the distance, you can see the cluster of red brake lights on the 404 as you pull into the next lane and gear up. Up ahead, you see a familiar bike trailer and realize it's your friend taking his kids to daycare. Pulling into the slow lane, you say hi to the kids and chat with your friend for a few minutes before they get to their off-ramp.

A few minutes later, the bikeway opens up and widens to six lanes as you pass the GO station. As hundreds of GO riders merge into traffic on their yellow bikes, you are getting warm, so you strap your jacket on the back of your bike. Further on, you notice a hint of fragrance, which quickly grows into a field of odour and colour as you pass through the orchids growing in one of the greenhouses located along your route. Just around the corner, you cross the Don Valley as the sun breaks through the clouds. In no time, you are passing by the market stalls, making a mental note to pick up some organic bananas at the fruit stall on your way home that night. Shifting down, you take the next off-ramp to work. Checking your watch, you notice you are early again.

Welcome to Velo-city.

Velo-city is a viable strategy for helping bikes commute through the city. It is a highway for bikes, a network of elevated bikeways that connect distant parts of the city. The bikeway has three lanes of traffic in either direction, for slow, medium and fast travel. Riding through Velo-city is like riding through a long atrium because the bikeway is enclosed by a glass roof. Each direction of travel in Velo-city has a separate bikeway tube. The separation of direction reduces wind resistance and creates a natural tailwind for cyclists. The reduction of air resistance increases the efficiency of cycling by about ninety percent, allowing for speeds of up to fifty kilometres per hour. Velo-city increases speeds, reduces spent energy and eliminates intersections to produce total travel times that rival any other form of high-speed transit.

Upon initial examination, Velo-city might sound like another expensive public expenditure that no one would use. While it *would* require a dramatic change in lifestyle for many, compared with other transportation options Velo-city has significant and far-ranging economic benefits. Velo-city fits into spaces that trains, subways and roads simply can't fit into due to their size, noise or pollution. And because Velo-city is elevated, it can be located in already existing highways, power and railway corridors; it does not require any additional real estate. Velo-city produces no noise or pollution so it can be built right into, through or beside buildings. On streetcars, buses and subways, riders are effectively controlled and ridership determined by the space of the individual car, but Velo-city users can determine their own speed and level of congestion.

A bicycle takes one-seventh the space of a car on the road. That means that the equivalent width of the bikeways in Velo-city has seven times the capacity of a highway. Velo-city takes no additional space in the city, and

it relieves our transit system and highways of congestion. It also, of course, saves seven times the amount of parking space required at home, work and retail centres. The resulting land savings in the city could be used for more productive and economically advantageous uses. The average bicycle post costs $250. The average underground parking space costs $25,000. Reducing parking spaces is essential to reducing the cost of housing. In commercial terms, a typical shopper takes up seventy times his or her own personal space when driving and parking a car. More important, fewer parking spots creates a proliferation of active streets, with thriving businesses, cultural activities, restaurants and so on. The real-estate value of the consequent land savings alone would offset the capital cost of building Velo-city. Maintenance costs for Velo-city would also be relatively low. The weight and vibration of bicycles is considerably less than that of automobiles or railways. And because Velo-city is covered, it would be sheltered from weather distress. The staff required to maintain Velo-city would be less than that required for road maintenance or transit use.

Recent studies in Canada show that the average family spends twenty percent of its income to own and operate just one car.[1] With rising oil prices and the threat of peak oil, we desperately need a more affordable alternative to the motor vehicle. Not only is Velo-city a cheaper form of transport, but it also causes no pollution and requires no energy use. Transportation of all types accounts for more than twenty-five percent of the world's commercial energy use, and motor vehicles account for nearly eighty percent of that.[2]

1 Carmen Mills. *Driving Home the Costs - The Real Price of the Automobile.* (Better Environmentally Sound Transportation. Emerald City Communications. 1999), http://www.best.bc.ca.

2 World Resources Institute, 1998-1999 *World Resources: A Guide to the Global Environment* (New York: Oxford University Press, 1998).

The Ontario Medical Association estimates that air pollution is responsible for 5,800 premature deaths annually across Ontario.[3] According to the OMA, such pollution is estimated to cost the province more than $1 billion a year due to hospital admissions, emergency-room visits and absenteeism. When the costs of pain, suffering and loss of life from polluted air are factored in, the total annual economic loss is estimated to be $7.8 billion a year. This amount is expected to increase to $9.8 billion by the year 2015.[4] Ironically, people who exercise outdoors, such as cyclists and runners, as well as children, animals and the elderly, are most susceptible to pollutants. With the real-estate, social, environmental, health, agricultural, tourist and cultural costs of our present auto-oriented society, we can't afford not to build Velo-city.

3 Ontario Medical Association, 2005-2026 *Health & Economic Damage Estimates,* June 2005. http://www.oma.org/Health/smog/report/ICAP2005_Report.pdf.

4 Ibid.

Toronto is one of the biggest biking cities in North America. The popularity of the bicycle is growing rapidly at the grassroots level. Yet, despite the strong support by the cycling community, the City of Toronto has provided little infrastructure or support beyond bike posts and bike lanes painted on the sides of designated roads. A quick look at a Toronto bike map shows that there are no continuous bike paths that are suitable for long-distance commuting. According to the 1999 Toronto Cycling Survey, cyclists who ride to work number almost 159,000. These cyclists make approximately 573,000 work trips per week.[5] The City of Toronto Bike Plan has the ambitious goal of doubling the number of bicycle trips made in the city by 2011 and reducing the number of bicycle collisions and injuries.[6] However, the rationing of the width of our streets remains a contentious issue, and recent City of Toronto decisions belie the Bike Plan's optimism. The City of Toronto removed the bicycle route designation along Spadina in 1994, and then, in 2004, along St. Clair West and Queen West, rather than trying to physically accommodate bike lanes. A close examination of the Bike Plan's proposed 1,000 kilometres of bicycle routes shows that they are conveniently located along wide streets and open spaces rather than actively creating a strategic commuter network. Velo-city offers an alternative: a parallel infrastructure that acts in support of other modes of transit. The bikeways are connected to the subway, railway, highway and parking lots, thereby offering more commuting choices. Regardless of the law, the most vulnerable vehicle now gets the least protected position in a shared roadway. Velo-city simply gives bicycles the same level of dedicated infrastructure that other modes of transit enjoy. Trains have dedicated corridors, cars have highways and most of the roads, streetcars have tracks, and pedestrians have sidewalks. Velo-city provides the environmental conditions that would allow many more cyclists to bike year-round.

5 Decima Research Inc., *City of Toronto 1999 Cycling Study*, February 2000.

6 City of Toronto, *Toronto Bike Plan*, 2001. http://www.city.toronto.on.ca/cycling/bikeplan/index.htm.

Ironically, bicycle groups were the first civic groups to lobby for good roads. One hundred and twenty years ago, bicycle maps of Toronto showed an extensive network of bicycle routes extending in a hundred-mile radius around the City of Toronto. In the late nineteenth century, the Canadian Wheelman's Association created the Good Roads Movement to lobby for the first paved roads to be built in the city for bicycles – long before automobiles were even on the scene.[7]

One hundred years ago, there was a brief moment in history when the bicycle was seen as the future of transportation. Around this time, H. G. Wells wrote two books that featured the bicycle. In *A Modern Utopia*, Wells describes his vision of a world in which the bicycle was a primary mode of transportation. *The Wheels of Chance* is a quixotic romantic comedy that follows its

7 Glenn Norcliffe, *The Ride to Modernity: The Bicycle in Canada, 1869–1900* (Toronto: University of Toronto Press, 2001).

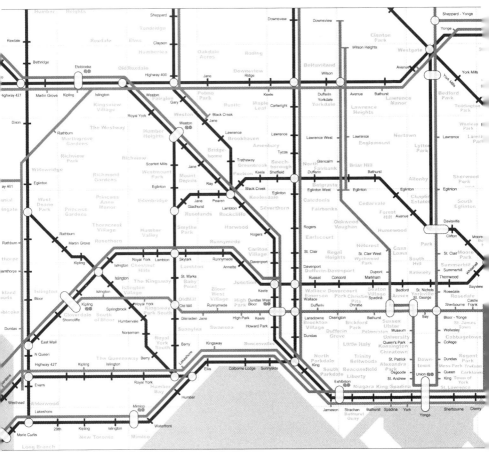

cyclist hero biking around the villages of southern England in order to save a cycling damsel from a cycling cad. In that novel, Wells uses the bicycle as an illustration of the newly discovered freedom of mobility. This brief period of liberty disappeared as soon as the automobile took over the roads. The bicycle left science fiction and was replaced by cars, flying cars and spaceships.

The culture of a city is often defined by its transportation system: yellow cabs in New York City, bicycles in Beijing, streetcars in San Francisco, highways in Los Angeles, double-decker buses in London, scooters in Taipei, canals in Venice, cyclos in Ho Chi Minh City and the Metro in Paris. Often, transportation systems create interdependent relationships with urban form and culture. Think of the interrelationship between highways and shopping malls, arterial roads and strip malls, subways and skyscrapers, streetcars and main streets, scooters and roadside stalls. Over time, Velo-city will create a cycling culture for Toronto: kiss 'n' rides, shower

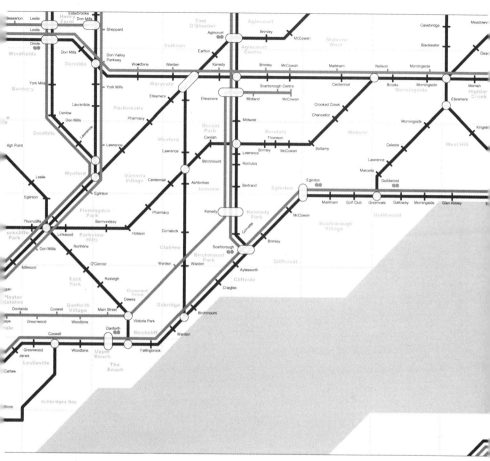

facilities, velodomes, bike parks, health clubs, cycle-path stalls, repair shops, bike couriers, bike picnics, car-free housing, inter-modal stations and cycling fashions. Above all, it would encourage active, healthier lifestyles and, consequently, better lives for all Torontonians. The more we learn of the environmental harm caused by the automobile, the more we see the fiction of its benefits. Suburban areas that are difficult to traverse by walking or cycling report higher incidents of obesity and heart disease. Urban dwellers, choked by pollution, suffer increased respiratory diseases. All other modern modes of transit are passive – cars, trains, buses, subways and streetcars all take users for a ride. We ride to work and then we ride to work out. Velo-city is like a long gym between your house and your job. Why not just ride to work?

For more information about Velo-city, please visit www.velo-city.ca.

Luis Jacob
Flashlight: public art and the mothership connection

The message 'EVERYBODY'S GOT A LITTLE LIGHT UNDER THE SUN' appears one day in the Toronto Sculpture Garden. This message is written upon an LED sign that frames a climbing dome situated beneath a large mirror ball. The electric sign and the mirror ball's motor are powered by two different sources, which are contingent both on the climate's variations and the activities of the garden's visitors: solar panels capture available sunlight and convert it to electrical energy; alternately, bicycle pedals attached to hidden electrical generators also transform visitors' muscle power into electricity. The solar source powers the motor of the rotating mirror ball suspended above a geodesic climbing dome that is the central focus of the entire installation. This dome – and the playful behaviour it elicits – is observed from a platform equipped with seating and the bicycle pedals that transform the energy voluntarily exerted by visitors into electricity to power the LED sign overhead: EVERYBODY'S GOT A LITTLE LIGHT....

Flashlight is the site of a utopian proposal. Its LED message is derived from the Parliament song 'Flash Light,' written by George Clinton, Bernie Worrell and Bootsy Collins. This message establishes a relationship between the installation as a whole and the aspirations for self-transcendence and social union embodied in funk culture from the 1970s. Installed in the Toronto Sculpture Garden from May to September 2005, this sculptural ensemble proposes that playful personal interaction is a source of power that is parallel to the natural power of the sun under which we are all equal. The sun shines in the same way for rich and poor, for citizen and alien, for bodies black, brown, red, yellow and white. Equally, we each

carry within us an inner spark – an innate agency to manifest individually and to concentrate collectively within that regulated and regimented terrain known as the public sphere.

Flashlight is a hybridizing work where two relatively autonomous systems are made to energize and to arouse a new third system. In the first place, there is the cosmic system formed by the earth in rotation around its axis and in orbit around the sun, from which it receives energy in the form of solar rays. This system is of particular importance for us, of course, since it is the foundation of all organic life on earth, including our own.

This cosmic system comes into contact with a second system that is social in nature. This second system is composed by constellations of public and private uses of territory – land in the cities – that, in the form of social norms, express interests that mutually conflict, endorse and transform one another. To enter a public park is to enter into this social system, this constellation of personal interests expressed by behaviour and structured by law. For some of us, this experience of entering a public park is free of troubles and conducive to leisure, fun and relaxation; for others of us, this experience is frequently vexing, even intolerable.

These two systems are made to touch upon each other in *Flashlight*. The cosmic system enters the project *from above*, and its point of entry is the solar panel. The social system enters the project *from below*, and its point of entry is the platform equipped with the bicycle pedals, from which are visible the playground climbing-dome and the myriad of relations the park's visitors establish with it. In both, the lit-up LED message and the activated rotation of the mirror ball, this overlaying of systems energizes a third, now-emergent presence: funk culture that came to prominence during the 1970s, and that, in the mutating forms of electro-funk, post-punk/no-wave, hip-hop, Chicago house, acid house and Detroit techno, remains a resounding message in both the popular and mass/corporate music cultures of North America. Funk culture strives to produce a social experience of unity that weaves through racial lines and other divisions between people, by prioritizing a bodily, interpersonal and spiritual identification with rhythm. This form of identification is understood to be innate – that is, already present within all people regardless of background, and thereby forms the basis for communality. Funk is primarily an *experience*; it is something you perceive – not by observing it at a distance, but *by taking part in it with others*. The experience of funk can certainly produce a high, but a high that comes from below. It is a high that emerges from our bodies in action, and from the lowest part in harmonic music – the rhythmic bass. From this lowliness, funk uplifts.

But a peculiar theatricality appears in *Flashlight*, arising in the form of a variety of props. The LED sign serves as backdrop or caption to the activities unfolding on the geodesic play structure below, and these activities are observed from the comfortable seating of a viewing platform. Whatever play may occur between visitors upon the climbing dome, it occurs in fictional form, as a kind of performance. *Flashlight* is premised on the idea that, in the time between the 1970s and today, we have become the children of a new, colonized form of experience – the everyday experience of a certain kind of social space *that is itself based upon fiction*. In privatized 'public' amenities – of which the recent development of Dundas Square provides a striking instance – our experience of being social is fictional in a way that today is eminently common and everyday. More and more, this is what we recognize as public space – the staging of the commons, the management of the experience of being with others, the fiction of being public.

The message that funk culture thematized in the 1970s was one of togetherness, spontaneous generative interaction, shameless bodily expression and self-transcendence. If any of this appears in *Flashlight*, it comes to light as a utopia – a fleeting and unstable apparition – in the sparkling of a mirror ball, and the ephemeral illumination of an LED. The geodesic climbing dome, around which all the other elements of the installation are oriented, is a cipher – a spherical non-site, a place holder

like the number zero in a sequence of digits – that designates the possibility for something to happen.

What is this something that is also an unregulated event? We call it *play*. The performance of play within the confines of the city and its routines – the enacting of child-like abandon and collective pleasure – can perhaps manifest itself today in our docile bodies only theatrically, as a fantasy. *But this fantasy is up for grabs.* It can be shaped into customized interaction and managed conviviality, or else into a spontaneous moment of experimental action. The third system of funk arises in this context to appear *almost like* the non-conformism of artistic autonomy and freedom, and *not quite as* an affirmation of a bureaucratized notion of 'arts in the community.' Funk must be born freakishly, arising as if from the earth itself in the form of a weird geodesic mothership. It calls for a collective act of cultural misappropriation and a transformative botched rehearsal performed in the service of the promise of liberation, pleasure and togetherness.

In *Flashlight*, playful participation occurs beneath the rhetorical presence of a mirror ball that scintillates and spins in a revolution that is daily renewed and powered by an indefatigable cosmic source. Our collective performance of playfulness takes place in front of the declarative presence of an LED sign lit up by the social power of our own active bodies. If collective play is ever to occur within *Flashlight*, it will be born twisted, but as its own reward. Feet, don't fail me now!

Flashlight was installed at the Toronto Sculpture Garden from May 4 to September 15, 2005.

TOmorrow

Bert Archer
Making a Toronto of the imagination

The University of Toronto held a little conference in 2004 called Cities of the Imagination. It brought together scholars from around the world to talk about the way cities exist outside of themselves, whether through literature, film or mythology. I was invited to deliver some general remarks on the subject, and the first thing that came to mind, and the first thing I said, was that I wasn't sure whether it was fascinating, ironic or simply a little sad that a conference entitled Cities of the Imagination was taking place in Toronto – a city that exists in no one's imagination, neither in Toronto, nor in the rest of the world.

Evidence of the former fact, I said, is to be found in the tittering you hear at movies when Toronto is mentioned – this does not happen with Niagara Falls, which, for various reasons, does exist in the imagination – and in the disbelief among those who noticed that, in 2005, the *Utne Reader* declared Toronto the best city in the world for magazine culture. Torontonians are always more than vaguely amazed that we're mentioned in anything other than a domestic context, whether positively or negatively. Evidence for the latter point comes to any Torontonians going more or less anywhere in the world and telling people they're from Toronto. The greatest reaction they're likely to get, and in fact the most likely, is that the person they're speaking to knows someone who lives there, very likely a family member or friend who moved here. Toronto is a place people live, not a place where things happen, or, at least, not where the sorts of things happen that forge a place for the city in the imagination.

Some of the cause has to be the city's place in the imagination of our nation too. The Rebellion of 1837, for instance, which has all the potential to be the sort of building block every city of the imagination needs, is just rubble, neglected even by the curricula of many of the country's schools.

Upper Canada's (and therefore Canada's) first parliament buildings are actual rubble, right around the foot of Parliament Street (go figure). They were the subject of a brief activation of Toronto historical spirit in 2003 and 2004 that quickly withered. They're under a Porsche dealership now. The root problems here are the lack of a sense of the importance of such things in Canada when confronted by much more firmly and narratively entrenched stories from Britain, the U.S., France, India and Germany; and the sometimes latent, sometimes not so latent, anti-Toronto sentiment in the rest of the country, where its cultural and financial centrality has been unchallenged at least since the Montreal exodus of the late seventies and early eighties.

Montreal has a much larger place in the imagination of its own residents, and of people abroad, than Toronto. The reasons for this are manifold, and include the extremely low tuition rates that, for several decades, attracted many Americans, who then went off and became a sort of alumni diaspora, and the fact that Montreal, unlike Toronto, is significantly different from the mainstream of American culture. It's a handy tourist destination: European, but without the expense and bother of transatlantic travel, and so it sticks – at least with Americans. It resides so comfortably in the imaginations of its own people largely because of the mentality that springs up when a place is culturally threatened, as French Canada is by English Canada and the United States, and as English Montreal is by Franco Quebec. Anglo Toronto doesn't have this problem. We're not linguistically threatened, and we relate directly enough to the rest of Anglo culture that we don't, except sometimes rhetorically, feel culturally threatened enough to install ourselves in a Quebec-style garrison.

Quebec has some cultural relations with the francophone world, whether it be France, Haiti, Belgium or the former French colonies in

Africa, but Ontario and Toronto's natural historical cultural connection is to England, a country that is far more concerned now with the centre of the English-speaking world – the United States – than it is with Canada. The royal family may come to Canada on slightly more frequent official visits than it does to the States, but that's about the extent of our preferred status. At least culturally speaking. The Commonwealth is of very little significance. And so Toronto (and most of the rest of the country) has nowhere to look but south.

Which is precisely the problem. Most of Canada has gone from being a British colony to being an American one, with only a very brief interim, round about the time of Diefenbaker, Pearson and Trudeau's first term or two. Laurier declared that the twentieth century would belong to Canada, and if Woodrow Wilson and FDR hadn't come along, perhaps it could have. But they did, and it didn't.

In any case, our continued devotion – in theory to Britain and in fact to the U.S. – makes us like nothing so much as a child who's moved back home to his parents' empty nest, looking for love and recognition he's just not going to get.

My Toronto includes a Sneaky Dee's on Bloor Street that's open twenty-four hours a day. It includes a cinema called the Roxy, way out in the east end at Greenwood, that shows the *Rocky Horror Picture Show* every Friday at midnight, and a Christian Science Reading Room – beside what used to be a Beaver gas station at Bloor and St. George – where you can buy cheap, pretty, gold editions of the *Bhagavad Gita* and the *Dhammapada* to get your undergraduate fix of world religion before chucking the entire concept altogether. It also includes another little bookstore with no real sign, underneath an otherwise featureless government building. This shop is the Bob Miller Book Room; it's like a bookstore for a small, liberal-arts grad school, except it's not. It's across the street from the U of T campus, but it has no affiliation with it. It has display tables out front, just like the big bookstores do, except they're stocked with the latest life of Saussure, and Bob Miller's newest best-seller might be, as it was recently, *Minimal Theologies: Critiques of Secular Reason in Adorno and Levinas.*

Everyone has a Toronto like this, made up of a combination of places from the past, little nooks and crannies they find charming or unique, or that have some personal resonance. They'll also include bigger places, if you ask them, like the Eaton Centre or the Church of the Redeemer or Pusateri's. We have many Torontos. We have our neighbourhoods, which residents invariably describe as being like little villages (they'll also, I've found, usually tell you the neighbourhood's a great place for dogs, even in Riverdale, where dogs have been known to get poisoned). Cities exist in layers, and this is the layer that includes your house, your neighbours' houses, the corner store where you get your last-minute bread and your late-night chocolate, the schoolyard where you take your dog for a walk and the place you like to go for brunch or hangover recovery. This is the insular, inward-looking layer that has a lot in common with those developments you see in Whitby and Ajax and Pickering, where people move when their domestic lives become more important than their social ones.

The next layer is the often barbell-shaped home-work continuum, two blobs of familiarity – the work blob being very much like the home blob, only with more food courts and take-out coffee places – linked by a commute, whether it's along the Queen streetcar line, up and down the lanes of Avenue and University, or across the 401. There are a hundred things we're familiar with along the various commutes we make daily. Along the Gardiner, for instance, there are these hillside flora ads for Manulife, the United Way and a few others (there used to be one for Arthur Andersen before it ran into its difficulties), that R. J. McCarthy school uniform building on the QEW with the schoolbus on top; Big Al's aquarium store with the shark feedings north on Kennedy; the Hav-a-Nap motel on Kingston Road; or those halal pizza places (with names like Mecca and Madina) in the Muslim section of the Danforth that you're always intending to get a slice from, just to see. It's in this layer that our disconnection from the city begins. Even though hundreds of thousands of us are familiar with the same particulars of these bits of city we travel through, they have in all but the broadest cases (the CN Tower, the Eaton Centre, the ROM and AGO, maybe Upper Canada College) failed to become common points of reference among us. We don't talk about them.

And nothing happens before conversation. If we don't consider these sorts of things, our local loci, important enough for conversation, we certainly won't consider them important enough to write down, or to film, or to otherwise record, and, without that, places – regardless of their population, density or legal status – remain towns, not cities.

There's a reason this is as it is, and there's a way out of it.

I remember, as many do, reading Michael Ondaatje's *In the Skin of a Lion* for the first time. I had just moved to Toronto and was getting to know the city, the bits I mentioned above, staying mostly around where I was living, at Bay and Bloor. My Toronto at the time didn't extend west of Bathurst or north of Yorkville or really east of Yonge, but it was a big, exciting city (I'd come from Victoria). I didn't know much about it before moving here. I saw it on the news every once in a while, but *In the Skin of a Lion* was not only the first thing I read to have a Toronto resonance since I moved here, it was the first decent thing I'd ever read or seen that considered Toronto important enough to incorporate into art the way Paris or London or Berlin or New York have been for centuries. It was unapologetic, but also unselfconscious. Ondaatje, possibly because he came from somewhere else, was treating the city he lived and wrote in the way a writer would in any one of these other global cities (as Saskia Sassen calls them). It's as a result of this book that the R. C. Harris water filtration plant just east of the Beaches has the resonance it does. Ditto the Bloor Street viaduct. It's been outside itself. It's been in a book. A good book. A widely read book. It's important.

There's a feedback loop that gets set up when someone does something good with one of our places or things, or even people, this way. The artist pulls something out of apparent obscurity, except, of course, she's working from one of those frames of reference shared by thousands of locals. So when those locals read or see it, they're reminded that, yes, they know that place and isn't it cool that, say, Ondaatje knows it too? Then they might talk, eventually, to someone else who's read or seen what they've read or seen and, suddenly, the person, place or thing has become communal. But even better than that, the next time they see the noun (let's call it), it resonates not only with whatever direct personal experience they have with it, but with the added significance of its transmogrification into art, and its promotion from private to communal or public point of reference.

But in the years since *In the Skin of a Lion*, there's been very little first-rate follow-up (it was preceded by Morley Callaghan's stuff, but no one reads that anymore; Hugh Hood's series would have been great if it'd ever caught on). We've had plenty of movies filmed here, obviously, but even the ones that are set here too, such as, to take a couple of decent ones at random, *Eclipse* (Jeremy Podeswa, 1995) and *Sugar* (John Palmer, 2004), aren't confident enough in either themselves or the city to reify it. (I use this word a lot, but it's really not that useful, since every time I do, I feel compelled to explain that it means, roughly, to thing-ify, to conceptualize and then to present something as a thing worthy of conceptualization and presentation. There.) We see no references to College Street or Roy Thomson Hall (or Roy's Square or the Annex or Yonge and Eg). People in the audience of both these movies pointed and either giggled or mumbled when they recognized a storefront or a street corner, but the movies themselves never did. No filmic pointing, no mumbling. Toronto's as much of a stand-in in *Sugar* as it is in *Chicago*.

But we're getting ahead of ourselves. I'm not too concerned at the moment with offering suggestions about how to portray the city in film and literature (except possibly to mention that grants with strings and CanCon regulations are absolutely not the way to do it. One real, unassisted mention of Bill Barilko by the Tragically Hip is worth a dozen NFB films about Yonge Street). What I'm interested in is that conversation, and getting us into it.

It can be a circular sort of a thing at first. People consider cities important enough to talk about and use bits of them as assumed points of reference when the cities are generally thought to be important enough to talk about and refer to. The question is, how do we get from here to there? Since the two main routes to establishing a place in the popular imagination – history and a dominating presence in contemporary mass culture, whether through traditional cultural product or through being the subject of globally significant or interesting news (Hiroshima, Lockerbie, Waco) – are not immediately open to us, the only practical suggestion is that we follow the leads already on the ground.

New York, contrary to apparent popular wisdom, is not one of those leads. New York has become the city it is in the imagination of New Yorkers and much of the rest of the world in fits and starts. *King Kong* (the 1933 and the 1976 versions), *Saturday Night Live* and Woody Allen certainly helped it along, as have the *New Yorker*, the Algonquin, Broadway (especially once it started feeding Hollywood), Times Square, Andy Warhol, *Midnight Cowboy*, *Taxi Driver*, Basquiat, Spike Lee, *Seinfeld*. The list is prodigiously long. But before they even got to Fred Astaire singing 'on the avenue / Fifth Avenue,' or Deborah Kerr standing Cary Grant up at the Empire State Building, the locals had to be impressed enough with themselves and what they'd wrought to put it in print and on film.

The differences between New York and Toronto far outnumber the similarities: population, history, geopolitical importance as the centre of the ruling culture of the twentieth and, at least so far, twenty-first centuries. Though New York has the highest degree of global centrality of any city since London in the nineteenth century, its domestic significance is not singular. It shares the spotlight with L.A. and D.C., and sometimes Chicago and Boston. In Canada, Vancouver is no more than a San Francisco, Montreal a Santa Fe. Toronto is New York, D.C., Chicago and Boston all rolled up into one and in that way is a lot like Paris and London. And yet, we have this problem.

But one of the biggest dissimilarities, one that I've spent hours trying to figure out in conversation (I'm not much for private meditation, me), is the fact that at no point in American history does the rest of the country seem to have begrudged New York what it had or was in the way Canada has Toronto; as a result, New York has had an entire nation celebrating its achievements, pleased with its biggest city, proud of it, eager to claim it as its own and have New York represent it to the world at large. I've heard no grumbling from Utah about the fact that the NBC headquarters are in New York, no cavilling from Washington that the UN is there and not in the nation's capital. Our political ideologies and even personal practices may be more communally minded than the Americans', but when it comes to urban matters, we're all lobsters, pulling each other back down into our trap. Perhaps Americans realize that people come from all over the country to make their mark in New York. As they do in Toronto. Like Dublin, London and Paris, Toronto is a cross-section of the nation. It's a magnet for domestic immigration, which makes the rest of the country's disdain for us even more ridiculous. Torontonians are Calgarians; we're Vancouverites and Winnipeggers, Montrealers, Hamiltonians, Haligonians and Reginans.

But, as I say, for all that New York has done right or stumbled into, it's not that city's lead we should be following first. We have our own to follow now, thankfully. New York's won its races and retired to its hall of fame, and we, at last, seem to have made our way to our starting block. For years, probably more than a couple of centuries, Toronto, like every place, has had its boosters, chamber of commerce sorts who shake their pompoms because civic pride is seen as a virtue, like school spirit. That is useless to us. But more recently, there has been a different sort of city spirit, rising from people who get off on Toronto not because they should, or because it happens to be where they live, but for the city's inherent qualities. It's a Zeitgeisty sort of a thing that's finally wafted into town – and not the result of any particular organization or movement, though, in the way of such things, people have congregated around the casually cohesive groups such as those responsible for *Spacing* magazine or the Toronto Public Space Committee or the [murmur] project. It's the precipitating force behind this book.

This particular geist was also coincident with *Eye Weekly* starting up its City section, used largely to investigate the city and reify it with stories about urban shadows, profiles of writers in exile who'd chosen to live in Toronto, stories about particular shops and neighbourhoods. It was a necessarily modest, corporate version of what Gabe Sawhney (*Eye*'s webmaster) and Shawn Micallef (who's written for *Eye*) have been doing with [murmur], an audio project that records people's stories of very particular places (this house, that patio) and erects markers in front of them with phone numbers people can dial to listen right there. Matt Blackett (an

Eye cartoonist) continues to do similar, though more overtly ideologically minded, things with his quarterly *Spacing* magazine.

Former mayor John Sewell (once a *NOW* columnist, and later at *Eye*) and Don Wanagas (once a *National Post* columnist, now a *NOW* columnist) are both a certain kind of city booster, and, on the surface of it, they – along with the *Star*'s Royson James and the *Globe*'s John Barber – might seem to have a lot in common with Micallef, Meslin et al. They're all mad for the particulars. But Sewell, Wanagas and friends – though they've achieved a great deal in the city – are wonks. The *Spacing* and [murmur] folks are geeks. Huge difference. Wonks get things done behind the scenes and spend a good deal of their time behind those scenes. In the course of reporting on and trying to change the city, they make it their business to know the inner workings of committees and subcommittees, to be familiar with budget line items and municipal administrators. Wonks, for the most part, can inform (and all four of these do that prodigiously well), but they cannot popularize. Geeks, on the other hand, though socially pretty similar, are all about popularizing. It's the music geeks who let us know about Sigur Rós and Broken Social Scene, the ones who took the Velvet Underground above ground, who brought the Kinks to vanilla society. It's the film geeks who laid the critical and, more important, the video-store-buzzing groundwork for the recent Japanese horror crossover, as they did for the French New Wave, the New New Wave, Dogme, etc., etc. The geeks are the focused few who act as prisms for their manias, refracting their components and letting the rest of us see how lovely it all really is. Which makes them very valuable.

And it means we should be watching them. I'm sure they're explaining themselves in other parts of this book better than I could here, so I'll let it suffice to say that realizing that those little ringed bicycle posts are a Toronto design, taking long walks in neighbourhoods you've never been through, and trying to find the oldest sidewalk stamp in the city are all important, essential first steps in transforming our relationship to Toronto from that of a mildly embarrassed child to his parents, into something more like Kate Hudson's with Goldie Hawn (a house on fire, those two).

As I say, though, they're geeks, amateur urbanologists; it's not necessary that we all be. Our version of [murmur], for example, would be to simply cease ignoring – and as a result wasting – the parts of our days we tend to consider white noise: the going-to and coming-from, the getting and the spending parts. Notice the details, the patterns; we've got some of the better examples of mid-eighties po-mo architecture around here, for instance – notice that when you walk by the tumbly police headquarters on College, or the even more tumbly Scotia Tower, especially the bit that backs onto Adelaide.

But more generally, it involves getting a handle on, as our friendly neighbourhood geeks have, what Toronto is, rather than what it is not. It's an extensive city for one, and an extraordinarily dense one, even outside what most people consider to be downtown (Ossington to the Don Valley, Harbourfront to Eglinton). You could walk, as some folks do, from the outer edges of Etobicoke to the inner circles of Scarborough and not run out of stuff to see and do. It's an extraordinarily interactive city in this respect, more than any other in the country. More, in fact, than almost any other city in the Western world; we just don't tend to interact with much of it. Been to Roncesvalles recently? How about Long Branch? Bendale? Unless you live there, I'm going to guess no. So let's start there, shall we?

Jonny Dovercourt
Making a green scene

Toronto, 2025

Jade is one of the few people in this scene who can legitimately say, 'I was here first.'
A south Annex kid from birth, Jade went to kindergarten at King Edward
before it was shut down in the big school-board consolidation of 2010.
Most of her friends in the crowd, and even those nerds onstage, moved
downtown from the suburbs. Jade is here to see the band Avatar – it's their
first gig and they sound awesome. She knows them from all their other
projects, and she's not the only one; the Brits and Germans and Chinese
are here. It's one of *those* nights. The rockers onstage don't seem fazed by
the pressure – this is old news to them.

The mains are pumping out a viscous sonic attack that reverberates
around the walls of the former gymnasium. Jade's uncle might have recognized this as rock 'n' roll when he was her age. The musicians up on that
high arched stage pummel their instruments with joyous force. Before
them, the 400-strong throng bounces up and down on the hardwood
floor, shimmying around the big red and green circles that were left there
by design. Once the markers for intramural sports teams, now they serve
as a reminder to the spectators to *participate*. And cordoned off by rope in
the corner of stage right are the über-geeks, sitting in folding chairs and
stroking their chins, trying to figure out who in the band is plugging into
the network and who's going directly into an amp.

Jade is twenty-one. She was born shortly after Miller became mayor
in what is now referred to as the Great Toronto Renaissance that led to
province status in '17. She came of age as a teen during the teens, and
watched nonchalantly as our entire civilization's way of life came to a
end. Toronto was one of the few world cities that was ready for the change
to the new economy.

The Show Space (it had a real name once, but everyone just calls it that now) provides electrical power to the band's miniaturized, energy-efficient amplifiers via an array of solar panels installed on its roof. Its rainy-day generator consists of hydrogen fuel cells that store extra solar. When it opened in '14, it was the first facility of its kind to be run entirely off the grid. Now that the grid's been taken offline, this is how everything's run. But the Show Space – they were the first, they were the leaders.

Down the hall from the main auditorium, old classrooms house a recording studio, workshop spaces, a café, library and office space. No one's getting rich working here, but everyone gets a salary. Outside, the old schoolyard is lined with trees. As for those twenty-, thirty-, forty- and, yes, fifty-something kids playing outside, half of them might be lounging out in the May sun sipping a beer and enjoying a non-carcin smoke, but the rest are getting some much-needed exercise on the soccer field.

Just around the corner is College Street, whose central avenue provides a thoroughfare for a leisurely flow of cyclists and streetcars. At thirty feet wide each, its sidewalks house a comfortable spread of patio tables at each of the strip's fabled brunch spots – where no one seems to be working but everyone's getting something done. Families of all formats are out enjoying the sun, and no one's hurriedly dodging others. Every twenty feet or so is another ever-growing circle of random pedestrian encounters. And, if you can make your way to the Bathurst car, it'll take you down to the lake. And as you approach the railway bridge south of King Street you'll see a row of windmills, turning innocently like children's toys in the sunlight. It's a nice day – let's go swimming.

Toronto, 2005

The preceding narrative is not the introduction to an aborted science-fiction story. It is, rather, an entirely believable, if entirely naive, vision for the future of our city. And since 'naive' is one of the many meanings of 'green,' I believe this stance is a crucial one if we are ever to create a 'Green Scene.'

What I am proposing is a vision of Toronto based – in part – on the synthesis of the city's independent music scene and the environmental or green-energy movement. The two streams of activism do have a lot in common, but at the present time there is little in the way of substantial crossover. I hope that this essay will serve as a modest proposal for effective collaboration and co-operation between these two communities. The music scene has harnessed and unleashed much creative energy in Toronto, and, with the emergence of climate change as the primary eco-threat of our age, energy has become green's number one concern. This is not just a cute play on words – synchronicities are often indicative of profound connections.

Similarly, it was positively synchronous when I was asked to contribute to *uTOpia*, since a not-so-secret code word for the project that I and many other independent musicians have been undertaking for the past decade is 'Torontopia.' Though I have been environmentally aware since the eighties, independent music has been the primary focus of both my creativity and community activism since the early nineties. I don't know who originally coined the term *Torontopia*, but I first heard it from Steven Kado, a fellow musician and music-scene organizer, in 2002. Our community has been helping to create Torontopia through our work with institutions like Wavelength, Blocks Recording Club, the Music Gallery and the now-defunct Three Gut Records. In all cases that are identifiably Torontopian – and judging what counts as such is admittedly biased, subjective and possibly downright corrupt – our activities are driven by a defiant optimism. And this defiance has grown in reaction to the prevailing sentiment of the recent past – that is, the Toronto scene *sucks*. By contrast, Torontopia says, 'Toronto Is Great!!!' – not coincidentally, also the title of a compilation CD released by Kado's Blocks Recording Club. The idea of Torontopia is based on believing that your town is the best, or being inspired by those moments when you feel your town *could be* the best. Torontopia is not about fomenting civic rivalries; it's about making your town the best, *no matter where you live*. Improving the place you call home, rather than just complaining about how *boring* it is.

Case in point: at the end of the twentieth century, Toronto music had a reputation for being as grey and uninspiring as its architecture. This, of course, was totally unfair. In the past few years, the quality of music has certainly improved, but it turns out the real problem was a lack of support from the local media, and the audiences who depended on them for exposure to new music, which left many a talented sound creator languishing in undeserved obscurity. This personal frustration led to my involvement in the creation of the Wavelength music series and zine, which debuted in February 2000. Though by no means single-handedly responsible for the current revitalization, Wavelength definitely marked a turning point. I'd like to think it helped instil a sense of self-worth and confidence, and, most important, *possibility*, in Toronto musicians. Over five years later, Toronto boasts an impressive list of original, vibrant and internationally recognized artists, many of whom arose from our community: Broken Social Scene, the Constantines, Do Make Say Think, the Hidden Cameras, Peaches, Caribou (a.k.a. Manitoba), Death From Above 1979, Feist ... the list keeps growing.

Today, 'indie' music has become a cultural juggernaut. American acts like the Postal Service are shipping gold (over half a million copies) in the U.S. without the benefit of 'hit singles,' and getting name-dropped in popular network TV shows like *The O.C.* One Canadian group is joining these ranks: the Arcade Fire, signed to established U.S. indie label Merge Records, which has, at the time of writing, sold over 130,000 units of its disc *Funeral*, and was seen last April on the cover of *Time* magazine's Canadian edition – about as mainstream as recognition gets. (Note that although the Arcade Fire is from Montreal, its early following was equally developed in Toronto. This unexpected cross-pollination between the historically rivalrous cities has been referred to by some wags as 'Moronto.')

The question then arises: as Toronto indie musicians, success may be in our grasp, but is it sustainable? Artists who 'make it' to the international touring level are often forced to sacrifice the comforts of normality: jobs, relationships, apartments. People from our once underground community are now breaking into mainstream consciousness, but what does the future hold?

More important, is there a future *at all?* That's right, musicians, there's a bigger issue at hand than your band's review on Pitchfork: we're up against imminent eco-apocalypse, coming this century. Most of us Torontopians, myself included, live in an insular bubble. When so much of your energy is focused on making your band work, it's hard to pay attention to the bigger picture: we're making our planet uninhabitable for ourselves. Climate change is a direct result of the Western lifestyle – one rooted in the voracious consumption of hydrocarbons, or fossil fuels. This lifestyle is dependent on the supply of cheap oil, which is predicted to run out within the next generation. That might be good news for the atmosphere, but not for us – oil is needed for almost every modern convenience, from cars and computers to food production and electricity. The whole globe should be switching en masse to an alternative energy system *right now*, but we're not.

Let's not pretend indie rockers aren't part of the problem. I need electricity to power my amp. And the P.A., and the practice space, and the venues in which we perform. Our vans guzzle gas on the way to those out-of-town shows. Yes, I know what you're thinking, this is the mother of all bummers, and we prefer our blissful ignorance. But don't fret – I'm not saying the answer to the world's biggest problem is that the music scene unplug and turn into a bunch of bongo-playing hippies. I *like* making electric music. I also like writing on my laptop, living in a heated apartment, and making guacamole out of avocados that have travelled thousands of miles to get to my local supermarket. And I'm sure you do too.

There's nothing really wrong with our lifestyle, it's just that its power source is dirty. The number one environmental and economic issue should be the implementation of green, or alternative, energy systems. Though it's industry and policy-makers who are ultimately responsible, any change must begin with the public. Sadly, environmentalism is currently considered unfashionable, mainly because of the public perception of greens as nags or Chicken Littles. A green lifestyle has also been stigmatized by its association with bourgeois baby boomers – the only people who can afford organic produce and Greenpeace memberships. Programs aimed at reducing greenhouse gas emissions in Canada, such as the One-Tonne Challenge, beg consumers to take voluntary measures such as increasing home energy efficiency or buying a hybrid car. Unfortunately, there is little incentive for the public to change their habits, and little opportunity for public engagement in what is required: a radical transformation of our energy infrastructure.

In the spirit of 'think globally, act locally,' I would like to see Toronto become a world leader in this area, and members of the Toronto indie music scene become civic leaders within this movement. Though they may seem divergent on the surface, indie music and green energy have a lot in common: both are local, aim at self-sufficiency and are marginalized yet beginning to provoke some mainstream curiosity. Indie music is rooted in the DIY spirit of unplugging from the music industry apparatus, and making your own records, booking your own shows, publishing your own zines. Imagine if do-it-yourself electricity were a possibility as well. And despite the ubiquity of overly inflated egos in the music scene, the endless array of fundraisers and awareness-raising concerts – from Live 8 in Barrie to women's-shelter benefits at Sneaky Dee's – demonstrates that many musicians are driven by a sense of social responsibility. Promoting green power is less clearly a humanitarian cause than ending poverty in Africa, for instance, as it is more utilitarian and tech-driven. But musicians are often tech nerds, and the indie scene was one of the first to colonize the Internet. Maybe we are the ones who can put a human face on this cause.

uTOpia-building, 2005–?

My uTOpia begins with a building. A long-standing dream of the Toronto independent music community has been a collectively run space for performance, rehearsal, recording, organization and socializing. This could be more than just a music centre; it could engage other arts disciplines and encourage healthy lifestyles and physical exercise. I propose that this space be a 'green building' – one that produces its own power cleanly, affordably, efficiently and locally. With solar photovoltaic cells on the roof, and an electrolyzer and hydrogen fuel cells in the basement, the facility could be a self-sufficient mini-utility that not only covers its own energy needs but can also sell power to the rest of the city. A closed-down school would be the ideal space for this kind of adaptive reuse, and would suit the 'academic nostalgia' aesthetic on display in present-day Torontopian activities like Track and Field (a Participaction-styled camping and music festival near Guelph) and the Fake Prom (which allows indie scenesters to 'do their high school prom over again').

Torontopia is about making use of your town's specific *potentialities*, and it makes sense to envision this Show Space in the context of the city in which we currently reside. Toronto is a city with a walkable downtown and plenty of green space, and this may be its greatest asset. The Show Space could be safely located in a central neighbourhood such as Little Italy or Kensington Market and still be far from the congestion and hustle of the downtown core. (Creating it out of an abandoned school would turn a Harris-era casualty into another unexpected asset.) In this sense, viewing an indie music space as more of a community centre than an average rocker bar, it could be an integrated part of a healthy neighbourhood – or part of a network of healthy neighbourhoods. With a location making effective use of green space for recreation, it would be more open and accessible to more diverse segments of the community – ethnic diversity is another Torontopian strength.

As a green-energy building, the Show Space would be part of decentralized electricity grid based on distributed power networks – a coalition of similarly self-sufficient buildings, including hospitals, businesses and still-functional schools. This would reduce our dependence on nuclear and fossil-fuel stations to zero as we move to a more diversified grid consisting of a community-owned mix of solar cells, wind turbines and hydrogen fuel cells. The much-hyped 'hydrogen economy' is a few decades away, pending some crucial technological innovations. But the beauty of this system is its integration: hydrogen power is based on the electrolysis (splitting) of hydrogen and oxygen molecules in water. This process can be powered by electricity produced by solar and/or wind, and after its conversion to electricity, hydrogen power can be stored in fuel cells, which could be plugged into a car or returned to the local electricity network.

The problem, of course, is access. How do a bunch of scruffy musician types afford a bunch of solar panels and a hydrogen power system? As Thomas Homer-Dixon pointed out, many non-profit groups lack the organization or resources to go green on their own. This is where city government must step in. Generous tax breaks and subsidies must be offered to all who wish to convert to green power – especially non-profit arts groups. Artists and musicians' collectives must be proactive in pursuing partnerships with environmental activists groups such as EnerACT (the Energy Action Council of Toronto) in order to implement these goals.

Toronto is already a model for tolerance to the rest of the world – let's add cultural vitality and energy independence to the mix! We are close geographically to the United States, yet far enough from it politically to make the shift away from fossil fuels much less of a battle. That said, we rank far behind American states like California or Minnesota (to say nothing of Europe) in green-power conversion, especially in the area of wind power. The WindShare turbine at Exhibition Place may be North America's first *urban* wind turbine and a fine symbolic start, but this lone windmill only produces enough to power 250 homes – a drop in the trough of Hogtown's energy needs. Even worse, it took five years to get that one set of blades turning. Still, it's a thing of beauty, and we need more. I can think of no better way of revitalizing our waterfront than a windmill park stretching from Pickering to Mississauga (mixed use with affordable housing and public space, mind you). Space them a hundred metres apart and you've got four hundred wind turbines – that's enough to power 100,000 homes! Assuming four people per home as average, that covers twenty percent of Toronto's population.

Energy, of course, is not the only environmental issue at stake in Torontopia. This city is in the death grip of car culture. Mayor Miller should go one step further than 'Red Ken' Livingstone of London and ban cars completely from the downtown core. Even if there is a mass rollout of hybrid or fuel cell cars in the near future, the congestion, stress and danger to public space created by the automobile should still be done away with. My uTOpia would see only public transit, bicycles and shared delivery vehicles on the road. And by 'delivery,' I mean both my Marshall amp and my neighbours' kids to hockey practice. A large-scale, affordable and accessible version of the Autoshare network is necessary. Freeing up the roads will not only decrease smog but also will slacken the pace of our too-hectic city, while increasing safety for cyclists and pedestrians. The pedestrianization of certain key neighbourhoods, such as Kensington Market, Little Italy, the Bloor/Annex strip and Roncesvalles Village, will open up vital public space – which should also contain plenty of green space, such as community gardens and squares.

Our music scene here in Torontopia, to me, is sometimes defined by those moments when I'm wandering down Queen or College and I run into someone I haven't seen in a while, and while we are catching up, someone *else* that one of us knows comes along and joins our rapidly agglomerating circle. This is the organic way that communities grow, and to this end, I say widen the sidewalks! We need to create more opportunities for authentic street culture to develop in Toronto. I would like to see more guerrilla music jams, more indie magazine stands, more spontaneous happenings involving electricity and the unexpected energy of youth, more freaky ruptures of the flow of everyday life that make people stop and ask, 'What is going on?'

Still, the future may not be so rosy. If life after the oil crash is as dire as some doomsayers predict, then music and culture, politics and power, will all be forced to thrive on the local level. I do believe that the cities will save us, that heading to the hills is not the answer. The city is where people can help each other out, whether it be growing our own food when the trucks stop pulling in or entertaining each other with our own music when the lights go out. Our bands should tour the world now while we can, because the future will be local. And if we can take control of the (green) power switch, the Internet may continue making *everywhere* local. Yet people will remain attracted to vibrant localities, and that means places with a strong sense of community. In the future, the rest of the world will look to Toronto, for its music and so much more.

ACKNOWLEDGEMENTS

This essay took great inspiration and information from the book *The End of Oil* by Paul Roberts. I'd also like to credit Janis Orenstein with the school-retrofit idea, and to thank Kerry and Wolfgang for reminding me of the importance of the 'c' word ('community').

Barbara Rahder & Patricia Wood
A funny thing happened on the way to the future

A funny thing happened when we got out of the car. Let's be honest: we stopped driving because we couldn't afford it. The thought of cleaner air makes us feel better about it, but we still sometimes miss the comfort and convenience of our cars, not to mention the speed, the power, the status – the thrill of driving. But we've given all that up, like a drug addiction finally kicked. In its place is a whole new view of the city.

Walking down the sidewalk is an entirely different experience than driving down that same street. The colours, smells, textures and tempos of city life have been transformed. We see, as if for the first time, where people live, where they work, where they play and where they just hang out. From flyers on mailboxes and hydro poles, we learn about local theatre and missing dogs and garage sales. We get the local gossip and good gardening advice. We learn which children live in which houses. Without even trying, we have developed a rich collection of relationships to people and places.

In retrospect, we can see that getting out of our gas guzzlers was a good change for more reasons than simply saving money. Here is a pace and quality of life we can enjoy *and* sustain. Why in the world did we think that mad rush of earlier times was so seductive? The social benefits of a relatively car-free society are such a pleasant surprise that we almost forget the obvious economic and environmental gains.

In our own older 'inner-city suburb' near the downtown, it takes two minutes to drive to the nearest major intersection, eight blocks away, and fifteen minutes to walk. From the car, we see other cars, traffic signals, pedestrians crossing the road, and billboards on the rooftops of low-rise buildings. From the sidewalk, we see all that, plus the headlines of newspapers in their boxes, the fruit that's in season at the grocer's, local workers waiting for the bus, seniors enjoying the garden in front of their retirement villa, parents pushing strollers, young nannies with toddlers, dogs lapping at bowls of water while their owners chat over coffee – and we can smell the freshly baked bagels, hear the conversation about changing school districts. As we stroll, hundreds of threads of city life spin around us.

No doubt some of the most surprising developments have been in the suburbs. We used to risk life and limb by walking on the roadway because there were no sidewalks, but now the streets are filled with people walking, cycling, pushing strollers or wheelchairs. The occasional taxi, and the rare private auto, now crawl past us carefully. We finally own the streets.

How did this happen? In the early days of the climate change/energy crisis, we were myopically focused on maintaining a growing economy while making only minuscule efforts to address ecological issues. At some point, it dawned on most of us that our economy would have to change – and change dramatically – in order for life on earth to continue. Our efforts to understand and create healthy local ecologies kicked into high gear. But it took us longer to figure out that we also would need to reconfigure our social lives, expectations, networks and ways of seeing one another.

Luckily, social sustainability is now understood as the bedrock of our city. Local community organizing hasn't been this popular since Chicago in the 1930s. We experiment with different decision-making models, and through trial and error discover what works with which group of people. Most important, there is a much broader acceptance of principles of social and environmental justice than ever before. Everywhere across the city, groups are using notions of equity and justice to guide their efforts at reorganizing and redistributing public goods, services and facilities. Even privately owned spaces, like backyards, are seeing fences torn down so that neighbours can share organic gardens and quiet sitting areas. We are returning to the commons that was long ago taken away. The very fabric of the city has been transformed to reflect the rebirth of this new collective consciousness – one that celebrates social, cultural and ecological diversity and local economic needs.

When Toronto first put in the car-free zones in 2015, it gave us a chance to turn parking lots across the city into parks and community gardens. The enormously successful light rail system that now criss-crosses the landscape like a fine net also allowed many streets to become dedicated cycle and pedestrian paths. These changes have been a tremendous boon to local networks, markets, stores and services. Our neighbourhoods are no longer residential islands but a fine-scale mix of uses, including grocery stores, clothing shops and all kinds of personal services. For most of us, our workplaces are also now within easy reach. The result is that we all have more time and more energy. We and our kids are in better shape than we have been, well, probably since the invention of the car!

Now that we have come to know our neighbours, it's fair to say that our differences have become more familiar – less scary. Some tensions remain, for sure, but we have opened lines of communication so that we can keep trying to find common ground. The diversity of Toronto's cultures may mean that the city faces more challenges than other cities, but it has also meant more opportunities. The cultural richness, flexibility and adaptability displayed by our diverse local communities has allowed us to create hybrid community organizations that adapt quickly and can effectively negotiate changes in the environment.

Toronto was lucky to avoid the kind of wide-spread violence common in other parts of the world. Our new national slogan, 'Peace, justice and good government,' has set a standard not only for peace at home, but for world peace. While it seems remarkable that notions of environmental and social justice have been so widely accepted in Canada, it calls to mind Brecht's old refrain of self-interest rightly understood. Once people realized that their own survival and their community's sustainability depended on the development of strong co-operative local relationships, suddenly CANDU took on a whole new meaning. Sure, we have disagreements. Even some fights. But we are, for the first time ever, really, seriously working at participatory democracy. Not every community in Toronto operates in exactly the same way, but openness and transparency keep it from being confusing. Good government is what we make of it.

These changes in our city didn't take force so much as political will and leadership. We had developed an urban landscape that accommodated our bad habits marvellously – everything was geared to the car and driver. But traffic and lack of maintenance were so bad that our streets and neighbourhoods weren't safe. Our children played outdoors less and less, became overweight, restless and increasingly angry and apathetic. Parents exhibited the same symptoms. We all felt powerless. We were exhausted from commuting, from the fifty-, sixty-, seventy-hour work-weeks, and from caring for children and aging parents at the same time. We stopped voting and focused on the things we could control, like our backyards. We had no time to demand changes in our schools, so we paid tutors and saved our own children. We bought alarm systems for our homes and our beautiful cars.

Even when we wanted to do better environmentally, it was too difficult to fit into our schedules and lifestyles. We tried to change things, to make a difference. We bought organic food and used our recycling bins. But when we tried to do more, we ran into walls. We wanted to take the sub-way, but it didn't go where we needed to. The buses ran too infrequently, and we couldn't get a stroller up the steps if we'd tried. Sure, we wanted our kids to walk to school, but the lack of sidewalks made it too dangerous, and too few other people we knew were out there to look out for them. We thought about biking to work, but it wasn't worth the risks. We tried to play with our kids at the local park, but the unleashed dogs and drug detritus made the experience too stressful. And where could you take a child to the washroom?

Until they started listening to communities, governments had spent virtually all of their time telling us what to do without giving us what we needed. Among the lessons we learned was that social sustainability can-not be imposed. It cannot be 'bought into' or sold. Only by participating in the processes of democratic decision making can people create their own socially sustainable communities and networks.

Local groups began by critically examining the ways our environment and our lives had been shaped by the car. We documented what needed to change in order to live and work comfortably without cars. Then we started to reshape our local communities and to lobby for more public transit and more public spaces, services and facilities close to home. Our councillors listened to us, and the mayor in turn listened to her council-lors. While suburban-style developments proved to be one of the most problematic designs to retrofit precisely because of that design's reliance on the car, physical and social transformations previously undreamed of did take place. We built up, instead of just out, putting residences, offices and daycares on top of strip malls, and gardens on top of that.

We have to tip our hats to the amazing crew of young urban environmental planners and designers who helped teach us about ecological processes, local economic trade systems and participatory community organizing methods. They helped us articulate our own priorities for change. All of the new 'alternative' forms of public transit, intensification and adaptive reuse are a result of these collective efforts.

So Toronto has once again demonstrated to the world that it is the most livable city, with the most diverse and most equitable social networks yet devised. The city's slogan, 'Diversity our strength,' has served us well after all. We could never have come this far without the wealth of knowledge and experience we were able to draw on. It has reminded us that a sustainable city is a diverse, creative and adaptive city, a city with compassion and imagination.

The view through that old windshield was not just smoggy and expensive; it was socially narrow and exclusive. We still need to remind ourselves that cars were an addiction we no longer need. We remain vulnerable to winds of fear that can still send us running for private cover. The city, by definition, will always be a cosmopolis full of strangers. But instead of giving in to this fear of the unknown, we need to be visible and active in our neighbourhoods. It's only when we get out there – frequenting the local shops and playing in the local parks – that we can see what and who our city really is.

Dave Meslin
2019

CITY HALL UPDATE
Get informed • Get involved!

Spring 2019

De-amalgamation continues
Voter turnout breaks all-time record

During the four years since the 2015 de-amalgamation referendum, City staff have been working night and day to undo the mess that was created by the reckless dismantling of our municipalities in 1998.

For seventeen years, millions of dollars were wasted trying to make Metro Toronto more efficient by downsizing democracy. Many citizens lived over 20 km away from their own City Hall while their overworked city councillor would be trying to fairly represent more than 60,000 citizens in his or her ward.

For the first time since 1994, residents of Etobicoke, Toronto, York, East York, North York and Scarborough were able

continued on page 2...

Garrison Creek returns

It's been almost a hundred years since the Garrison Creek saw daylight. Once the largest flowing river between the Humber and the Don, the Garrison became a victim to development and was buried in a concrete pipe that flows under neighbourhoods such as Hillcrest and Little Italy.

In an effort to acknowledge our natural environment, sections of the creek have been dug up and re-opened at Christie Pits and Trinity Bellwoods Park. Two buried bridges on Harbord and Crawford streets have also been revealed by new digging.

Garrison Creek
Re-Opening Celebration
Sunday July 21st • All welcome
Trinity Bellwoods Park • Free

INSIDE:

CITY HALL UPDATE
Editor: Dave Meslin
mez@publicspace.ca

Taxi drivers form metro-wide union

Taxi drivers across Metro Toronto have formed a city-wide union to fight for better pay and better work conditions.

The Metro Union of Taxi Drivers (MUTD) is hoping to work towards major change to address problems in the industry.

Taxi driver Belayet Meer was elected the first president of MUTD at its founding convention.

"Everyone has tried to fix the taxi industry," Meer said during his election speech. "The politicians, the company owners and the plate owners. Now the drivers will have the loudest voice. The days are over for the absentee plate owners to make

Metro Union of Taxi Drivers

millions of dollars from our labour while drivers work 18 hours a day to pay their rent."

Mayor Amita Singh has supported the union drive and has called on all stakeholders to come together to make the industry work. "The answers have to come from the drivers. We are happy to see a strong unified voice come forward."

De-amalgamation ...continued from front page

to vote for their own City Council last fall, a huge step towards revitalizing our local democracies.

But the hard part has just began. City councillors must decide if they want to keep the 'harmonized' bylaws created by the Megacity Council or return to Toronto's previous municipal code. Decisions are being made bylaw by bylaw with citizen input.

One of the highlights of de-amalgamation has been a surprising surge in civic engagement. The 2018 elections saw a dramatic increase in candidates, contributions, volunteers, and the highest voter turnout in the city's history (63%).

With new powers given by the province the mayor has established the Democratic Reform Task Force. Various split-system models are being looked at for the 202 election, with the hopes of increasing participation even further.

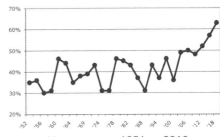

Voter turnout 1951 to 2018

How does the new federal marijuana law affect you?

The Canada Marijuana Act has just been passed by the NDP/Liberal coalition government. Phase One, effective immediately, allows all citizens to possess and consume marijuana as well as cultivate marijuana in a home garden.

 For more information - www.canada.gc.ca/potisokay

Last billboard removed from Toronto

On April 17th, local City Councillor Todd Irving pulled a lever on a yellow crane that lifted Toronto's last commercial billboard out of the ground near the Distillery District.

As dozens of local residents cheered, Councillor Irving and Mayor Amita Singh promised the citizens of Toronto that our public spaces would never be used as cheap advertising space again.

"Public space is not a resource to be auctioned off to advertisers," said the mayor. "It's for the citizens of our city to enjoy and share. This includes not only our publicly owned land but also the visual environment that extends from the side-walk to the sky. Televisions belong in living rooms, not at intersections. And billboards belong in the dump. Like hundreds of other cities across North America, Toronto is now billboard-free and is truly a beautiful city."

Work here, live here

City Council has endorsed the "Work here, live here" initiative that will require all senior planners and managers to reside within the City of Toronto. More info at www.toronto.ca

Car-Free Zones to be expanded

Toronto's Car-Free Zones are ready for another expansion. After playing catch-up to other cities for decades, Toronto is finally becoming a true leader in healthy urban planning.

"It was almost embarrassing in the early 2000s how behind we were," says Mayor Amita Singh. "While London was charging tolls and Paris was creating a Car-Free Zone, Toronto was doing virtually nothing. People with private cars were taking up too much space at the expense of everyone else's comfort, safety and health. Something had to change. Looking back, I'm not sure why this took so long. It's really a simple thing to do."

In 2009, cars were banned on Queen Street West for a six-month trial period. The results surpassed everyone's expectations. The Car-Free Zone became the most livable and enjoyable neighbourhood in downtown Toronto. Store owners experienced increased sales, tourists flooded the hotels and restaurants, and the air became significantly cleaner.

The current Car-Free Zones in Kensington, the Annex, the downtown core and St. Lawrence Market will all be expanded and seven new zones created over the next three years. The Car-Free Zones are part of the city's Green Mobility project which also includes new infrastructure for cyclists and rapid transit.

Your Taxes Your Choice
Community budget meetings

More library books? Longer hours at the community pool? After-school programs? What does *your* community need?

The next round of community budget meetings is about to begin. This is your chance to be a part of major budget decisions for the city-wide budget, as well as having a direct vote for your own community budget. Millions of dollars have been allocated to be spent directly by our city's 49 Community Councils. Neighbours will discuss options, ideas and solutions.

Translation and childcare available at all meetings.

Ottawa and provinces adopt One Percent Solution

The federal Coalition government and the provinces have agreed to double their spending on housing and shelter services across the country. The increase represents one percent of their total budget, an amount that housing activists have been suggesting since 1998.

"For over 20 years this country has had a homeless disaster and a housing crisis," said Toronto's medical officer of health, Cathy Crowe. "It's a tragedy it took so long for senior levels of government to respond humanely. Sadly, it took an investigation by the United Nations to nudge them along. Here in the city, we intend to create a permanent memorial at Nathan Phillips Square to honour the thousands of people who have died homeless in our city."

The new funding program will exceed $2 billion federally, and another $2 billion among provinces and territories. Plans include an emergency rehousing program with a commitment to reach targets in 12 months.

All provinces have also now adopted a Homeless Bill of Rights, guaranteeing affordable housing, medical care, training, legal protection and civic empowerment.

Budget Meetings:

Alexandra Park	June 7
Annex	June 10
Beaconsfield Village	June 9
Bedford Park	June 8
Bickford Park	June 7
Bloor West Village	June 9
Brockton Village	June 8
Cabbagetown	June 8
Casa Loma	June 9
Corktown	June 10
Corso Italia	June 8
Danforth Village	June 7
Davisville Village	June 9
Deer Park	June 9
Downtown	June 8
Dufferin Grove	June 7
Earlscourt	June 8
Forest Hill	June 8
Grange Park	June 8
Harbourfront	June 10
High Park	June 8
Hillcrest	June 9
Islands	June 8
Kensington Market	June 9
Lawrence Park	June 8
Leslieville	June 8
Little Italy	June 7
Lytton Park	June 8
Moore Park	June 7
Moss Park	June 8
Niagara	June 10
North Toronto	June 8
Old York	June 9
Queen West	June 7
Regent Park	June 7
Riverdale	June 8
Roncesvalles Village	June 9
South Annex	June 8
St. James Town	June 8
St. Lawrence	June 8
Swansea	June 10
The Annex	June 7
The Beaches	June 8
The Junction	June 8
Treffan Court	June 7
Trinity-Bellwoods	June 9
Uptown	June 7
Yorkville	June 7

Adam Vaughan
An age-old idea

Grand buildings, master plans and the love of a clean, safe city are all wonderful and necessary things, but what has always driven Toronto forward is something a bit more special: people. It is the people of this city who allow us to dream of – and perhaps even one day achieve – utopia.

Every time Toronto has embraced change on a human level, the city has blossomed. Long before multiculturalism was a value mouthed by politicians and measured by bureaucrats, it was an organic reality in this city. In fact, it predates the arrival of the French or the English. The local myth is that Toronto translated means 'meeting place.' It doesn't, but it would have been apropos.[1] Toronto was a meeting place and a place of trade for its original inhabitants. Even by the time John Graves Simcoe arrived in this city, there were already twenty-six different language groups present: Portuguese, French, Flemish, to name just a few. Toronto has always been defined by diversity. The struggle to understand and accommodate one another hasn't always been easy, but every triumph or accomplishment in the name of civility has moved Toronto closer to utopia. Magnificent old buildings may define our past and new monuments may house our future, but only people can give structure to structure. If we are to seek out a bold and beautiful future, we must look to each other. That's the lesson of Toronto's past.

1 There is no doubt that Toronto, with all its rivers, was a meeting place for several different First Nations people. From an archaeological perspective, the oldest evidence of settlement in the area suggests that the Mohawk used the port area and the mouths of local rivers as fishing camps. The Mohawk used to fish by staking the river with uprooted trees; the roots and branches acted like fences and steered the catch into waiting hands. The Mohawk word for this technique was *Tkaronto*. Literally translated, it means 'where there are trees standing in the water.'

In the 1950s, vagrancy laws were challenged. The growing Italian community socialized on the sidewalks. After church on Sunday, men would gather around the shortwave and listen to soccer games broadcast from overseas. Cafés sprung up with informal patios, and, with them, the smell of espresso made its way along College Street. The police often tried to break up these gatherings. Patio licences were unheard of. It took time, it took pressure, but sure enough the city changed. Not only was the practice tolerated, it became something to be enjoyed by every citizen. Toronto was the better for it. Try to imagine this city without cafés and espresso machines.

In the 1960s, Canadians with roots in Trinidad and Tobago gave Caribana to Toronto. Less than a decade earlier, people in the city were forbidden from going to movies or hockey games on Sundays. It was against the law. Within a decade of calypso and carnival hitting the streets, Gay Pride Day began. Imagine this city without summer festivals and dancing in the streets.

The 1970s gave Toronto heritage language. A groundbreaking program was developed that saw children whose mother tongue was not French or English receive instruction in their own language. Not only was a second or third language retained and developed, instruction in math or social studies was pursued so that immigrant children didn't stop learning while they picked up English. The city's school board also broke ground by integrating English as a second language (or ESL) throughout the public school system.

The 1980s saw an explosion of international culture in this city. Harbourfront found its groove, programming local and diverse artists alongside superstars from all over the world. The International Festival of Authors debuted, and, for every foreign-language writer who read in English on the mainstage, additional performances in the language of origin were happening in smaller, unofficial venues. To our credit and amazement, such culture flowed both in and out of Toronto. Musicians like the Parachute Club, writers like Michael Ondaatje and architects like Jack Diamond were all local icons with international reputations. All these people were products of our immigration system. The Toronto International Film Festival, which started in 1976, flourished and thrived through this period. A dynamic, tolerant and curious mix of people, all of whom called Toronto home, formed the foundation on which the festival grew. Films from every country had an audience that was as plentiful as it was culturally literate.

Of course, we had problems too. In the late eighties, we became focused on trying to become 'world class.' We chased the Olympics, we built the Skydome. In the nineties, we started to chop and slash at the very institutions that nurtured citizenship. Schools, public housing, transit, health care, even multiculturalism itself, were attacked. We lost our way. When we began to neglect the people of our city, we also started to neglect the buildings, sidewalks, parks and back alleys of the city. During that same period, it was not surprising that violent crime became more gruesome. Litter and vandalism became more prevalent. As we ignored the homeless sleeping on the streets, the buildings on the same streets also seemed to lose their beauty.

Toronto's wealth can be hoarded or squandered. Its vitality can be buried by bureaucracy as easily as it can be blanketed by snow, but its most inspiring characteristic, its people, will never be driven from the city. The utopia being searched for lies here. So what's next? Toronto's modest but determined embrace of same-sex marriage gives us the clue. At the height of the SARS crisis in 2004, one event managed to divorce Toronto from the dreaded disease. It was the image of two men kissing after being officially married by the state. We might have had a serious problem in our hospitals but, without much notice, we had suddenly become the best place in the world to fall in love and get married. Not just anyone, but *everyone* was allowed to do it.

For thousands of gays and lesbians, it was monumental. In fact, people from all around the world flocked to Toronto, and, to our credit, we welcomed them. Who knows where this may eventually lead? What's important is that in creating space for others, others arrived, and, with them, came untold benefits. Last spring, two doctors got married in Toronto. They had more than thirty people in their wedding party. Many were medical professionals. They spent a week in this city, and *spent* is a key word. But beyond the cash, they may have also made another contribution. The married couple met while studying at an Ivy League school. One of the people who visited was also a doctor trained at the same university. The guest loved the city. That doctor is now moving here. Human rights isn't just good economic policy; apparently it can be good for your health too.

Toronto needs to search out, explore and embrace the next frontier of human rights. In seeking to create utopia on the shores of Lake Ontario, we have to put people front and centre. The city needs to lead debates on these issues and not simply follow developments elsewhere. And what might the next wave be? For Toronto it should be accessibility. Toronto needs to become the world's most accessible city for people with disabilities. Smaller municipalities like Victoria, where ramps and dipped sidewalks predate Toronto's efforts, and European cities like Stockholm or Copenhagen can provide inspiration and lessons. This goes way beyond just ramps and elevators. It's about finding ways to make this city the most extraordinary place in the world, regardless of how extraordinary a person's needs are. It should be exhilarating to live in Toronto if you are someone who relies on a wheelchair. The blind should be dazzled and the deaf amazed.

In making every corner and building of this city more accessible, more dynamic, more automatic, safer and easier to use, we might accomplish something truly great. The transformation could be a marvel in and of itself. The city could construct a series of fantastic parks for kids in wheelchairs. Perhaps an accessibility festival could be staged annually in Toronto. Major roads could become wheelchair-only boulevards, significant buildings retrofitted and international activists honoured. Our city would be the first place in the world where the visually impaired could see. Significant buildings and historic neighbourhoods could have listening posts where the location would be described for the blind. Noted actors or writers could bring the communities to life through taped readings of their site-specific work. The transformation could also be small: property-tax breaks for people who renovate their houses with accessibility as a goal. Wider sidewalks, more benches, solar-battery recharging posts for electric scooters and wheelchairs. The list of possibilities is long. We would be left with one thing, though: Toronto would suddenly become an amazing city to grow old in. Toronto would nurture wisdom.

Think of the social benefits. Cultural isolation could be reduced, health-care costs minimized, multigenerational families more common. We would retain the experience of the old while challenging the ingenuity of the young. Economically speaking, we'd be able to export our technology and innovations to cities around the globe. Tourists who are older or disabled would make pilgrimages to Toronto, and thousands of people who face barriers to self-sufficiency would suddenly have the opportunity to live better, fuller and more engaged lives simply by moving to Toronto.

Perhaps the best part of this utopian vision is that it doesn't prevent great buildings from being built or the waterfront from being developed. People would continue to be free to marry whomever they choose, and old Italian men on College Street would still be able to sip espresso and watch soccer from the sidewalk. All we have to do is to keep finding ways to let more people live here. And we need to keep finding ways to let those people's lives enrich ours.

Mark Fram
Situationist Toronto: three mappings

The zone of uncertain definition  Let's take a short walk in the middle of the 'topia.' This is a sort of architectural tour, but you needn't pay too much attention to the buildings. Rather, take a closer view, at the narrow strips of city at your feet and in your face along the edges of older streets, between the road and the building fronts. These strips are usually much more than mere sidewalk. They comprise an almost infinitely variable collection of the ordinary: bits of mismatched paving, lampposts, street accessories, tiny gardens, front porches and (even in the poshest neighbourhoods) parked cars. Trees, shrubs and patches of green are everywhere, too, this being Toronto.

On major streets, even where this strip is mostly concrete, there are defiantly utilitarian impediments in the footpath itself (the Latin root of *impede* means, literally, to shackle the feet): parking meters, trash bins, transit shelters, fire hydrants, you name it – even a few old Metro artifacts like dirt-filled concrete boxes with stunted saplings. And despite recent

> Whenever More mentions his book in his correspondence, he refers to it as 'my Utopia,' and in the course of successive editions and translations, all that has remained of the original lengthy title is the name of the island. This name, derived from the Greek *topos* ('place'), is qualified by the prefix U, understood by More as a contraction of the negating *ou-* ('non-place') and as the adjective *eu-* ('good-' or 'right-place'). Space therefore has been designated as the book's subject from the start ...
>
> *Françoise Choay*

> Revolutionary urbanists will not limit their concern to the circulation of things, or to the circulation of human beings trapped in a world of things. They will try to break these topological chains, paving the way with their experiments for a human journey through authentic life.
>
> *Guy Debord*

municipal declarations to improve matters – and space – for people on foot in the city, the sidewalk is shrinking. In addition to more and bigger trash bins and newspaper boxes, shopping strips in the central city are being freshly punctuated every few yards by clutches of pipes sticking out at shin level (a gas meter for every storefront) snatching away another foot of clearance.[1]

Even the widest sidewalks in Toronto are narrow[2] and getting narrower.[3]

On the other hand, on the vast majority of city streets the front wall does not sit right on the street line, and there is an indefinite zone where public and private realms overlap. What seem to the casual viewer to be rows of private front yards, thresholds, low fences and porches, are in fact a jointly held public/private domain. Private owners take care of both their own turf and the city's, most often quite seamlessly. This is true not only in the older parts of the old Toronto, but in almost every part of the big new Toronto; it's just that in the newer parts, the front yards (and parking pads) are much bigger and blander than the condensed frontages of the 'historic' parts.

Throughout the metropolis, the city owns a public street 'allowance,' which is more than roadways and sidewalks. Both the apparently sedate two-lane side streets off older major routes and those busy arterials were surveyed to the same width, most commonly sixty-six feet (one standard surveyor's chain – close to twenty metres

1 The new gas meters are arriving even at the same time as the new water meters get to stay indoors, read wirelessly from outside. Apparently this has something to do with higher-pressure gas mains. Perhaps the utilities ought to bring in the design team from Terry Gilliam's movie, *Brazil*.

2 One shining exception to prove the rule is at the northeast corner of Avenue Road and Bloor, where what was a four-foot sidewalk on a six-lane road has been widened and the *roadway* is narrower.

3 There is a duel between two apparent 'goods' in the form of bicycle parking on the sidewalk. Old parking-meter stanchions converted to bike rings appear at first sight to be an astonishingly happy coincidence of public objectives that certainly makes the city more bicycle-friendly. But the rings and the bikes make many busy sidewalks even more congested and pedestrian unfriendly. Which good ought to prevail, and where?

for those who think in those units). For instance, in the middle of the city from Queen north to St. Clair, Bathurst Street, with its four lanes of rumbling streetcars, regularly clogged traffic, syncopated metered parking – and narrow sidewalks – has the same legal width as those sedate, tree-lined, two-lane, traffic-calmed streets on either side. Bathurst was, once upon a time, a sedate two-lane street too.

Like most older 'arterials,' Bathurst's current frontages comprise fragments of that older street, most frequently as blocks of houses of varying size and status. But what is no less interesting – and easily overlooked, quite literally – are the seams between sidewalk and front wall, as well as the intermittent expansions of building frontages out to the sidewalk line – an incremental and disordered project to redefine the street as 'main street commercial,' like, say Bloor Street through the very middle of the city. (For that matter, stretches of midtown Bloor still show a few patches of their former domesticity, some even within a few steps of Bay Street.) To some, this looks too much like a city incomplete, improperly decorated, lacking finish appropriate to the proper modern metropolis. It's *bush* (now there's an ironic Canadianism). To others, it's like the stubborn weed struggling through the cracks in the sidewalk, a sign of genuine life poking through to remind us that life does still flourish despite 'control.'

Why should this commonplaceness be *interesting*?

Well, because it's *useful*. Let's give eu-topia its due, and allow an experiment in topology in honour of the quixotic but prescient Guy Debord. These supposedly messy in-between places right at your feet are regarded by most orthodox planners as needing control in almost the worst way because they're, so, well, *right there in front of you*. Maybe this is the urban-landscape version of the city's so-called 'homeless problem,' presumably

to be dealt with by zipping the seam up tight with building facades tight to the public realm and no ambiguity whatsoever, just like the central business district, whether old-style, modern or even 'post'modern.

These commonplaces are interesting because they are evidence of a sort of urban ecology that needs to be better understood and used to give 'topia' a little more 'eu' and a lot less 'ou.' Utopia needs a great many more sites of urban co-operation, and a great deal of this messiness (not all of it, mind you), because that's what makes the city *livable* rather than merely acceptable, and the indeterminate frayed bits are the evidence of decades of private effort to do just that. If these small places look worn out, maybe that's because decades of public operation to clean them up have made it hard for its citizens to keep co-operating.

liv·a·ble or **live·a·ble** adj: 1. comfortable or suitable for living in; 2. endurable and worthwhile; 3. enjoyable to live with.

uTOpia has to get past 'suitable' and 'endurable,' and aim for 'comfortable' and 'enjoyable.' And to do that, city rulemakers need to encourage (not just 'keep open') the possibilities for better options than the usual uniform buffers of distance and bland cushions of grassland and sprawl and separation by wide arterial roads, and give the public and private some room at the interface to accommodate each other a little bit. To park bikes out of the pedestrian's way, say, while acknowledging that riders are pedestrians when off the saddle. To have civic gardens on public streets, not just in sheltered ravines, and to have civic gardeners, too, not just parks employees. To clean up trash, but to pre-empt it too.

This takes time, maybe a long time, and as much (or more) attention to maintenance as to creation. It takes citizens acting like citizens. Official action can help speed things up (or slow them down), but it's the citizenry that *produces* the livability over the long term, not just consumes it.

And the topology of this messiness? Imagine a Möbius strip, twisted, impossible in normal planning space, but essential to the city. That's really what lines all the most 'livable' streets. Just when you think you have the rules for its assembly figured out, you are faced with its other side, courtesy of time and human activity – that is, the activity of real humans. This twisted interface makes older neighbourhoods valued and valuable.

Why can't planners work up something like that for the newer parts of the city? Unhappily, there's nothing usable about that in the Official Plan. Some talk about buffers maybe, but too much along the lines of soft padding to keep things at a distance from one another, regulated and uniform. For evidence of the results, look at what's been built on the so-called brownfields, the tracts of land in the middle of the city where people used to make stuff. The old industrial tracts are full of monotone townhouses and squat apartment blocks that, no matter the skill of their builders, look like so much inner-city sprawl, certainly more densely occupied than Markham or Brampton, but hardly any more urban for that. Curiously, in those rare instances where these infills have back lanes, there really are interesting signs of life. Perhaps the lesson is to be very cautious about those back-lane housing schemes – beware the temptation to overfill the infill.

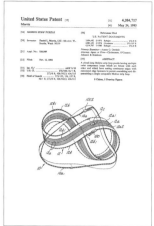

Simultaneity It is customary, in any crowd outdoors, to see dozens of people chatting on their mobiles (isn't 'cellphone' *so* twentieth-century?). To support these wanderers there is an obvious geography of relay towers and stations that facilitate these 'connections,' and there are a few locations where the signals don't work very well, punctuating the ostensibly boundless ether of the wireless. But there is also an invisible geography of those conversations – imaginary lines that radiate from those walkers and drivers to other walkers and drivers, and to those in their chairs who often wish they were walking or driving.[4]

Unitary urbanism consisted of making different parts of the city communicate with one another. They did have their experiments; I didn't participate. They used all kinds of means of communication – I don't know when exactly they were using walkie-talkies. But I know they were used in Amsterdam and in Strasbourg.
Henri Lefebvre

4 Speculation, for further investigation: in public, cellphones really are mobile, since it appears to be but a minority who stand still while talking.

The conversations rarely have much to do with the physical environs of the talkers, except when arranging meetings ('You're where? I'm there too, but I can't see you … '), and their usefulness for automobile safety is counterbalanced by the increasing evidence the same conversations can lead to car crashes.

But when cellphones and portable audio devices are made to correspond to their environs, something quite magical can happen. There's no need to look very far: such performances include those Unitary Urbanists wandering Amsterdam with walkie-talkies (how terribly *avant-garde* way back when!); the interaction of audio, video and the where-you-are in some of the works of Janet Cardiff;[5] and, of course, the exquisitely local cellular narrations of [murmur].[6]

5 http://www.collectionscanada.ca/women/002026-505-e.html http://www.publicartfund.org/pafweb/projects/04/cardiff_J_04.html

6 http://murmurtoronto.ca

7 http://www.psychogeography.ca/ http://www.socialfiction.org/psychogeography/dotwalktoronto.html.

These psychogeographical performances,[7] especially the 'mediated' ones, all work with what is already in front of you to reveal, well, something you're looking at but not really seeing, at the same time as you're hearing and not at all seeing. These

displacements are technological and their effects almost telepathic, though in truth they follow the psychic displacements that storytellers have known since even before the *Odyssey*. We are, however, cycling through the media to augment these experiments with increasing speed. Our great-grandparents in the early twentieth century took a couple of decades to really absorb the capabilities of radio and telephone, but we're all up to speed on podcasting already, aren't we?[8]

That you can stand or walk around in one place and 'be' in some other place may be to some folks profoundly spiritual. They're not wrong. We are creatures of linear time, but we can get some very unlinear pleasure in trying to harmonize other people's timelines with our own.[9]

If the city is filled with distractions that we must tune out all the time simply in order to survive, there is no small delight in *seeking out* distractions that can make the place more livable, in the 'worthwhile' and 'enjoyable' parts of the definition. Substance abuse not required. So, go seek 'em out.

8 Is it possible that [murmur] might be *obsolete* already? Sigh.

9 The panoramic views here are assembled from a series of digital photographs taken at different moments, not quite in 'real' time; so that (for instance) while the billboards in the view above make up a matched set that changes in synchronization, the software that assembles the pictures 'decided' to insert one out of synch. It also merged at least one human being with at least one automobile. Simultaneous? Not *quite*.

WSB . . . the montage method is much closer to the actual facts of perception than representational painting. So that's it. Life is a cut up. Every time you walk down the street, or even look out the window, your consciousness is caught by random factors and it was a question of bringing that back into writing. That was the point of the cut up, and making the cut explicit with a pair of scissors.

GPO What's the difference between the cut-up and the fold-in technique?

WSB Essentially. The fold-in technique is simply a simple way of doing a cut up. You just fold a page and read across, just as you read across columns in a newspaper. There are any number of ways in which you could randomise your material or cut it up. And None, that's just one of them. There's no difference.

William Seward Burroughs, interview with Genesis P-Orridge, 1981

Cut up, fold in, white out 🄐 Most utopian maps are uncomfortably neat and tidy. There are certain exceptions, of course, but the more modern and more resolutely architectural utopias seem to look more like organization charts than the impassioned visions of yore.

Alternatively, ponder the future according to a rather different kind of map: Guy Debord's and Asger Jorn's Situationist maps of Paris: the 'Guide psychogéographique' and 'Naked City.' [10]

10 'Guide psychogéographique de Paris: discours sur les passions de l'amour; pentes psychogéographiques de la dérive et localization d'unités d'ambriance [sic]' of 1956, which spawned in its turn the somewhat better known 'The Naked City: Illustration de l'hypothèse [sic] des plaques tournantes en psychogeographique [sic],' published 1958.

11 Simon Sadler, *The Situationist City* (Cambridge MA: MIT Press, 1998), page 61.

Both versions look like pieces of an old-style city plan thrown down haphazardly on the table and linked with bold directional arrows. The arrows might represent those walkie-talkie exchanges, or taxi rides, or simply the *idea* of connectivity across empty voids. That's certainly the way in which the maps have tended to be used for illustrative purposes over the last half-century. But they aren't actual cartographic versions of Burroughs's cut-ups; they're *white-out* maps[11]: 'areas of central Paris threatened by redevelopment, retaining those parts that were still worth visiting and disposing of all those bits that they felt had been spoiled by capitalism and bureaucracy.'

Which means that the impression of Debord's 'Naked City' as a conceptual displacement of parts of the city into little islands with short-hop boat connections (like the fantasy of an Aegean paradise) is, sad to say, wide of the mark. Too bad. It

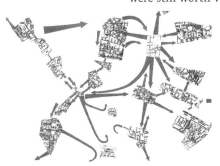

was disappointing to have that particular image deflated. It turns out that Debord was simply practicing urban renewal; white them out and the spoiled bits will be gone.

By association, the idea of the cut-up map is probably just as wrong-headed as a suitable conceptualization of the city. And it is certainly so if those juxtaposed bits of the city along its streets are what *makes* the city.

Of these three techniques of cartographic violation, that leaves the fold-in map (not to be confused with the fold-*up* map). After due consideration, the fold-in seems much more analogous to the actual city, if at a somewhat reduced scale. The rest of that city is still there under the folds of the conceptual short cuts across the so-called spoiled bits.

So, with apologies to WSB, there *is* a difference.

The actual city, that is, with both the bits 'worth visiting,' and all the rest, is also folded. Though, to be precise, the city is rather more crumpled than neatly creased. But with careful folds, and different map readings across those folds, there ought to come some fresh and useful urban understanding.

You can never have too many maps – and creases – because, like their creators, they all tell both truths and untruths. Maps are entertaining and edifying – perhaps most especially when you *mis*read them. We must ensure that global-positioning gizmos don't replace maps. Rather, GPS ought to provoke more and better illustrations and demonstrations of where we are (and who we are) in all our topias.

And refolding the maps should be encouraged, just so long as no parts – even the spoiled bits – are cut out. Because those can be refolded and restored to view. And with some effort, even to life.

Perhaps even folded up into a Möbius strip.

REFERENCES (PAGES)

257   Françoise Choay, 'Utopia and the Philosophical Status of Constructed
      Space.' In Roland Schaer, Gregory Claeys, Lyman Tower Sargent, eds. *Utopia:
      the Search for the Ideal Society in the Western World*. New York/Oxford:
      New York Public Library/Oxford University Press, 2000. p 346.

      Guy-Ernest Debord, 'Situationist Theses on Traffic' (#9), 1959;
      online at http://www.bopsecrets.org/SI/3.traffic.htm.

259   Dictionary definition from Encarta World English Dictionary, Microsoft Word 2004.

261   Daniel L. Morris. Mobius [sic] strip puzzle. U.S. Patent 4,384,717, issued March 24, 1983.

262   Henri Lefebvre. Interview with Kristen Ross, 1983. Published in *October*, Number
      79, Winter 1997; online at http://www.notbored.org/lefebvre-interview.html.

264   Axis Archive. Transcription, 1983, of taped interview with William Burroughs;
      online at http://www.brainwashed.com/axis/burroughs/wsbint01.htm.

      'Naked City': http://www.luxflux.org/n9/drills3.htm#.

267   Daniel L. Morris. op.cit.

LOCATIONS

Streets throughout Toronto: Clinton, Bathurst, Bloor, Major, Dupont, Sammon, Steeles.

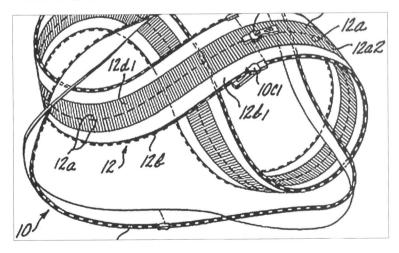

Deanne Taylor
Between utopias

Utopia is a destination so beautiful and beneficial for all that quite a few must be hideously sacrificed en route. The city of Toronto does not dream of such perfection.

Its civic imagination is shaped by generations of immigrants unfit for utopias around the world: people who fled Divine Monarchs, Great Oarsmen, Beloved Leaders, Infallible Clerics, Infamous Tyrants and Obscure Social Engineers, war, famine, assimilation, reservation, pogrom, gulag, holocaust, apartheid, genocide, conscription, torture – endless utopian techniques of great evil for a greater good. Toronto's collective anthem or civic prayer might be 'No megalomania, please, we're *between* utopias.'

Between Isms, between Ideals, between Paradise and Hell, Torontonians are free from the weight of a purely racial, religious or ideological destiny, and relieved by the relative lightness of being Canadian. Thanks to centuries of creative resistance by Aboriginals and *les Canadiens français*, Canada's nationality is not based on the simple solidarities of ethnicity but on shared political ideas – liberty, justice, enfranchisement – complex principles and instruments that evolve with use. Once acquired, these legalistic entitlements may not fire the blood, wet the eye, set armies marching, unleash collective passions as flags, martyrs, national myths and hymns can do, but that's the idea. Citizens are free to be as English or Irish, American or Iraqi, Indian or Pakistani as they can, as long as they don't blow up each other's discos.

Toronto's messianic potential is tempered not only by a cool nationality but by an even cooler climate. The city's natural antidote to old crusades and new insurrections is winter, when all Torontonians are created equal and made peaceful by wearing parkas. Shivering in slush, reaching home before frostbite, thawing out, ensuring supply lines; the tyranny of winter demands alliances with neighbours and co-workers on the ecumenical and apolitical basis of a war against cold. The city unites in puffy coats and runny noses; newcomers are woven into the ancient rhythm of shovelling snow for people who threw their backs out while shovelling snow; all are linked for survival in mitt borrowing and boot lending without regard for race or creed. In spring, Torontonians are filled with gratitude for the return of light and warmth, and are not the fodder of grandiose missions, but more inclined to cultivate their own gardens, water their neighbours' yard while they're away and pick up litter in the local park.

Toronto is a young metropolis in the parental grip of the provincial government. Whenever the city threatens to mature, it is restructured or vastly expanded, arresting its sense of city-hood. Now comprised of 640 square kilometres, a hundred languages and five or ten centuries of custom, the city is almost unknowable. To manage the scale and cultural dissonance, generations of residents have created hundreds of village-neighbourhoods, beginning in the nineteenth century with what is still a densely residential downtown, spreading east and west along the shore of Lake Ontario, and then northward, where the compact roadways and architecture eventually gave way to mid-twentieth-century ring roads and dispersed suburbs. Most Torontonians live within the crescent of older and denser neighbourhoods and are socialized by their human-scale buildings and byways. A few of these neighbourhoods are monocultural, or homogeneously rich or poor, but most embrace residents of many cultures and means, and feature modest homes and apartments, good public schools, parks, community centres, garbage and snow removal, tree doctors, wildlife rescuers and a billion dollars worth of policing to discourage sociopaths and illegal parking. Vitally, at the physical centres of these neighbourhoods, are low-rise main streets where the social, entrepreneurial and recreational energies of the community may gather, recombine, evolve.

Blessed with laws, humbled by climate, unburdened by history or destiny, Torontonians remake the world in their small communities, adding yoga, sweat lodge, dim sum or doughnuts to their lives. Neighbours meet easily and frequently in local schoolyards, parks, markets, diners; they transcend private beliefs to share common aspirations – healthy children, peaceful streets, helpful neighbours, mutual respect. Toronto's genius for hyper-local improvisation and collaboration sustains social peace and economic stability in hundreds of organically grown neighbourhoods. Here, Toronto fashions small miracles of civilization: multiple urban eco-systems of social and entrepreneurial imagination, the DNA of civic life.

To live in Toronto is to live in two cities at once: one real, one virtual. For most people, the real city is a few neighbourhoods, the familiar places of home, work and play, experienced with feet on the pavement, hand on a tree, eye on a sunrise, ear to the street, nose in the bakery, talk in the café. Beyond the body's intimate knowledge is a virtual city of words and images, a city built on shards of history and avalanches of media, a city of myths, brands and mega-plans. Those who create the virtual Toronto, who spin virtu-topian stories of its gifts and possibilities, who frame the city's history and therefore its future, are always those who own the biggest microphones. Toronto's most amplified mythmakers are the oracles of media, business, politics and city planning.

In the mirror of the local mass media, Toronto glimpses its cutest, saddest, proudest, most horrifying features, and wherever a little is magnified, much is hidden. Some journalists seek to reflect the city's true character, but most publishers and broadcasters are faithful to Toronto's colonial tradition of emulating or importing, rather than creating, and derive the bulk of their advertising and content from the American infotainment empire. So complete is the local habit of self-effacement, many broadcasters, columnists, editors and reporters are proud to call Toronto 'Hollywood North' – to honour the city's numerous encounters with foreign celebrities. 'Hollywood North' and 'Broadway North' are the simu-topian dreams of those who see Toronto as a sequel to a really successful utopia. Industriously, they shape the city as a local backdrop for the foreign superstars of mass-market TV, movies, music, sports and fashion, and much profit is made without risk by those with no need to invent, develop, produce and distribute original goods.

Imported vision is the preference not only of the media but of all the higher echelons of Toronto's corporate class. In the boardrooms and conference rooms of big business and banking, the ideal city is a franchise, based on the magic formulae, branding, attractions, ideas and investment of a mightier power: this is the City That Goes Ka-Ching. For these corporate utopians, Toronto is real estate and ad space, citizens are consumers, city hall is a business facilitator, and politics an extension of deal making. To make their dreams come true, they groom political candidates, finance and run election campaigns, write and promote public policy for private profit, with an enthusiasm for civic politics that literally knows no bounds. These civic leaders see the promised land and the betrayals required to get there. With the passion of soothsayers, they urge Torontonians not to hoard public property as their grandparents did; not to pass on to their children the natural infrastructure of the city, the waterfront, green space, sky, sunlight, vistas; not to bequeath public space, public services, public institutions: but rather to unload these assets quickly to stave off the virtual bankruptcy of the virtual city.

The ideal Toronto conjured by media and big business is well represented at city hall. Most planners and politicians support or merely modify the rules of the virtual city. No one challenges the basic models of Hollywood North or the City That Goes Ka-Ching; indeed, the better to serve these visions, city hall has replaced the old language of the public interest with the language of business and promotion. The idea of taxation as a collective investment in social harmony has been succeeded by tax phobia, causing the city government to downsize, sell off and lay off. Understaffed and underfinanced, Toronto's public servants now depend on big business as a source of studies and statistics, as a purchaser of fire-sale public assets, as a provider of the low-cost services that non-unionized workers are said to ensure. With think-tanks and summits, with Power Point spiels and ad-buys, with campaign financing and editorial endorsements, with job offers and junkets, Toronto's most powerful private interests engage the hearts and minds of the city's public servants, and move them ever closer to the utopian ideals of business and media. And city hall, grappling with hundreds of thousands of microdecisions, is all too grateful for the language of utopianism, language that orders the chaos of democracy, language that conjures the common good while justifying particular evils.

Constructed of news, hype, branding, polls and other rumours, the virtual Toronto is a comforting home filled with flattering portraits of the city's leaders and board members, a glamorous home visited by globally famous salespersons, a secure home fortified against indie criminals. Through years of practice, Torontonians are capable of ignoring the contradictions between this virtual home and their tangible city-neighbourhoods. They may mock but would rather not challenge the virtual city of 'World-Class Tax Relief,' 'Globally Competitive Wages' and a 'Business-Friendly Environment.' In fact, Torontonians would rather not challenge any part of the status quo, *if* the precious equilibrium of their neighbourhood eco-systems is left undisturbed. But Toronto is well supplied with disturbing forces – the mega-schemes and ideal models of builders and planners, which always require the sacrifice of a treasured aspect of neighbourhood life, a sunny main street, a lakefront, a vista, the natural or architectural grace of a heritage area. At city hall, where dreams become bylaws, where abstractions become all-too concrete, Virtu-topia meets the Neighbourhood in a contest of urban vision.

This contest plays out continuously at city hall for stakes great and small. On one side are the corporate lobbyists and strategists, paid by the year, friendly with politicians and bureaucrats, fluent in laws and loopholes, armed with the civic goods of Progress, Growth, Development, Investment, Tourism, Intensification, Renewal. On the other side of the contest is the volunteer neighbourhood group, funded by bake sales, composed of a few veterans of earlier wars and all the raw recruits they can muster, armed with the civic goods of Stability, Harmony, Beauty, Preservation, Conservation, Heritage. Some might call this no contest, but Toronto calls it the tough love of democracy. For every neighbourhood battle lost or won, new citizens with civic muscles are created. For every condo towering over heritage buildings and eclipsing the sunlight in a thousand beauty spots, for every threat of an expressway, airport, incinerator or Olympian mega-project, new political energy gathers in quiescent neighbourhoods. As long as planners, developers and politicians blueprint perfect cities, real communities resist.

When previously apolitical residents have activism thrust upon them, they form or expand neighbourhood groups, and discover they've joined allies across the city in a long history of local resistance to invasive ideas. There is honour in becoming a member of the unofficial government of the verifiable Toronto, the City of Small 'Hoods, but the price of voluntary participation in politics is dear: thousands of life-hours for meetings and mailings, for reading studies and bylaws opaque in their specialized idioms, for making deputations at city hall to inattentive councillors, for being smeared as NIMBYs, or Selfish Interests, or A Few Malcontents Standing In The Way Of Jobs, Market Forces and Other Inevitabilities. Neighbourhood residents are not in the right until proven wrong, but immediately charged as Enemies of the Common Good and forced to defend what Arundhati Roy calls the Greater Common Good, the officially unrecognized Good that does not sacrifice the small, real and irreplaceable treasures of nature and culture.

Such citizen-governors stand in the path of the utopian bulldozers and cranes that would plunder the land and sky, diminish community wealth for the benefit of a few, and call it 'growth.' As victories are usually temporary and losses usually unjust, citizens rarely return to their apolitical state, but rather are propelled deeper into the mysteries of nominating and electing city politicians, providing them with evidence and direction, learning to cultivate a neighbourhood one meeting, one councillor, one voter at a time. Most political battles are local and unsung, but occasionally the city-at-large is aroused by good leadership to defend a shared interest. Notably, in the 1970s, people across the city joined forces to protect the residential heart of their downtown by restricting high-rise development, and by stopping an expressway from destroying Spadina and Kensington Market, the vibrant immigrant areas that survived to cradle the city's arts community.

In Toronto's 2003 election, 'neighbourhood-ism' rose up to defeat many of the incumbents and candidates of the virtual city, and to stall the political machine which had constructed that phantom edifice over much of three decades. Against great odds, former councillor David Miller won the mayoralty by rallying the city around a vision of the lakefront as an extension of everyone's neigbourhood. To restore the lake to the public imagination, Miller had to demolish years of promotion for a waterfront airport, a boondoggle endorsed by all newspapers, and touted to make Toronto a world-class destination worth X billion dollars over Y years by capturing millions of Lost Tourists theoretically not able to find their way from the nearby international airport to the city's cash registers. Much of the research and strategy Miller used to bury this faux-topia was gathered one democratic step at a time by a handful of waterfront residents and their network of long-range thinkers around the city. With the Miller campaign, they defined the waterfront and the city-at-large in neighbourhood terms, and succeeded in showing a plurality of Toronto voters that giving away their lakeshore was too high a price for the utopian myth of a Tourism Paradise.

City hall's enthusiastic support for the theft of the waterfront (and for other deals equally scandalous, more expensive, and the subject of a public inquiry) revealed that top public servants were in thrall to very private interests and übermyths. Miller's mayoralty campaign captured the larger issue eloquently, calling the citizens to apply the wisdom and values of their neighbourhoods to the whole city, calling them to defend Toronto's natural infrastructure, public space and public interest, calling them to create a city where beauty, harmony and civility took precedence over profit. They acted, they voted, Miller won, and time passed. The airport retreated, but like all truly bad ideas was merely refitted for a new attack; public space and neighbourhoods were newly threatened. No doubt, the hero of the 2003 municipal election is a man of great integrity attempting to fulfill his committment, but foes of the public interest are too powerful to be reformed by one election.

Their narrow, kleptocratic vision of the virtual city is entrenched in city budgets and bylaws, and enshrined in the latest Official Plan, a utopian blueprint seemingly guided not by city planners but by accountants. The plan describes an imminent Torontopia that does not aspire to be a greater society or more civilized city, but a bigger and cheaper tax base, a magical place where a million new taxpayers can be acquired for 'free' by wedging them into the already-paid-for public infrastructure on Toronto's mainstreet grid. Developers, who helped the city's tax-starved bureaucrats design this policy, are rushing to maximize the windfall by stuffing cheap condo towers into modest-scale main streets across the city, instead of fitting the profile and profits of their buildings to the long term interest of these successful neighbourhoods. The iconic heritage-scapes of Queen West and other core city neighbourhoods have been assaulted by a development rush that evicts successful small businesses for global franchises, wrecks architectural scale and heritage, and steals natural or publicly owned goods.

Toronto's oldest buildings and neighbourhoods nurture the oldest civic DNA *and* incubate the newest mutations, as Jane Jacobs first revealed about New York. It was in the mature neighbourhoods of Toronto's core where multiculturalism began to fuse into a true local culture, where the tribes mixed in street markets and music clubs and saw that it was good, where the world came to enjoy the harmonious polyrhythms of this urban jam. Just as each successful neighbourhood depends on an energy-transforming main street, Toronto-at-large has always needed this thumping heart at its centre, neighbourhoods where inventors and newcomers can afford to live, collaborate and provide a market for the new. This urbane downtown has been shaped and defined by heritage buildings, sociable streets and views of the sky's endless dance – non-renewable public resources now being ravished by developers. Like farmland or wildland threatened by lateral sprawl and the attendant pollutions and extinctions, Toronto's urban eco-system is a fragile mix of nature and culture, endangered by vertical sprawl and the destruction of rare urban life forms. In the next decade, the city will decide whether it wants a heart or a mall, whether to protect the older downtown neighbourhoods for their priceless socio-cultural value or tear them down as sacrifices to the latest one-size utopia.

In the venerable Cameron House on Queen West hangs a simple sign made by sculptor Tom Dean: it reads THIS IS PARADISE. Most of Toronto's residents know that in their comfortable neighbourhoods they have found the 'good place,' found the sweet spot, found as perfect a 'topia as possible under the circumstances so far. They enjoy and renew the city's heritage of built forms and social values, shaping the prosperity and harmony of their communities and the city-at-large. The same cannot be said of Toronto's leaders, who are blinded by utopias from another place and time and cannot see the golden neighbourhoods for the glittering towers. Toronto can only aspire to be great by deciding to be itself – by cherishing its own heritage and values, its own thinkers and artists, its own small-business owners and residents, its own funky skylines and safe streets, its own live-and-let-live/all-in-the-same-canoe ethos. Perhaps one day the city's leaders will tear themselves from their simu-topian fantasies, fall deeply in love with the real Toronto, and help to cultivate the true-topia no one could have dreamed.

uTOpians

HOWARD AKLER is a co-author of *Toronto: The Unknown City* (Arsenal Pulp Press) and wrote *The City Man*, a novel from Coach House Books.

ANDREW ALFRED-DUGGAN is a freelance cartographer based in Toronto. Working for International Travel Maps (ITM), he has mapped approximately forty world centres. Many of these cities prioritize planning for a livable city, which always includes expansive transit systems. Toronto has always been Andrew's favourite city, and he believes that with some smart planning and transitification we can build the perfect city.

JACOB ALLDERDICE, graduate architect and urban designer, interned with Steven Holl Architect and Edward Larrabee Barnes Associates in New York City, and with William Hurst Architects in Toronto. He teaches interior design at Toronto's International Academy of Design and Technology. Past work includes running a charrette in Chicago that proposed removing a highway from the waterfront (replacing it with lagoons, waterside cafés and bicycle infrastructure) and an award-winning (but unbuilt) scheme for the Labrador Innu, for the Newfoundland and Labrador Housing Corporation. One current project is a pedestrian-oriented redesign of Coxwell Avenue in Toronto to include a 'bridge of houses' over the Don Valley (carrying trams, pedestrians and cyclists but no cars) and a new ferry terminal (linking Toronto with Rochester and other Lake Ontario destinations). As a member of ARC (Advocacy for Respect for Cyclists), Allderdice campaigns for bicycle lanes in Toronto. His work includes a 'weblob' at www.allderdice.ca, where he makes the argument that all automobile advertising should be deemed illegal.

BERT ARCHER has been an editor at and writer in the *Toronto Star, NOW* magazine, *Eye Weekly* and *Quill & Quire*. Though he lived in Jane Jacobs's Annex for many years, he currently makes his home in the far east (out by all those halal pizza places on the Muslim Danforth) with the love of his life, the incomparable Jason Gilbert and – far less frequently than they'd like – their apprentice urbanite daughter, Melissa.

JAMES BOW was born and raised in Toronto until the age of nineteen, when he attended the School of Urban and Regional Planning at the University of Waterloo. He has maintained his childhood love for his hometown and the Toronto Transit Commission, and has put his skills to work as co-founder and co-webmaster of the information site Transit Toronto (transit.toronto.on.ca). He is embarking on a career as a freelance journalist and novelist. His works have appeared in *Business Edge, Metro* and the *Record*. He is looking forward to the publication of his first young adult fantasy novel with the Dundurn Group in spring 2006.

NICOLE COHEN has lived in Toronto for six years. She is the co-founder and co-editor of *Shameless*, a progressive magazine for teenage girls. A graduate of Ryerson's journalism program, Nicole has worked as a staff writer at *Eye Weekly* and has written for the *Toronto Star, This Magazine, Herizons, Broken Pencil* and *Spacing* magazine. She is currently a graduate student in political science at York University.

DEBORAH COWEN is a postdoctoral fellow at York University and is appalled by the obsessions with economy and morality that govern the production and regulation of public space in Toronto. UTE LEHRER teaches at York University and finds herself regularly contemplating the meaning of 'public' in spaces, and its increased co-optation by private interests. ANDREA WINKLER studies planning at York University and is interested in the 'public' of space. Deb, Ute and Andrea are all members of Planning Action in Toronto. They would like to see this city become a place of justice, welcome and care. (www.planningaction.org)

Currently guitarist/songwriter with 'utiliopian' punk quintet Republic of Safety, JONNY DOVERCOURT has been making noise with such Toronto bands as Three Ring Circuits, the Magnetars, the Frankfurt School, Christiana, Kid Sniper, Secret Agent and A Tuesday Weld since the early nineties. He is co-founder of the Wavelength music series and zine, and has recently been named interim director of the Music Gallery, Toronto's premier venue for avant-garde music.

DALE DUNCAN is the managing editor of *Spacing* magazine. She also writes about politics, events and people in Toronto as a staff writer for *Eye Weekly*.

PHILIP EVANS is a project architect at ERA Architects Inc. in Toronto, with four years of post-graduate experience specializing in heritage building conservation. He has been involved in a variety of cultural policy–based projects, ranging from a comprehensive study of Toronto's cultural facilities and waterfront to the preservation of public art installations by local artists. Philip's private work deals with a variety of installations within the city that have been featured in local exhibitions. His collaboration with the Culture of Cities, an international research project housed at York University, explored the identities of Toronto's neighbourhoods. He is currently practising in the United Kingdom.

MARK FRAM is a designer, architectural consultant and urban planner whose *Well-Preserved* (3rd ed., 2003) is the standard text for historic preservation practice and educational programs in North America. He is a member of the academic communities in geography and architecture at the University of Toronto as both instructor and almost-completed PhD scholar. He is the primary author and the designer-photographer-typesetter of the recent Coach House book *4square* (2005). A born-and-bred Torontonian still in his native habitat after travels to faraway places, his preferred mode of transit is walking.

MISHA GLOUBERMAN is the host of the Trampoline Hall Lecture series and the Room 101 Games series. He is also the founding member of the Queen/Beaconsfield Residents Association.

CHRIS HARDWICKE studied fine art, environmental studies and architecture at the University of Waterloo. Chris founded the Informal Connective in 1997 to explore new urban economies that allow our health, environment and culture to have value in the design of our cities. The Connective is a network of researchers, engineers, planners, artists and designers allied in the pursuit of making cities more natural, healthy and vital. The Informal Connective is currently working on Ravine City, a project for extending an artificial ravine system through Toronto, and Farm City, a self-sustaining living skyscraper. (www.informal.ca)

SHEILA HETI is the creator of the Trampoline Hall lecture series, and is the author of two books, *The Middle Stories* and *Ticknor*. She was born and raised in Toronto.

ALFRED HOLDEN is a journalist, an assistant business editor of the *Toronto Star* and a keen observer of city life. He is a regular contributor to *Taddle Creek*, a Toronto literary magazine, where his writing on city building has been nominated for a National Magazine Award and recognized by Heritage Toronto. He also writes a monthly column for the *Annex Gleaner* community newspaper. He has lived in Toronto since 1981.

LUIS JACOB is an artist and writer living in Toronto. Recent exhibitions of his work include the solo exhibition Open Your Mouth and Your Mind Will Follow, which travelled to Articule (Montreal), Artspace Gallery (Peterborough), AKA Gallery (Saskatoon), and The New Gallery (Calgary); Downtime: Constructing Leisure, New Langton Arts (San Francisco); Koch und Kesslau Gallery (Berlin); Curb Appeal, Confederation Centre Art Gallery (Charlottetown); Meniscus, Artspeak (Vancouver); LTTR Explosion: Practice More Failure, Art in General (New York); Towards a Theory, Het Wilde Weten (Rotterdam); Tomorrow's News, Gallery Hippolyte (Helsinki); Better Worlds, Agnes Etherington Arts Centre (Kingston); Art Is Activism, Fine Arts Building Gallery, University of Alberta (Edmonton); Voices in Transit, Cape Town Central Station (Cape Town); and House Guests: Contemporary Art at the Grange, Art Gallery of Ontario. Upcoming exhibitions include 18 Illuminations, at the Tom Thomson Memorial Art Gallery (Owen Sound), and the solo exhibition Habitat, at the Art Gallery of Ontario. Luis Jacob is represented by Birch Libralato, Toronto.

LORRAINE JOHNSON's interests include native plant ecosystems, sex laws, gardening, censorship, environmental theory and travel – all of which she's written about in her nine published books.

Toronto writer EDWARD KEENAN works days as the city editor for Eye Weekly. He lives with his wife in the north Annex, in the shadow of a castle.

MARK KINGWELL is Professor of Philosophy at the University of Toronto and a contributing editor of Harper's magazine. He has held research posts at Cambridge University, the University of California at Berkeley and the City University of New York, where he was Weissman Distinguished Visiting Professor of Humanities. The author of eight books of political cultural theory, including A Civil Tongue (winner of the Spitz Prize for political philosophy) and the national best-sellers Better Living and The World We Want, Kingwell writes for many academic and mainstream publications and has won two National Magazine Awards. His latest book, an iconographical study of the Empire State Building, will be published in the spring of 2006; he's also at work on a book about cities and consciousness.

JOHN LORINC is a Toronto magazine writer who specializes in urban affairs and the environment. He is the author of *New City: How the Crisis of Canadian Cities Is Re-Shaping the Nation*, to be published by Penguin Canada in April 2006.

JASON MCBRIDE is an editor at *Toronto Life* magazine. The former managing editor of Coach House Books, he is also a filmmaker and freelance journalist, having contributed to *Lola*, the *Village Voice*, *Cinema Scope*, the *National Post* and *The Believer*. He is the editor of *From the Atelier Tovar: Writings by Guy Maddin* and *Everybody Loves Nothing* by Steve Reinke.

SALLY MCKAY is a Toronto artist and writer who co-owned and co-edited *Lola* magazine with Catharine Osborne. Her multimedia project on quantum physics, *The Trouble with Oscillation,* is online at www.sallymckay.ca/oscillation. Watch for Up and Anti-Up, Sally's regular column on art and science in *Kiss Machine* magazine.

HEATHER MCLEAN is currently pursuing a PhD in Environmental Studies at York University and is often active with Planning Action. She has worked on a range of community development, affordable housing and urban planning projects in southern Africa, British Columbia and Toronto. She is interested in urban environmental and social justice issues and the privatization of urban and rural spaces.

DAVE MESLIN was born in beautiful Toronto. His hours are spent trying to fill the intellectual potholes inside City Hall with the assistance of a small army of municipal dreamers called the Toronto Public Space Committee. His work is driven by the possibility that at some moment the boys and girls of Toronto may suddenly say, 'Hey, this is ours! What should we do with it?'

SHAWN MICALLEF grew up in Windsor, Ontario. He worked at the mall and in a factory and completed an MA in Political Science while living there, but he always wanted to move to Toronto and has an old miniature CN Tower to prove it. Since heading up the 401, he attended the Canadian Film Centre's Habitat New Media program, where he co-founded the location-based cellphone documentary project [murmur] that is spreading through Toronto neighbourhoods as well as other cities (www.murmurtoronto.ca). Shawn writes the Stroll column in *Eye Weekly*, and sometimes writes for nice publications like the *Globe and Mail* and *Broken Pencil*. He is an editor at *Spacing* (www.spacing.ca) and *This* (www.thismagazine.ca) magazines, and a co-founder of the Toronto Psychogeography Society, a group of flâneurs who drift through and explore Toronto, sometimes living to blog about it (www.psychogeography.ca).

DEREK MURR's writing has appeared in *Spacing* and *Broken Pencil*. He lives and works in Toronto. It is unlikely he will ever leave.

NINJALICIOUS spent more than a third of his life exploring the nooks and crannies of Toronto's most – and least – notorious buildings. His adventures in the urban landscape are well documented in *Infiltration*, the zine he produced from 1996 until his death in 2005, and on the website infiltration.org. He is also the author of a guidebook to urban exploration, entitled *Access All Areas*, which aims to help the average city-dweller open his or her eyes to the many hidden worlds the urban playground has to offer.

DARREN O'DONNELL is a writer, director, social acupuncturist and artistic director of Mammalian Diving Reflex. His shows include *A Suicide-Site Guide to the City*, *Diplomatic Immunities*, *pppeeeaaaccceee*, *[boxhead]*, *White Mice*, *Over*, *Who Shot Jacques Lacan?*, *Radio Rooster Says That's Bad* and *Mercy!* He has organized *The Toronto Strategy Meetings*, a durational project focusing on self-responsibility as a social act, *The Talking Creature*, a continuing experiment in public discourse and the upcoming *Haircuts by Children*, an event offering free haircuts to the public by children aged eight to twelve years. He was the 2000 winner of the Pauline McGibbon Award for directing, the 2000 Gabriel Award for broadcasting, and he has been nominated for a number of Dora Awards for his writing, directing and acting, winning for his design of *White Mice*. His first novel, *Your Secrets Sleep with Me*, was published on May 6, 2004, and has been called by the *Chicago Reader* 'a bible for the dispossessed, a prophecy so full of hope it's crushing.'

BARBARA RAHDER is a professor and graduate program director in the Faculty of Environmental Studies at York University, a Fellow of the Canadian Institute of Planners and former co-chair of Planners Network. She has a BSc in Psychology and an MSc and PhD in Urban and Regional Planning. Her research focuses on participatory planning with communities marginalized by gender, class, race/ethnicity, disability, age and experiences of violence. Her publications span the continuum from academic articles on planning theory and education to professional reports on planning, housing and community services for diverse communities. Her current research explores issues of social sustainability, diversity and urban public space. She is currently a guest co-editor for a special 30th-anniversary issue of *Women and Environments International* on women and urban sustainability, and an active member of the York University Faculty Association Community Projects Committee, which promotes university/community partnerships in the Jane-Finch neighbourhood.

DYLAN REID is an associate editor of *Spacing* magazine. He is also simultaneously an alumnus, an employee and a research fellow of the University of Toronto. He first arrived on the St. George campus twenty years ago to live there as an undergraduate, and after an excursion to another campus in Oxford, England, he returned first as a Fellow of the Centre for Reformation and Renaissance Studies at Victoria College, and later also as a staff member at the law school, where from his office he can see his old residence room. While he passes through the St. George campus most days of the week, he also delights in exploring the rest of Toronto, sometimes in the company of other walkers and lovers of the city.

ERIK RUTHERFORD moved to Paris after his studies in literature at McGill and Oxford Universities. In Paris, he made several short films and produced a radio program called *L'Oeil de la Mouche*. Now back in Toronto, he is developing a web-based radio project.

JEFFERY STINSON is the former associate dean of the Faculty of Architecture, Landscape and Design at the University of Toronto. He is a practising architect in Sydney, Australia; London, England; Montreal and Toronto. He has a post-graduate degree in Conservation-Industrial Archeology and held a post-graduate fellowship at Imperial College in London. The winner of local, national and international awards for building and urban design, including the City of Toronto Award for original research (Port Industrial District), Stinson is currently at work on laneway housing and projects for the Department of Civil Engineering at the University of Toronto (all with Terence Van Elslander) and prototype squatter resettlement housing in Cebu, Philippines.

DEANNE TAYLOR is a playwright and director with the award-winning VideoCabaret, which has performed in theatres and taverns from Vancouver to Montreal, from New York to London, and mainly from Bathurst Street to Spadina Avenue in Toronto. She once ran for mayor with the art trio the Hummer Sisters, winning ten percent of the city-wide vote and a landslide in the true-topian neighbourhoods of the Toronto Islands. Since then, she has dramatized the tragi-comedy of contemporary politics in many multimedia cabarets and plays, including *City For Sale* (2004), about the theft of an election and a waterfront by lobbyists and financiers.

CONAN TOBIAS is the editor-in-chief and founder of *Taddle Creek*, a Toronto literary and city-loving magazine. He has lived in Toronto since 1991.

ADAM VAUGHAN was born and raised in Toronto and has been working as a broadcast journalist since 1982. His career started at CKLN, a community-based radio station at Ryerson Polytechnical University. By 1985, he was managing the station. In 1987, he left CKLN for Citytv to produce *CityWide* with Dini Petty and later with Judy Haliday and Greg Rist. During this time, he helped out with federal and municipal elections as well as producing news serials, and did a set of free-trade debates during the 1988 federal campaign. Adam left Citytv in 1989 to return to community broadcasting – this time to sit on AMARC's board of directors for three years (the international association of community-based radio broadcasters). In 1990, he joined CBC Radio's *Metro Morning* as a segment producer. He took on reporter duties for the coverage of the municipal election in 1991, and by 1994 he began doing part-time work for CBC *Evening News*. In 1995, he switched from radio to television and was assigned full time to city hall for CBC. Adam joined Citytv in 2000 following the death of his father, Colin Vaughan. While most of his experience is in the electronic media, he has also written for *Toronto Life* and the *Toronto Star*.

STÉPHANIE VERGE was born in Finch, Ontario, and has lived in a variety of places, but keeps coming back to Toronto. She is an assistant editor at *Toronto Life* magazine.

ALANA WILCOX is the senior editor of Coach House Books. She is also the author of a novel, *A Grammar of Endings*, published by the Mercury Press.

PATRICIA K. WOOD is Associate Professor and Chair of Geography at York University. She does research on citizenship, diversity and identity politics, particularly in cities in Western Canada. She is the author of *Nationalism from the Margins* (McGill-Queen's, 2002) and co-author, with Engin F. Isin, of *Citizenship and Identity* (Sage, 1999). She lives downtown and prefers not to drive.

MARLENA ZUBER is a freelance illustrator and artist. She graduated from the illustration program at the Ontario College of Art and Design in 1997. Her illustrations have appeared in the *Washington Post, Boston Globe, Chicago Tribune, Ms., Spacing, Broken Pencil* and *Print* magazine. She has shown her personal work in numerous group shows. In addition, Marlena is a vocational rehabilitation arts councillor at Creative Works Studio, an outreach program serving individuals dealing with mental illness and socio-economic barriers. She has taught art classes in community centres, to both children and teenagers. She is a board member of the Toronto Public Space Committee and a founding member of the Toronto Psychogeography Society. Marlena is interested in creative community building projects and has recently cultivated an interest in maps. She has drawn a number of maps for [murmur], a new media storytelling project, and has sketched and painted personal maps based on urban explorations. The *uTOpia* map is definitely the most ambitious one she has created thus far.

uTOpia: TOWARDS A NEW TORONTO

EDITED BY JASON MCBRIDE AND ALANA WILCOX

THE BOOK

uTOpia was designed and typeset by Mark Fram, with the inevitable and irreplaceable contributions of Stan Bevington and Rick/Simon at the Coach House.

The text faces are ITC Mendoza Roman, designed by José Mendoza y Almeida, and H&FJ Whitney, designed by Tobias Frere-Jones. The titles are set in Home, from Canada Type, designed by Patrick Griffin.

THE COVER

The cover art was created by Jay McKay (collage on painted board, 2005; 37 x 52 cm); www.jaymckay.ca.

The cover was designed by Mark Fram.

THE MAPS

The large folded map was created by cartographer Andrew Alfred-Duggan after his own map of Toronto.

The smaller folded map was created by artist Marlena Zuber from her own imagination and that of some fellow uTOpians.

Coach House Books
401 Huron Street on bpNichol Lane
Toronto, Ontario M5S 2G5

416 979 2217
800 367 6360

mail@chbooks.com
www.chbooks.com